Praise for *The Unsettlers*

"A fascinating, timely, and deeply personal examination of what it means to be a non-conformist in the modern age." —*Outside*

"If talk of politics makes you pine for a life away from Twitter and cable news and the rest, Mark Sundeen's *The Unsettlers* offers a few tips for how to build a sustainable future."
—*The New York Times Book Review*

"In-depth and compelling . . . These homesteaders show us how the other other half lives."
—*Los Angeles Times*

"A well-crafted, intimate portrait . . . Sundeen is a sympathetic, self-deprecating, imperfect Virgil, and thus a perfect, humorous, yet earnest guide on a foray into uncompromising outposts where people are striving for purity in a deeply compromised world."
—*San Francisco Chronicle*

"[A] deftly written study." —*Nature*

"An enlightening read . . . [and] exceptional reporting on a topic that we'd all be wise to familiarize ourselves with." —*Paris Review*

"You say you want a revolution? These stories of 'unsettlers' striving to lead more simple lives are an inspiration as well as a dose of reality on how difficult that can be. This is an important book." —Yvon Chouinard, founder of Patagonia

"[A] carefully and affectionately reported account of idealists working not to leave the real world behind, but to make it better." —*BookPage*

"[A] contemporary twist on Wendell Berry's 1977 classic, *The Unsettling of America* . . . Sundeen finds beauty in each of the couples' lives, he doesn't flatten them into human Instagrams. . . .[They] are weird, stubborn and strong, and Sundeen provides a nuanced picture of their beliefs."
—*High Country News*

"In this deft, impeccably reported book, Sundeen offers a fresh look at the recurrent American urge for the 'simple' life . . . gain[ing] personal insights that feel honest and weighty."
—*Los Angeles Review of Books*

"This fallen world has quite enough wannabe farmers, and long may they thrive. But it's frankly hard to imagine the bunch of carrots, however lovingly husbanded, that would be more nourishing than the body of work Sundeen is building." —*Missoula Independent*

"A mix of social history and well-crafted journalism." —*USA Today's Green Living*

"A seriously fascinating and inspiring read. It's a book for anyone who has ever wondered how to live more sustainably, more consciously, and also a bit more crazily. . . . I was absorbed by every page of this deep, insightful examination of the lives of a handful of Americans who choose to live differently." —Cheryl Strayed

"Sundeen captures a balance between idealism and realism that leaves the reader feeling inspired, introspective and, at the very least, a little bit unsettled." —*The Missoulian*

"By framing the book as a search for answers, not arguments, Sundeen fills [*The Unsettlers*] with empathy and curiosity. Each section is distinguished by strong reporting, and Sundeen's admiration for his subjects is clear." —*The Rumpus*

T0201754

"A mix of social history and well-crafted journalism, this book relays the deeply personal stories of today's pioneers." —*Living Green*

"Simplicity is a relative matter; there is no one path or goal in that quest, and the degrees of simplicity one might achieve vary widely from one person to another. . . . Those who seek the simple life that Mark Sundeen presents in *The Unsettlers* reflect that diversity. . . . But all of these simplifiers have been roaring successes in one simple way: they have, through their devoted work, gained true joy in their lives." —*Missouri Historical Review*

"In captivating detail, [Sundeen] explores what it takes to live off the grid, survive without government intervention and live a sustainable life. . . . Charming, self-deprecating and honest."
—*Coachella Valley Weekly*

"Well researched, immediately engaging, immensely readable, and ultimately inspiring. This is the perfect read for DIY-types with dreams of saving the world, or at least their own backyards."
—*Booklist*

"From dirt roads in rural Missouri to Detroit's foreclosed streets, Sundeen reports how people throughout the United States have chosen to live simple but never simply . . . these pages will leave any reader with a penchant for sustainability to question their own carbon footprint."
—*Library Journal*

"Engaging, honest, and deeply personal . . . Provocative reading for anyone who has ever yearned for a life of radical simplicity." —*Kirkus Reviews*

"Sundeen . . . ask[s] important questions about technology, the economy, and the moral implications of being both critic and participant in our society." —*Publishers Weekly*

"Rigorously reported and utterly enthralling. With candor, wit, and live-voltage curiosity, Sundeen profiles pioneers who have developed better ways to live in our overdeveloped world. *The Unsettlers* isn't in the business of guilt or shame mongering, but it will certainly—if you have a pulse and a laptop, or even an electrical socket—make you question how you live in the world as well." —Leslie Jamison, author of *The Empathy Exams*

"With his chronicles of modern-day American visionaries and iconoclasts who have opted out of the mainstream culture, I've come to think of Mark Sundeen as our poet laureate of a new era of alternative lifestyles." —Bob Shacochis, author of *The Woman Who Lost Her Soul*

"*The Unsettlers* portrait of six true-hearted heroes of husbandry pitted against the Corporate Person would put the fear of God in that monster if it had a pulse. Sundeen's opus combines fierce reasoning, romance, impeccable research, the narrative pull of a thriller, and the subliminal magic of some wondrous old myth as he takes the measure of America's betrayed yearning for a living, thriving earth."
—David James Duncan, author of *The River Why* and *The Brothers K*

"There is a fullness and complexity to each of these tales that is impressive and illustrates a feat of cerebral strength on the part of Sundeen." —Albuquerque *Weekly Alibi*

"*The Unsettlers* is not an exploration of trendy food movements—it is a profile of sociopolitical renegades who are trying to disrupt the means of production." —*The Santa Fe New Mexican*

"In a time where progressives rage against an American system seemingly out of control, it's hard to know how to live. Author Mark Sundeen has found himself uniquely fascinated with people who decide to live as far outside that system as possible." —*Salt Lake City Weekly*

ALSO BY MARK SUNDEEN

Car Camping
The Making of Toro
The Man Who Quit Money

The Unsettlers

IN SEARCH *of the* GOOD LIFE

IN TODAY'S AMERICA

MARK SUNDEEN

RIVERHEAD BOOKS

NEW YORK

RIVERHEAD BOOKS
An imprint of Penguin Random House LLC
375 Hudson Street
New York, New York 10014

The Library of Congress has catalogued the Riverhead hardcover edition as follows:

Names: Sundeen, Mark, author.
Title: The unsettlers : in search of the good life in today's America / Mark Sundeen.
Description: New York : Riverhead Books, 2017.
Identifiers: LCCN 2016026360 | ISBN 9781594631580
Subjects: LCSH: Self-reliant living—United States. | Sustainable living—
United States. | Alternative lifestyles—United States. |
Simplicity. | United States—Civilization—21st century.
Classification: LCC GF78 .S86 2016 | DDC 640—dc23
LC record available at https://lccn.loc.gov/2016026360
p.   cm.

First Riverhead hardcover edition: January 2017
First Riverhead trade paperback edition: January 2018
Riverhead trade paperback ISBN: 9780735216082

Printed in the United States of America
1   3   5   7   9   10   8   6   4   2

Book design by Amanda Dewey

For Cedar, who showed me what to say

The danger of civilization, of course, is that you will piss away your life on nonsense.

—*Jim Harrison*

The only way to deal with an unfree world is to become so absolutely free that your very existence is an act of rebellion.

—*Albert Camus*

They love our milk and honey but they preach about some other way of living.

—*Merle Haggard*

Contents

Introduction

By the time the train approached the station, night had fallen. Sarah gathered her bags and descended the stairs to the luggage rack. Her husband helped slide an unwieldy cardboard box toward the door. The steel floor rocked beneath her shoes. The conductor's voice crackled over the loudspeaker: "This is not a smoking stop, folks. Unless this is your final destination, please stay on board the train. The next smoking stop will be Kansas City." Sarah peered out the window but saw only her reflection. She turned to the woman beside her.

"Are you from here?"

The woman said she was.

"Can you see the stars here?"

"Oh, yes," said the woman. "They're beautiful."

Sarah and Ethan had spent two nights on the train. First they rode the Silver Meteor from Fort Lauderdale to Washington—a twenty-two-hour haul. Then nineteen hours to Chicago aboard the Capitol Limited. Had she sifted through newspapers discarded on seats by fellow passengers, Sarah might have seen an item concerning the bankruptcy of the nation's second-largest subprime mortgage lender, the most recent in a string of nearly fifty such failures. In other news, a senator named Barack Obama had announced a bid for the presidency. Steve Jobs had unveiled a device called the iPhone, its failure quickly forecast: *Nothing more than a luxury bauble that will appeal to a few gadget freaks.* Sarah had slept some, lulled by the clicking of the rails and the muffled *whump* each time a bridge flexed beneath the car.

She was hungry. During these final four hours, aboard the Southwest Chief, she had eaten the last of the peanut butter from Florida. The train had smelled of disinfectant when it left Chicago, but as the passengers began to snore beneath blankets, sprawled in their seats, the air had thickened and gone stale. Through Illinois, Sarah had gazed down at backyards and country lanes, but once the sun had set, the window allowed no glimpses of her new home. She was as giddy as a bride.

The train shuddered to a stop, and the conductor slid open the steel door and placed a set of portable yellow stairs on the platform. An icy wind nipped Sarah's ears as she stepped into the white pool of light. Sarah and Ethan wrestled the cardboard box off the train, piled it with the rest of their belongings. The train whistled and chugged into the night. The smattering of departing passengers was whisked away by waiting cars. The frozen air smelled of wet wood.

Sarah cut open the box with a pocketknife. Inside were bicycle parts. Resting a frame upside down on the concrete, she attached the wheels and brake cables. Her breath hovering in clouds, she flipped the bike and threaded the seat post into its orifice and tightened the clamp. By the time both bikes were ready, the station was empty. Fingers of trees stretched toward the dark sky. The whole place could be swallowed by the night. They hung panniers and fastened backpacks to the racks. Sarah zipped her jacket, snugged a wool stocking cap beneath her helmet, inserted her hands into warm gloves.

After studying a folded photocopy of a map under the lamps of the platform, Sarah and Ethan crossed the tracks and pedaled into town. They glided between the plain white clapboard cottages, a distant streetlight shimmering in a halo of mist. Sarah felt awkward, as if she had misassembled her bike. With each pump her knees bumped against her belly. But it was not her bicycle that had changed. It was her body. She was in her fifth month.

Three months earlier, she and Ethan had compiled a list of twenty criteria for a home, a place to begin their family. Among other things, they intended to grow as much of their own food as was possible, so they listed:

Year-round drinking-water source
Long growing season with ample rainfall

Those requirements alone had eliminated huge swaths of the country: the northern plains were too wintry, the Southwest too dry.

Another goal was to live without electricity and petroleum. That did not mean they would generate power with solar panels or wind turbines. They simply would not have it: no hot-water heater, refrigerator, furnace, washing machine, computer, or cell phone. No lightbulbs. They added to the list:

Existing structures not wired for electricity
No building codes, to allow building with natural materials

Sarah and Ethan would not use cars or airplanes. They would rely on walking, bikes, and public transport. They wanted to be:

Fewer than five miles from a train station
Within biking distance of a college town

They also listed criteria of purely personal preference. Sarah was a classically trained soprano and wanted a town where she could sing opera. As for Ethan, a former marine biologist raised in a Massachusetts fishing town, he hoped to be near the sea.

Ethan and Sarah already knew of a place that met most of their criteria: the forested hills of Cottage Grove, Oregon, where they had rented a homestead for five years and Sarah had sung in the chorus of *Carmen*. A generation ago, they probably would have bought the thirty-acre compound of forest and garden, with its long summer days and cool, dry nights. But back-to-the-land havens in Oregon and California and Vermont had long since been discovered. The property would have cost half a million dollars. And so one essential criterion effectively precluded ocean and opera:

Affordable land

Their pickings were slim: the parts of America without national parks and bike paths and natural food stores. Ethan had cycled across the United States and not found Missouri to his liking—flat and buggy and landlocked, humid summers and bitter winters.

Alas, Missouri it was. A friend found an eighty-acre Amish farm for sale: a hundred-year-old bungalow, barn, shop, two ponds, a hardwood forest, plenty of pasture and fertile soil. Devoid of tide pools and bel canto, the sparsely populated northeastern corner of Missouri, shoehorned between Iowa and Illinois, nailed the other eighteen criteria. And the bubble of land speculation had not reached it. Ethan and Sarah paid $160,000 cash, sight unseen, for the house, barn, and all eighty acres.

Which is how they had come to arrive on an April night in La Plata, Missouri, population 1,467, a once prosperous trading post along the Santa Fe Railway, now fallen on hard times. They cycled through the town square, doorways dark, wind rattling the leafless trees. The upstairs windows of the storefronts were boarded with plywood and corrugated fiberglass. Tacked to the door of an auction house was a list of farm implements and an inventory of tools and appliances with a brief preamble: *As I am residing in a nursing home will sell the following items*. In the window of one of the few functioning enterprises, the Christian Ministries Clothing Center, was taped a terse hand-scrawled note: *No TV's*.

Sarah did not share her husband's aversion to the Midwest. Although born and raised a city girl in Houston—singing at a performing arts school, speeding over freeways to coffee shops, working out at the gym—Sarah came from deep Iowa stock. Her parents were born there. Her great-grandparents had been farmers, and their parents homesteaders, just like in *Little House on the Prairie*. Sarah had graduated from Grinnell College, a hundred fifty miles north of here. Moving to Missouri felt like coming home.

The beam of her headlamp projected a meager saucer of gray on the asphalt. After a series of left-hand turns, the couple had to admit they were lost. They pedaled toward a glimmer, which materialized into a gas station bathed in neon along a highway. A police cruiser idled out front. The couple went inside to ask directions and the officer told them that all they needed to do was cross the highway to a gravel road named Mockingbird Hill. They mounted their bikes and inched to the shoulder. But Sarah could see no outlet on the far side of the four lanes. A truck roared past, rattling her teeth.

"I don't see where we're supposed to go," she said.

Just then the red lights of the cruiser flashed behind them. The officer crawled forward, the big engine purring, and Sarah saw him smile from the open window.

"Follow me," he said.

He escorted them across four lanes to where, sure enough, a gravel road descended from the embankment past a graveyard and into farmland. Keeping a respectful distance in front, he chaperoned them through rolling hills and fields. Sarah rode in silence, sucking in the cold air, trying to keep up, scanning each hill for the house she had seen only in pictures. It was like a treasure hunt. The frozen road beneath her tires was as smooth as clay. Lit by starlight, the dark earth of unplanted cornfields was milky with frost. A dog ran snarling from a farmhouse but left them alone.

It was an odd parade: a crawling police car, lights ablaze, and a man and his pregnant wife pedaling bicycles across the winter prairie. This was not the way they'd expected to begin their new carless, electricity-free life! Sarah looked at Ethan, and without warning laughter erupted. Not a rising giggle or a modest chuckle, but an instantaneous wail, a one-note aria, the kind of laugh that startles animals and delights children and causes stage actors to flub their lines—her laughter rang in the night.

Fifteen minutes later Mockingbird Hill teed against a paved road whose sign said simply "E." The deputy waved them close to the window, pointing. "It's just a few miles out that way," he said. At the first intersection they should take a left and they'd be there. With that he gunned it back toward town. Sarah and Ethan rode on into the night, rising and falling through the contours of the countryside, stars lighting the way.

I WISHED I'D BEEN on a train like that. I had long dreamed that around the next bend awaited a life more simple and purposeful than the one I actually led, cluttered with forms to fill out, machines that beeped, and pointless tasks performed for money.

As a teenager I'd escaped the suburbs of Los Angeles and fallen in with the packs of rock climbers who dwelled in vans in Joshua Tree and Yosemite Valley. Within a year of graduating from college I was living in my car in the Utah canyonlands, working as a river guide and a fry cook, drawn to the windshield and the wilderness. For most of a decade I instructed Outward Bound courses.

Trite as it sounds, backpacking made me understand my essence. My body was a simple machine. I carried the food I ate, which allowed me to keep walking. Extraneous items were not only useless but detrimental: dead weight. What drew me most was the wonder and beauty of the landscapes I crossed. Then I loved the freedom of being outside, of not having what appeared to be a job. I loved the satisfaction of learning useful skills, the kinds that I had somehow not been taught in college: how to cook and make shelter, to find my way across canyons by map and compass, to navigate river currents, to splint a broken arm. And last was the most difficult to describe: that oceanic feeling of belonging to the world, of being one of its creatures.

And then one summer in Alaska, day fifty-one of a fifty-two-day expedition, I found myself bushwhacking up a slope, fifty pounds on my back, and although it was not raining, soaked to the skin from the dripping head-high alder brush. I drank water that tasted of iodine from a plastic bottle, its lip caked with the dried residue of powdered soup, tea, and hot chocolate.

I didn't want to live like that anymore. I wanted to cook my meals indoors and eat them at a table, no more powdered milk, powdered potatoes, powdered whatever. No more snowballs: I was ready for toilet paper. A month later I sat in a cubicle writing copy for a political campaign. When I felt that my unkempt beard kept me from being taken seriously, I shaved it, and bought a pair of office shirts at the mall. It seemed so innocent at the time. But the comfortable life is a slippery slope toward the consumer life.

I suppose a more practical person by middle age would have outgrown my fascination with dropping out, but my case only worsened. I wanted fewer bills and fewer rules, less stuff and more freedom. For another decade, instead of a regular career I cobbled together an income through teaching, writing, and tinkering with old houses, sufficiently entangled with civilization to pay a mortgage but with my eye always wandering toward an exit.

My aversion to getting a regular job was not the result of being lazy—although sometimes I am. Nor was it that I simply don't like being told what to do—although I don't. What I have never been able to tolerate is the prospect that my few years on earth will be frittered away filling out the form to verify that I filled out the previous form, or worse, toiling in the service of some enterprise that perpetuates the things I hate: war, corporate bullying, bureaucratic hoop-jumping, plunder of nature, and more hours tethered to electronic screens. I was willing to work, but I wanted my work to matter—to repair land and cities, to cultivate peace and justice. I wanted not the frazzled anxiety that follows eight hours of chair-bound button-pushing, but the bodily satisfaction of employing hands, legs, and lungs in concert with the mind. I often felt helpless at the state of the world—climate change, racism, species extinction, poverty, war—and I wanted ways to address these things with my very life, to live in a way that was not just ethical but joyful.

Looking around, I saw that I was not alone. Anxious at the erosion of their freedom and security, Americans hungered for alternatives. A movement was afoot—local food and urban farms, bike co-ops and time banks and tool libraries, permaculture and guerrilla gardening, homebirthing and homeschooling and home cooking—a new twist on the back-to-the-land movement of the previous generation.

I decided to go find Americans leading lives of radical simplicity. Yet it wasn't just a matter of going without electricity. The real power matrix was the economy. I'd grown skeptical of government, universities, even the nonprofits that I had long thought held the solutions to our problems. They seemed too dependent on the organized money that they professed to fight, and their personnel often seemed especially mirthless and desk-bound.

I wanted to see if living along lines of radical simplicity brought a deeper, truer relationship to land, livelihood, economy, and spirit. I wanted to learn the old-fashioned concept of household, a meaningful mix of work, family, and home. How far might we go in rejecting the compromises of contemporary life—and what did we gain or sacrifice? What I wanted to learn was how to lead a good life.

As I delved deeper, I saw today's movement was part of a stream that runs through our history—a stream that has not yet prevailed but refuses to die. The willingness to forgo the comforts of civilization for some imagined rustic freedom, after all, was one factor that brought Europeans across the Atlantic, that spurred pioneers across the frontier. "Let us Eat Potatoes and drink Water," declared our second president, John Adams. "Let us wear Canvass, and undressed Sheepskins, rather than submit to the unrighteous and ignominious Domination that is prepared for Us."

It took me more than a year of searching to know whom I was looking for, exactly. Among the dozens I found, the three families I wrote about were not just living an alternative life. They had each taken on a fundamental aspect of how the world is broken, and had attempted, with all their might, to address it—in ways that felt sustainable, maybe even replicable. They inspired me. They challenged me not to quit my own dreaming just because my visions could never be made perfect.

THE SEARCH REALLY BEGAN at the fried-chicken case in the deli aisle of a supermarket, across a shadeless avenue from a Taco John's drive-thru and a B-grade big box called Shopko. The hot, bland haze could have been anywhere in America, but it happened to be on the outskirts of Missoula, Montana, where I had stopped on my way home to pick a brick of butter.

As I clicked down the cool aisles, I was hungry. I had worked later than I'd meant to, and it was already seven, and I hadn't eaten since lunch. I steered the cart into the zone devoted to natural foods. With organic this and artisanal that, including butter coaxed from cows presumably allowed to bed with their masters and stream Netflix, the place provided a haven from the consumption bonanza that ruled on the rest of the floor. I perused the butter, each box bedecked with competing visions of pastoral harmony. Let me be clear: I felt bad about the state of the planet, and I was willing to pay extra if it supported an actual farmer instead of the bovine gulag.

My life had reached a turning point. At age forty-one I was engaged to marry. I had vacated my house downtown and moved to my fiancée's ramshackle cottage on the banks of the Bitterroot River, where we grew vegetables and canned peach jam and from our bed watched bald eagles nest in the cottonwoods.

It felt like the natural conclusion to some journey. Six years earlier I'd been living in a room in Brooklyn, hustling to connect paychecks as a freelancer, spending every cent on yoga and beer, often in quick succession. The yoga and beer made me feel bodiless—a state I had previously attained paddling whitewater, descending canyons, skiing off mountaintops. But attaining that weightless sensation in the city required one crucial adjustment: I had to pay for it. I had begun to imagine myself as a money-lung, an organ whose sole purpose was to inhale dollars, transform them into pleasure, then exhale a stream of carbon into the air, feces into the sewer, and plastic containers into the landfill. When my furnished sublet ended, I faced the prospect of finding my own place, which would require doubling my income. Wandering through SoHo hungover and near broke one Sunday morning, I pressed my face against the window of a boutique and thought, Yeah, I'd pay two hundred bucks for those sneakers. I mean, they were made in Spain.

Luckily, the store was closed. I moved back West, hoping to live more simply, less tangled in money and simulated entertainment, more connected to nature, people, and spirit—or to put it in a single earnest word that's embarrassing in these ironic times, I wanted my life to be *authentic*.

I landed in Missoula, bought a small house whose payment I could afford, met Cedar. This was my first engagement, indeed the first time I had ever lived with a woman, and it signified not only the end of my two-decade bachelorhood but an initiation into a world I found marvelous and exotic. In case it isn't obvious from the fact that she was named after a tree, my wife was raised by hippies, home-birthed in a barn in the northern wilds of Montana—candles, wood-stove, outhouse—then homeschooled and homeopathed, unvaccinated and uninsured. She and I could not banter about the corny sitcoms of our youth because she'd never had TV. She was raised vegetarian and had never sampled a Big Mac or a leg of fried chicken.

Cedar hailed from a separate America, and as I fell in love with her, I fell in love with it, too. I had spent my adulthood fleeing the plasticky pop culture of Southern California, and Cedar appeared to me deeply connected to the things I deemed more consequential than, say, the WaterWorld show at Universal Studios. She knew the names of nearly all the plants and flowers and birds in the state of Montana. She knew how to grow her own food and cook it, too. She had encounters with wild animals that I could think of only as mystical. A regular element of her botanist job was detecting and avoiding grizzly bears.

Our first decision together was where to live, and I agreed to her place partly because of its rangy pastoralia and partly because she flatly refused to move to mine, citing my close neighbors and loud traffic. The rewards were bounteous. Her rented shack abutted twenty acres of pasture where horses and coyotes frolicked, and beyond them, a stand of willows along the river. When the spring floods receded, we claimed a private sand beach for skinny-dipping and sunbathing and sucking cold pink wine from the bottle.

We harvested lettuce and arugula in June, peas and raspberries in July, onions and garlic in August, corn and tomatoes in September. What we didn't devour fresh off the stem we pickled and preserved: crocks of sauerkraut and kimchi, gallons of tomatillo salsa with our own garlic and peppers, dried pears from the orchard, rhubarb-huckleberry pies. We foraged morels along the river and stuffed them plump with fresh-cut chives and goat cheese. We dried Indian corn and stored the hard kernels to boil for pozole. We grew a year's worth of garlic and a winter's worth of onions and stored it all in the cellar. I, who'd seen farmers only on TV, buried beets in buckets of sand so that they'd last the year.

We dined at ten. Nothing is as sublime as a Montana summer night, the sun finally sinking behind the hills at nine but the sky still glowing till eleven. There was no other place we wanted to go or people we wanted to see. A herd of mule deer bedded in the pasture. We saw a fox out there. Sometimes we packed dinners into a wicker basket and hauled them through the thicket to picnic on the beach. Cedar bought a fifty-gallon horse trough that we perched atop cinder blocks, filled from a hose, and heated with a fire beneath to make a hillbilly hot tub under the stars.

We were living in Arcadia and eating like aristocrats, and for rent paid just six hundred forty dollars. Yet our days there felt numbered. We didn't know how long the lease would last. Even if the property came up for sale, it was beyond our means. Meanwhile it was too small for both of us to work there, which is why I kept an office in town. I biked the seven miles between in spandex shorts, a DayGlo vest, and shoes with clips on the soles, considering my commute a feat of athleticism and danger despite the fact that Cedar had been pedaling this stretch for a decade in cowboy boots and a dress. After a few months of it, sitting in a car for even twenty minutes had come to feel cramped and stupid. Still, it seemed that if we had a baby we would have to move, giving up our idyllic life and taking on the high mortgage and other encumbrances we'd carefully avoided thus far.

In the grocery aisle, I tried to push all that out of my mind and consider dinner. Our plan was a curry of squash, peppers, and eggplant, and so in addition to butter for morning toast we needed canned coconut milk, limes, and a bunch of cilantro, as our own had already bolted in the summer heat. What lay ahead was a feast: harvesting the vegetables, washing and chopping, concocting the sauce from scratch, and celebrating each phase with a clink of cold beer glasses. By dinnertime there would be puddles on the floor and dirt clods in the sink.

But now I hesitated, my hand hovering over the dairy case.

For the first time in human history, I was aware, the appetites of our species exceeded the resources of the planet. From climate change to deforestation, extinction to depleted fisheries, we were devouring our nest. As a result, we had come to equate consumption with morality: buying one brand of butter was more ethical than buying another. It seemed bizarre that this should be so, but hadn't the agrarian Wendell Berry written, "How could we divorce ourselves completely and yet responsibly from the technologies and powers that are destroying our planet? The answer is not yet thinkable."

Not even thinkable!

I had long wrestled with Wendell Berry's prophecies. I swooned to his song of the simple life: horses pulling a plow across his Kentucky farm, forsaking a computer and lightbulbs for typewriter and candles, boycotting fossil fuels. In an era buffeted by news of killings in Ferguson and Baltimore, gender inequity and sexual assault, and a new hysteria over immigration, it's tempting to dismiss Berry and his donkey as a quaint fantasy. Yet I still thought of him as one of the radical thinkers of our times, one who flatly contended that our brand of capitalism had laid waste to our land, our homes, and not least of all, our souls.

Unlike most activists, Berry blamed our state of crisis not merely on government or corporations, but equally on our individual appetites. He seemed unique in understanding that the "environment" is not a place we vacation to gaze at warblers, but our home, the one and only garden that feeds us. In his vision of small farms, neighbor economy, and local governance, he lay in a tradition that germinated far before the back-to-the-land movement in which Cedar was raised, before the simple-living blueprints drawn by Thoreau at Walden Pond. It went all the way to the founding fathers, especially Thomas Jefferson. "Cultivators of the earth are the most valuable citizens," Jefferson wrote (and Berry approvingly cited). "They are the most vigorous, the most independent, the most virtuous, and they are tied to their country, and wedded to its liberty and interests by the most lasting bonds." In contrast, Jefferson considered manufacturers the "panderers of vice, and the instruments by which the liberties of a country are generally overturned."

In a society based on the premise of unlimited freedom, how could we live within limits? I knew that signing petitions and writing officials and reposting strongly worded editorials on Facebook solved nothing. What was required was action, finding new sources of food, fuel, and finance. And yet, as I was an English major raised on a skateboard, the action that was available to me—happy, happy butter—was not adequate. My hand continued to hover, indecisive. Which brand to buy? Valuable citizen or panderer of vice? I wanted to spread upon my toast the cream that made me neither victim nor executioner.

I laid my hand on the gilded cube of righteous cream. But my frugal fingers refused to clutch it.

Here's where my pastoral fantasy ran aground: the pound of organic butter cost six dollars and fifty cents. The ceiling for buying my way into grace was about five bucks. Especially if I ever wanted to save enough cash to buy my own homestead.

I marched out of the health haven toward Consumeria, a journey that bypassed the deli counter, where a whiff of the newly fried chicken stopped me in my tracks. Oh, how I love fried chicken! I soldiered on through the gauntlet of pink-frosted cookies by the baker's dozen, where I gaped at my fellow Americans piloting barges with logs of ground beef and pallets of frozen pizza, suitcases of Mountain Dew and pillowcases of Doritos, all of which they would winch into tanks that cost more than my yearly income and could barely cross the street on a gallon of gas.

Finally I arrived at the pulsing cold vaults of conventional cream, three bucks a box. But as I perused the ingredients and noted their place of origin, I balked, spun, and retreated toward the organic nook, suddenly faint with hunger in my fluorescent vest, drawn like Odysseus to the siren song of the battered breast.

I did not grow up eating junk—no Cokes and Cap'n Crunch—but neither did we eat what was back then known as "health food." We ate spaghetti with Ragú. Born in the Great Depression and raised during the war, my parents remembered sugar rations and were frugal and moderate. But from my Southern mother I'd inherited a love of fried chicken. Not that my parents, college professors both, were going to fry it themselves. And so from time to time we went to the man who did chicken right: Colonel Harland Sanders, whose red-and-white-striped Kentucky Fried Chicken kiosk on Sepulveda Boulevard remains what the shrinks might call my happy place. And to this day no memory evokes my childhood more fondly than beach picnics with a bucket of the Colonel, cheery styrofoam bowls of gravied mashed potatoes, a sporkful of slaw.

Intoxicated with nostalgic reverie, I found my feet carrying me toward the deli case. Now, I knew about chicken factories. I knew about the lightless cages, the clipped beaks, the overhead drizzle of shit, the poison-laced corn and soy shoved down their gullets, the farmers bullied into serfdom. I knew about growth hormones and preservatives and artificial flavors, the obscene categorization of body type by cooking method: fryer, broiler, roaster. I knew that I had built a life around better choices and that one definition of well-adjusted adulthood was restraint. I also knew that my future held no more buckets of KFC, although in truth I hadn't had so much as a wing of it since I'd read *Fast Food Nation*.

But between me and dinner lay another three miles of bike path and at least an hour of harvesting and chopping and cooking. Every meal Cedar and I cooked required at least three saucepans and two skillets, plus a battery of cutting boards, a quiver of knives, a grater, and a salad spinner. The downside of garden-to-table gourmet was that to get dinner from garden to table took For. Fucking. Ever. And who would be the one to do all those dishes, to shovel those dirt clods out of the sink? Me, that's who, doubled over in the windowless galley, sweeping the pocked and curling linoleum, with its black-burned ring where someone had oopsed a skillet, the floor the landlord wouldn't replace, and who could blame him given how little we paid? Cedar's love of cooking didn't extend to washing dishes.

Nearly all my friends were married, and they had shared some secrets, but none had warned me about this niggling sensation: that despite how good life was, everything that irked me—the dirt clods in the sink, the cracks in the windowpanes, the price of organic butter, the gnawing in my belly—would make me feel confined. When I'd been single, it had been easier to maintain my illusions of possibility.

There would always be another fling, I would never need money, I would never grow old. But now that I was engaged, I glimpsed the future: monogamy, mortgage, parenting, paychecks. And then, after all the years of worry:

Death.

If I actually began to live within the limits of marriage, of household, then I also had to confront the limits of mortality. This was some heavy shit for a honeymoon. Because no matter how good we have it, we always want more—more food, more beer, more car, more life. And those deep desires were in direct conflict with the ideas I admired, about simple living, living within the limits that sustained life—all life. Enough never seemed to be enough.

I rushed toward the checkout aisle, and as I reached for my wallet a voice said: *There's nothing wrong with the way you already live. You're an American. You don't need to change.*

Simple living was not so easy. It wasn't even simple. What was simple was hot 'n' ready Chester's fried thighs.

When I emerged into the blistering parking lot, hidden like a tumor amid the health food in my pannier (*No bag today, thanks. Brought my own!*) was the white breast of some young fryer, its dead heart pounding in a plastic sack. I leaned against my bike and tore the meat from its wrapper, gnashed at it with my fangs, the first bite gaining purchase only on skin, which I ripped off in a single sheet and huffed into my throat. In my youth I'd messed around with hard drugs, and let me tell you, none hits the blood as hot and sweet as whatever they inject in fried chicken these days. Explosions of salt-fat ricocheted in my skull, my eyes rolled into their sockets of grease, and with my free hand I steadied myself on the saddle. When I'd peeled away the meat with my teeth, I chewed the tiny bones and spit the pulp into the plastic.

Only then did I slide the provided mini wipe from its sealed envelope, its lemony bouquet taking me back to a picnic circa 1978. I wiped my lips, cheeks, nose, forehead. I scrubbed each finger. Domesticity would require compromise and restraint. It would also require, now and then, cover-ups. Would my fiancée judge me harshly for my meat snack? I did not want to find out. I stuffed the soiled tissue into the bone bag, dropped the whole mess into the bin. I mounted my bicycle, newly fortified, and lit out all carbon-neutral for the edge of civilization, for the simple life.

PART ONE

Missouri

One

I was looking for people freed from commercial civilization, who might give me direction for doing it myself. Yet after a full year, everyone I'd met fell into one of five categories, none of which was exactly right.

First were single men. These guys had achieved self-reliance, but in cutting ties with the economy, they had also severed family bonds, the opposite of what I was on the verge of doing. I wanted blueprints for cohabitation, not hermitry.

Next I met people who, after leading a simple life for some period of time, decided to quit—Cedar's parents, for example. After years of eking out a living growing food and selling stained glass at craft fairs, they both got full-time jobs and eventually replaced the barn with a beautiful on-grid home. "We took poverty as far as we could," her dad told me with a laugh. A friend of mine who birthed a baby in a school bus in a snowstorm on a mountain told me that tripping in the snow on the way to the outhouse one night—pregnant, shitting herself— was not what had finally nudged her and her husband to abandon the homestead. It was the prospect of driving the kids forty minutes to school each day. People who quit the simple life were the rule; I wanted the exceptions.

In the third group were people who had launched their vision with considerable wealth or inherited land. I met a family who had deftly flipped a house in the suburbs before the crash, paid cash for acreage, and built an off-grid straw-bale house. I envied and admired them, but I couldn't afford to replicate what they'd done. Perhaps the most famous modern homesteader is Ree Drummond, who spun her massively popular Pioneer Woman blog into a series of books and TV shows that extol home cooking and homeschooling. But Drummond acquired her piece of paradise by marrying into a family that ranks among America's largest landowners.

There were also those from a tradition of simple living, such as the Amish and the Mennonites. But you had to be born into such a culture. You couldn't just join.

And then there were the moonlighters. Western Montana and southern Utah, where I'd lived for two decades, were meccas for back-to-the-landers, as were Vermont and Northern California. But those places were all expensive now, and buying in these days—or even staying afloat—required working an outside job to support a homestead hobby. I admired the commitment of those who'd figured out how to make it work. But for me a crucial motivation for living simply was to gain more freedom, not to sprint on some treadmill just to pay the bank.

"What can I actually do?" asked the British economist E. F. Schumacher in his 1973 book *Small Is Beautiful*, in the face of intractable tentacles of industry. "In the excitement over the unfolding of his scientific and technical powers," he wrote, "modern man has built a system of production that ravishes nature and a type of society that mutilates man." Meanwhile, the wealthy were stripping the world of its cheap fuels at such a quick rate that poor countries would never get a fair share.

Schumacher's solution: "We can, each of us, work to put our own inner house in order." He viewed economics through a Buddhist lens, asserting that "the essence of civilization [is] not in a multiplication of wants but in the purification of human character." Instead of productivity for its own sake, Schumacher heralded the Buddhist ideal of "right livelihood," whose function he defined as threefold: to excel at one's craft, to overcome selfishness by working in common cause with others, and to create useful goods and services.

Wendell Berry echoed this: "How can a man hope to promote peace in the world if he has not made it possible in his own life and his own household?"

So after a year of searching for the people who had taken Wendell Berry's challenge to quit destructive technology, I found that I was equally interested in finding people who had taken his challenge to put their households in order.

Where to find homesteaders more radical, more committed, yet less isolated than the ones I'd met thus far? Not personally knowing any, I launched my search—where else?—on Facebook. Through a short chain of acquaintances I learned about a place in Missouri, the Possibility Alliance. Some people I met at an anarchist collective told me they had gone there to launch a monthlong bike ride devoted to service—a ride they'd all done dressed as superheroes. But in these instantly searchable times, it was surprisingly hard to find out more. The alliance was shrouded in analog mystery: no website or social media, no major press coverage. Was it a commune or a school or an ashram or a summer camp or a training ground for revolutionaries?

Gradually I gathered this much: Members of the Possibility Alliance used no electricity, cars, or computers. They lived by candlelight and grew their own food and rode bicycles and horses and trains. They lived in voluntary poverty rather than pay an income tax that financed war. Knowledge of the place spread by word of mouth.

I eventually obtained a phone number—landlines don't require electricity—and after a series of messages spoke with Ethan Hughes, who, along with his wife, Sarah Wilcox, had founded the Possibility Alliance after they'd disembarked that Amtrak train in La Plata in 2007. He told me that the alliance hosted 1,500 visitors per year, some for a two-hour tour or a half-day course in canning or knitting, others for a weeklong natural-building workshop or a two-week permaculture course.

"People pull up in the train and are picked up by horse and buggy or by bike," he said. "We call it 'necessary simplicity.' I don't know how to build another planet, but I know how to simplify. It creates a myth. In the age of the Internet, people get bored. There's this mystery. People track us down."

I asked what sort of people showed up.

"All kinds. Catholic Workers and anti-religious anarchists, permaculturists and Buddhists." At present they were so inundated with visitors that they could accommodate me only during "Experience Week."

The price for the nine-day visit: zero. They operated strictly on the "gift economy." I asked what that meant.

"I see objects and money like water," he said. "It's flowing. If in nature one tree kept all the water, everything downstream would die. By studying nature we see—" He stopped mid-sentence.

"The bell of mindfulness just rang," he said. "Do you mind taking a moment of silence with me?"

DAYS AFTER OUR WEDDING and our honeymoon in a lake cabin, I left Cedar in Montana and set out, alone, for the Midwest. Summer of 2013 had lasted to September and it was hot and muggy. I drove through La Plata's shuttered downtown and along the edges of farms where rows of soybeans were marked with signs advertising their peculiar brand names, which sounded more like erection enhancers than vegetables—Syngenta, CruiserMaxx, Touchdown Total—and then onto a long, straight dirt road that led to a wooden cottage.

The Possibility Alliance looked precisely like what it was when Ethan and Sarah had bought it: an Amish farm. An early-century Craftsman bungalow rested in the shade of big trees. A barn housed two draft horses, and inside a tin warehouse dozens of bikes hung from hooks. Behind the house, chickens clucked in a hutch, herbs flourished in a garden, and someone was cooking over a fire in the shade of an outdoor kitchen.

Ethan himself looked about as normal as a guy could look. He wore shorts and a ragged T-shirt and river sandals. Hair: brownish, thinnish, shortish. Likely he cut it himself. He told me where to park my car, where to pitch my tent, where to fill my water bottle.

The first order of business was trying to cool off. It was ninety degrees and humid, more of the same forecast for the week, and I was suddenly aware that there would be no air-conditioning, fans, refrigerated drinks, or ice cubes. Ethan invited me to cool down by jumping in the pond. "The only rule is you have to keep your clothes on," he said. He didn't want to offend the Amish neighbors.

I stepped behind a tree and changed into trunks, then beelined for the dock and leapt in. But instead of the heart-stopping chill of mountain lakes, the water caressed me like a lukewarm bath. I floated there, as if in a sensory-deprivation tank. Finally someone instructed that by diving deep I could reach the cold pockets, and I did, shivering joyfully in the deeps, then popping to the surface, finally refreshed.

So began Experience Week. There were twenty of us in all, some visiting from other intentional communities, some considering joining the PA, and others like me, the Luddite-curious. We attended classes on topics as wide-ranging as straw-bale construction, conflict resolution, organic gardening, civil disobedience, bow making, hand-saw forestry, and integral nonviolence. We rode bicycles to La Plata to sing in a nursing home. Four or five times a day we flopped off the dock into the tepid pond and floated there, slightly and temporarily cooled. There was holding hands in a circle, singing, naming things we were thankful for, icebreaker games: it felt just like the dozens of Outward Bound courses I had loved leading.

Like her husband, Sarah gave no outward indication of radical-ness, in cargo shorts and sandals and a tank top, her dark hair brushed straight to her shoulders. While Ethan led many of the workshops and games, she mostly retreated from the group. She seemed to have her hands full with their two daughters, six-year-old Etta and two-year-old Isla (pronouncd *I-la*), beautiful, precocious girls who had hardly seen a television screen or the inside of a store. In addition to Sarah and Ethan, there was one other permanent member of the alli-ance and three full-time residents considering committing. It wasn't a light decision; joining the PA required giving away all your savings—not giving it to the community, but donating it elsewhere. Another six apprentices were camped in tents for the season. The men at the PA were mostly clean-cut, shirtless Midwestern boys who split wood and milked the goats. If not for the rap about permaculture and yoga, I might have thought I had landed in a frat house.

Ethan and the others gathered us around and said, "Now it's time to receive your superhero instructions." They passed around a basket of folded paper notes and we each picked one. "Before the end of the week," Ethan said, "you must complete this mission." I opened mine. It read, *Tell somebody a secret that you're afraid to tell*.

It was becoming clear that, as guests, we were not passive observ-ers but rather subjects of the alliance's mission: to open our hearts and minds.

"It's easier to radicalize an institution than it is to radicalize your-self," Ethan said.

This struck me as some bull. I was already a good-enough person.

I recycled. I paid taxes. I voted Democrat. I didn't need to change. I just needed to persuade other people to change, to live a little more lightly, to live, well, a little more like me.

That night, lying in a pool of sweat in my tent, I had a chance to reflect on exactly what sort of life I led. I thought about my own household. At home, as dishes piled up in the sink, I had Googled myself and found that someone had posted photos of me on his Tumblr page. I clicked, assuming I'd find some parade of literary excellence. Instead it was a collection titled "Balding Men." I ran my fingers across my scalp. It's actually called a high forehead—a Scandinavian trait. It connotes wisdom. I searched for "bald authors" to confirm that I had not made *that* list. But was that because of my adequate hair or my obscurity? I examined the hair of literary stars. Jonathan Franzen, David Foster Wallace: full heads of it. The Norwegian Karl Ove Knausgård looked like a goddamn *hår modell* for Vidal Sassoon.

I was mid-list, mid-life, mid-forehead.

Amid everyone else on the Internet vying for acclaim, who would ever adore me? I surfed the websites of authors male and female: the lustrous hair, the bestsellers, the university appointments, the foreign translations. A fantasy of these recipients of Guggenheim grants formed in my mind, not an orgy but a Committee: in filtered sunlight behind lacquered diplomas they would encircle me like a panel of judges, praise my oeuvre, award me a fellowship, whisper sweetly that my life's work was worth the trouble. My appetite for this sort of acclaim had been repressed before the Internet, because finding an outlet was too laborious. Now it was easy. Infinite.

But the headshots instead of lavishing praise murmured the opposite: *Your career, your talent: so mediocre. And as for your marriage: Are you sure you made the right choice? Why didn't you find someone more successful, someone on the Committee who might introduce you to the right people?* Yet I kept coming back.

I had relied on a therapist over the years to condone whatever I wanted to do. Now he furrowed his brow and said, "Sounds like you're not being a good partner." He suggested that online voyeurism was the seed of infidelity. "Because here's the thing about being married," he said, "and this is the voice of God talking: *You can not fuck around.*"

"But it's not exactly *sexual*," I said.

Which was true. But what I was brewing was still a form of betrayal, more cowardly than outright betrayal. Despite having married the only woman I had ever wanted to marry, I still had something hollow in me, something that had been there all along and that I'd assumed would be filled by her love. For years I had chased love and acclaim, as equal rewards. But now that I had actual love, I saw that it was the opposite of acclaim. In the parlance of Schumacher, instead of purifying my character I was multiplying my wants. My longing for acclaim appeared to have no limits. Beneath my nonmaterialistic exterior, I was as driven to succeed as any salesman or stockbroker. Marrying the woman I loved would not move me up to the next career rung, and with a gasp of shame I had to admit that, somehow, I had hoped it would.

I resolved to disband the Committee. But when I sat at the screen and the link to some "Best American Essayist" appeared, I clicked it anyway. The Committee would not disband.

C. S. Lewis wrote of temptation, "No man knows how bad he is till he has tried very hard to be good." What a prig! In my two decades as a bachelor I'd considered temptation a fuddy-duddy myth. I partook in whatever I wanted: drink, drugs, daydreams. When I witnessed friends become drunks or problem gamblers, I was mystified. Because to me the amount I drank and gambled and caroused seemed just about right.

But now I saw that the reason temptation had never bedeviled me was that I'd never had reason to fight it. "Only those who try to resist temptation know how strong it is," wrote Lewis. "A man who gives in to temptation after five minutes simply does not know what it would have been like an hour later."

And me, a man who Googled that author whose debut book got a sparkly review in *The New York Times*: I learned how excruciating it was not to click on that link for five minutes, ten minutes, an hour.

IN MOST DISCUSSIONS ABOUT TECHNOLOGY, *Luddite* is a dirty word. Even the most committed activists embrace cars, planes, and computers as a means of furthering their cause, and begin their criticism of some specific innovation—fracking, pesticides, genetically modified organisms—by clarifying, "I'm not a Luddite, but . . ."

Not so at the Possibility Alliance, which had virtually excised itself from the industrial system of food, fuel, and finance. Ethan Hughes delivered the most coherent critique of technology I had heard. I was reminded that the original Luddites, the nineteenth-century weavers who smashed industrial looms, were not mere hicks who couldn't comprehend scientific advances, but rather principled resisters who correctly predicted that industrialism would end their trade and their economic independence.

At a picnic table in the shade of a walnut tree, Ethan Hughes proposed that we divide technologies into three types. First were those that required no industrial inputs. Dating back long before the industrial revolution, these included walking, horseback riding, knitting, weaving, candle making, hunting with spears and bows and arrows, and cooking over a fire. The next level included those technologies that required a one-time industrial input for their manufacture but afterward were powered by nonindustrial inputs. These included saws, hammers, bicycles, plows, and woodstoves. The last were those that required the constant industrial inputs of oil, coal, and electricity. In America, virtually everything we use falls into this category: lightbulbs, stoves and furnaces, internal combustion engines from chainsaws to lawn mowers to cars to tractors, electrical devices from cordless drills to clothes dryers to computers to cell phones. Ethan's goal was to use as much as possible of the first category, plenty from the second, and none from the third.

The result is that the PA had adopted much of the technology of the nineteenth-century American pioneers. Most of the food its members ate—and fed to their thousands of guests—was grown without tractors, petrol, or chemicals. In four large gardens they cultivated squash, tomatoes, beans, greens, cabbage, peppers, and a dozen other edibles. Pears and apples ripened in the orchard. They harvested herbs for tea, spices, and salves. They foraged in the forest for mushrooms and berries. Twice a day they milked goats and a cow, producing ample cream, cheese, and yogurt. A hutch squawking with dozens of chickens provided eggs and meat. They kept bees for honey and grew sorghum as a sweetener. They hunted deer and wild turkey, and fished the ponds for largemouth bass and bluegill and catfish.

With a pair of draft horses they plowed and planted wheat. One morning we threshed the wheat by hand, slapping it against the wall of the barn and collecting the berries in a tarp. Then we ground it to flour in a mill powered by a stationary bicycle. That night we baked challah in an outdoor wood-fired oven.

With Missouri's ample rainfall, the crops did not require major irrigation. The PA bought its drinking water from the county system, a dependency it was working to eliminate. In rooftop cisterns they collected rain for washing dishes and clothing. A gravity-fed filter purified some rainwater for drinking.

They supplemented their own crops with other local food. In the autumn they picked apples by the bushel at a nearby orchard. Their neighbor who bred cattle gave them beef when he culled the herd.

Lacking refrigeration, members of the Possibility Alliance ate what was fresh and in season and stored the rest. Apples, potatoes, beets, and squash wintered in the cellar. They canned hundreds of jars of tomatoes and string beans, and fermented crocks of sauerkraut. If they received more beef than they needed, they canned the remainder.

Items not available locally they ordered in bulk: vegetable oil, salt, oats, and flour. They insisted on purchasing rice from Texas instead of California. In an era of easy access to a range of upscale produce year-round, when nobody blinks at apples from New Zealand, avocados from Israel, and coconuts from Thailand, I tasted an actual locavore diet. At the Possibility Alliance there was no sugar, coffee, black tea, wine, chocolate, bananas, avocados, coconut milk, or peanut butter.

I asked Ethan if he missed any of those foods. "Coconuts," he said. "But I'm not going to eat them." One time, he remembered, some friends had arrived on the train from Los Angeles harboring a sack of California avocados, of which he had savored each bite.

The resulting meals ranged from the grim to the exquisite. Some breakfasts consisted of cold soaked oats and pick-your-own Concord grapes. Other mornings the cook scrambled eggs straight from the hutch. There were vats of soup and the occasional hamburger. On Friday night, when Ethan himself cooked, he roasted Italian peppers over hot coals. He tossed a salad of fresh greens, goat cheese, and pecans. Grilled tromboncino summer squash was laid over brown rice with a sweet-and-hot-pepper sauce. For dessert we had sorghum pudding and fried apples and strawberry jam. Although the PA was free of drugs, alcohol, and tobacco, we celebrated with a fermented "cup of joy," a mix of hard cider and water kefir. The feast was delicious, the kind of farm-to-table spread that would cost a fortune in a city.

The Possibility Alliance used no industrial fuels. Without gas or electricity, they relied primarily on wood and the sun. Without chainsaws or trucks, they felled trees with handsaws and hauled the timber across the eighty acres with handcarts or horse-drawn wagons. Before storing the wood for winter, they cut it into lengths of three feet, a practice to discourage gorging: the stove accepted wood in one-foot pieces, so if you wanted to feed the fire, you first had to cut the wood, which not only made you think hard about how much you really wanted that extra warmth, but also warmed you in the process.

Most of the year they cooked outdoors on "rocket stoves," highly efficient steel cylinders that burned finger-width kindling. They baked cakes and casseroles and heated pails of dishwater in solar ovens, steel boxes flanked by mirrors that when oriented south on a sunny day cooked food at three hundred degrees.

But their focus was not limited to the ecological. When I was there, members had just taken the bus to St. Louis to join the protests in Ferguson. Ethan had been arrested twice in recent years, for blocking the entrance to a nuclear weapons factory in Kansas City and for blocking fracking trucks in Minnesota. They got their news through newspapers and phone calls.

One afternoon Ethan taught a workshop on the history of nonviolence while his daughter Etta squirmed on his lap. A dozen of us sat in the shade of the walnut tree, partial relief from the muggy heat. It was boring stuff for a six-year-old. She wanted to go swimming. But when Ethan read a passage from Martin Luther King's "Letter from a Birmingham Jail," Etta climbed his shoulder and whispered a question.

"A prison is usually long-term," he told her, "but a jail is just for a weekend."

He gave an example of how nonviolence doesn't always work, at least not in the short term. A group of Jews in Germany were ordered to remove their clothing before being killed. They refused. They were gunned down fully dressed, holding on to their dignity. But their refusal humanized them to the soldiers.

"Tell me that story again so I can understand it," said Etta.

"Well, the people refused to take off their clothes when the Nazis ordered them to, hanging on to their freedom to choose," Ethan said. "They were killed but their courage impacted the hearts of the Nazis. Their murderers later put down their guns and left the Nazi Party because they knew they had killed a human being, not an animal."

Etta chewed this fact silently while Ethan continued the lesson. On a recent visit with family, Etta had watched a television report about three Iraqi children killed by a bomb. She wept. She could not understand how the grown-ups were able to carry on without grieving.

"We need millions of people," Ethan told us. "Gandhi's ashram took fifteen years to start the Salt March. We are midwives of the new world. It's going to be a bloody mess, but you are birthing your dreams."

AMERICAN HISTORY IS RICH WITH UTOPIAS. Most were religious—pilgrims, Quakers, Shakers, and Mormons—but some were secular, particularly the Transcendentalists. "To be yourself in a world that is constantly trying to make you something else is the greatest accomplishment," said Emerson, championing self-reliance over conformity. "Simplify!" said his protégé, Thoreau. "Live your beliefs and you can turn the world around."

Yet Transcendentalism did not provide much practical guidance. Even by Emerson's day, it was clear that the egalitarian nation of virtuous craftsmen and farmers was not to be. Rather, with the industrial revolution under way, a gulf between rich and poor was widening, just as it had in the monarchies democracy was supposed to replace. Americans would be submitting to the "ignominious domination" of the factory, leading lives, as Thoreau said, of quiet desperation. In the first major American backlash against industrialism, Transcendentalists celebrated wildness, imagination, and spirit. Emerson insisted that "the universe is composed of Nature and the Soul."

But how to manifest a life of nature and soul in a materialistic world? Not even Thoreau had been able to support himself at Walden Pond, and had notoriously hauled his laundry to town for his mother to wash. A smattering of utopian experiments attempted to embody Emerson's romantic simplicity. At Brook Farm in Massachusetts, idealists shared the labor and subsisted on their own farming. At Fruitlands, the commune founded in 1843, members bartered, grew their own crops, ate no meat or dairy, and wore no cotton that came from the slave trade or wool that was fleeced from non-consenting sheep.

A century later communes revived the spirit of Emerson. They were part of the back-to-the-land movement, that loose exodus in the sixties and seventies from cities to farms and homesteads. The movement charters were *Whole Earth Catalog* and *Mother Earth News*, which explained how to build compost bins and dome homes, and one of its oracles was the Zen poet Gary Snyder, who proposed living in "tribes" and moved his family from San Francisco to the Sierra foothills. "Young women and men with long hair joined the work camp for comradeship, food, and spending money," he reported. "Light was from kerosene lamps; we heated with wood and cooked with wood and propane."

Not all back-to-the-landers were hippies. The elder sages were a couple of Yankee curmudgeons, Helen and Scott Nearing, who left New York to homestead in Vermont during the Great Depression and stuck with it for six decades: building a home from local stone, growing vegetables, earning a small income by harvesting sap and making maple syrup. They cut their own wood for heating and cooking, used no electricity. They bartered with neighbors and paid no interest on mortgages or bank loans. Their book *Living the Good Life*, published to little notice in 1954, was reprinted in 1970 and sold a quarter million copies, becoming a bible for the disaffected.

And the movement's heartland prophet was Wendell Berry. Unlike coastal dropouts with their polyamory and dope, Berry was a prude. In his 1977 manifesto *The Unsettling of America*, he dropped phrases like "failure of character" and "absolute good" and "cultural degeneracy" that had fallen out of favor amid the day's moral relativism. Berry lambasted the me generation's quest to find yourself as "one of the genres of self-indulgence . . . the easiest form of self-flattery—a way to construe procrastination as virtue—based on the romantic assumption that 'who I really am' is better in some fundamental way than the evidence would suggest."

Berry preached restraint—and household. The antidote to irresponsible land use was to commit to one piece of land and cultivate it. To grow food was not drudgery but sacrament, "by which we enact and understand our oneness with the Creation."

Perhaps the highest expression of the back-to-the-land movement was the Farm, the Tennessee commune founded in 1972 that eventually swelled to 1,500 members, all locks and beards, tie-dyes and bellbottoms. It began when a caravan of fifty-four school buses filled with vegetarian Haight-Ashbury hippies fled the high rent and hard drugs of the city and, like the Pilgrims of yore, set out to re-create every function of civilization according to their own values. They grew soy and sorghum, repaired autos, installed and operated telephone lines, drove an ambulance, yoked draft horses, taught school, staffed a medical clinic, delivered babies, cooked, babysat, and dug graves. The Farm's founder Stephen Gaskin recounted, "And a bunch of people that were shiftless, most of them being English majors and kilo dealers and other worthless types that hadn't worked, learned how to run tractors and sawmills and learned how to farm."

Gaskin was six and a half feet tall, and thin as a skeleton, with wiry hair to his shoulders. He donned hip-hugging slacks and a turtleneck with beads, sat cross-legged on a pillow before a flock of followers. A combat vet of the Korean War who grew up on a ranch in the

Southwest, he rapped in a musical patois that mixed jive-talking guru with redneck shitkicker.

As a lapsed Christian drawn toward Eastern religion, I liked how Gaskin blended the two, and how in a neat twist he suggested that both the secular state and the stuffy old churches were conspiring to prevent divine communion. "If you was a materialist and you find out about spirit," he declared, "everything you knew up to then was a shuck."

He repackaged religion as rebellion against the squares and hypocrites. "If you want to be a follower of Christ, follow his teachings and do like he said, don't try to make puzzles and conundrums out of other things that other people said about him." He served up Buddhism as mere common sense: "Enlightenment is not so much making it to the never-ever land through the secret passageway—it's more like getting off your tail and doing something." Right livelihood simply meant "your work should not be a rip-off to the rest of mankind."

The Farm combined all three strains: the lefty frugality of the Nearings, the old-timey morality of Berry, and the West Coast mysticism of Snyder. And it had a streak of libertarianism more Thomas Jefferson than Jefferson Airplane. "Don't take over government," Gaskin exhorted, "take over government's function." And to a remarkable degree, they did, not only providing for their own but establishing satellites across the country that did good work, from an ambulance service in the South Bronx to disaster relief in Central America. "The beatniks can't retreat from society and turn on to an economy of roach clips," said Gaskin. "We gots to do better than that."

The Farm embraced personal conservatism. Stephen proudly called his brethren the Technicolor Amish. Couples were required to marry, and artificial birth control was banned. Gaskin said, "I think that abortions as a means to giving you more sexual freedom to ball more people with less responsibility are immoral."

The focus on marriage and sexual restraint reminded me, once again, of Wendell Berry. He had no patience for sexual liberation and decried promiscuity and birth control as tentacles of the same rapacious capitalism that plundered the earth. Berry likened the trading of partners to the exploitation of the land: both were ways of desecrating the sacred. The antidote to the irresponsibility of recreational sex, then, was the bond of marriage. The meaningful life required fidelity to both place and person. This directive embarrassed me. I professed a low-impact life, and yet in my two decades of adulthood I'd lived at thirty addresses in seven states. I'd had as many girlfriends as places of residence, never committing to any.

With this unlikely mix of personal restraint and political revolt, the Farm thrived. Stephen Gaskin became a hero of the counterculture, author of nine books, featured on television with Walter Cronkite and Tom Brokaw. Fifteen thousand visitors came to the Farm each year. Gaskin's wife, Ina May, revived the homebirth movement as her book *Spiritual Midwifery*, self-published in 1975, sold more than half a million copies.

As news trucks flocked to the Farm to lap up the zeitgeist, more and more hippies streamed in. Many were fresh-faced kids from the heartland, two decades younger than Gaskin, less enamored of the weed than the plow. The Farm opened its gate to the dispossessed and the mentally ill. Pregnant teenagers were given a place to birth, a home to raise their babies. Even the FBI seemed to approve. "The Farm believes in non-violence, is vegetarian in diet, spiritual in nature, and is a self-sufficient working farm," reported the agents after four years of spying. "It is a religious-type organization and is involved in no extremist or subversive activities."

Like most utopias, the Farm's lofty ideals collided with harsh economics. A decade with shoulder to the wheel, two or three families per school bus, subsisting on soy and sorghum, took its toll. Some Farmies pined for a truck assignment so that they could sneak a Dr Pepper in town. At the height of the Farm's fame, more than four hundred residents trickled out. When men began working construction on weekends for extra spending money, Gaskin decreed that the earnings be lumped into the general fund for nearby needs like property taxes as well as far-off causes like Caribbean disaster relief. The numbers of those working extra jobs quickly declined. The Farm fell into debt, largely because of medical bills, and a lien was issued on the land. The satellite farms shut down.

In 1983, with Gaskin abstaining, members voted to end the communal structure. And so began the "changeover." Residents were required to pay monthly dues. Hundreds of Farmies went looking for jobs, which, it turned out, were scarce in Summertown. Some pounded nails in Nashville or found work in local hospitals. The collectively owned Farm businesses were privatized. Hundreds more left, many deeply embittered. Having donated their savings or inheritance to purchase the Farm, and given up the prospect of a paying career to raise children or ferment tofu in a cashless community, they were now exiled because they couldn't fork over $130 per month.

Stephen Gaskin quietly abdicated. He ceased publishing and lecturing. He remained with Ina May and their three children on the Farm, whose population had settled at about two hundred. He did not change with the times. Running for president of the United States at age sixty-five at the Green Party convention in 2000, Gaskin, to my mind, stayed valiantly true to his creed, declaring: "We are a bunch of tree-huggers and mystics and peaceniks. My main occupations are Hippy Priest, Spiritual Revolutionary, Cannabis Advocate, shade tree mechanic, cultural engineer, tractor driver and community starter." By a vote of 295 to 10, he lost the nomination to Ralph Nader.

The Farm was no longer what it had been. Having been burned by pie-eyed idealists who couldn't earn a living, it no longer embraced deadbeats. Now the membership process was as rigorous as that for joining a Manhattan housing co-op, complete with a financial audit and years of probationary phases. Behind the Farm's electric fence, baby boomers with gray ponytails putt-putted in golf carts. "We are like a gated community of not-rich people," Gaskin quipped in an interview.

When I visited, I pitched a tent in the shadow of the rusted husk of a Caravan school bus, now used for storage. Over the course of my stay I sat through workshops on midwifery and conflict resolution and permaculture. Today most Farmies live in conventional on-grid homes, work full-time jobs (or have retired from them), and buy food at grocery stores. The Farm is not a radical communitarian experiment anymore, though what exactly it has become is unclear: it's part think tank, retreat center, housing co-op, birthing center, nature preserve. And yet I was struck by how many of its once far-out experiments—homebirths, tofu, soy milk, meditation, land trusts, conservation easements—have since been fully embraced by the mainstream.

And its radical spirit? Ethan Hughes and Sarah Wilcox were among the inheritors of the tradition I'd been able to trace to the earliest days of the republic. While they cite Shakers and Transcendentalists as influences, they don't think of themselves as utopians—a term that to them implies a sort of lofty detachment from society, instead of what they see as their direct grappling with its ills. "We are just imperfect people trying to help heal a broken world," Ethan told me.

Two

Ethan Hughes and Sarah Wilcox spent their very first night in Missouri in sleeping bags on the wood floor of the old cottage. They burned candles and lit a wood fire in an old coal stove. A friend had left them a box of food in the basement, so they dined on cereal and powdered milk. Sarah was far enough into her pregnancy that it was uncomfortable to sleep on a thin camping pad. Ethan knew he would have to get a mattress soon. There was not only no furniture; there was also no toilet, bathtub, sink, counters, shelves, or cookstove. In the pantry a single spigot sprouted from the floor like a weed, with no basin to catch the water.

They had stepped into a previous century, one without plastic, carpet, plywood, paneling, light fixtures, outlets, or switches. The doors and window frames and molding were handcrafted wood, the grain golden beneath antique lacquer, and the place had the sweet musk of an old attic. Sarah loved it. It was a blank canvas on which to paint their new life.

But Ethan was struck by the emptiness of it. Two days later Sarah left to visit her grandparents in Iowa. After the ride from the train station, she had decided her belly was too big for bicycling, so Ethan walked her the six miles to the train station. Then he pedaled back to the desolate homestead and wrote in his journal.

Questioning our decision. Overwhelmed by all that needs to be done to create a self-sufficient homestead. Afraid of being judged by the conservative Christian community nearby. I only thought about ticks and chiggers as I walked the land. Barbwire everywhere. How the hell did I end up in Missouri. Holy shitballs!

Ethan Hughes had not aspired to be a farmer. Or for that matter a homesteader. His path to La Plata started with a greater ambition. He wanted to uplift all life, to help humanity save itself! Or in the parlance of comic book heroes he had always loved, Ethan Hughes wanted to save the world.

Seven years earlier, costumed in a superhero's cape and tights, he had begun his quest to do just that. In May 2000, with Al Gore and George W. Bush having secured nominations, he and a group of friends pedaled away from downtown Seattle en route to his hometown of Gloucester, Massachusetts. The journey's purpose, as stated in a letter he distributed: "to DO GOOD!!!" In addition to raising money for Habitat for Humanity and the Center for Appropriate Transport, the bedecked riders would volunteer at schools, churches, and charities. And finally: "Along our ride where ever we see someone in need of assistance we shall stop and offer our humble and spontaneous service."

The crew was a ragtag assortment of superheroes, such as Hug Man, Velvet Revolution, and Turquoise Seeker. Ethan wore a red satin cape, shorts over long johns, and a red shirt emblazoned with the letters *BE*, for his superhero name, Blazing Echidna, inspired by the endangered egg-laying, spiny anteater that dwells in New Guinea and Australia. Their first heroic act: they changed a flat tire for a family sedan. Then they helped a man load furniture into his daughter's apartment.

None of Ethan's family or friends found this behavior odd for a thirty-year-old man. Since boyhood he had loved comics and even dressed as a caped crusader when it wasn't Halloween. He was drawn to the myth of the hero who risked his life—for free!—to save the world. As a lifeguard on Massachusetts beaches, he conscripted the younger kids to don towels as capes and compete to pick up the most trash. "He never gave a shit about what anyone thinks," said his brother, Sean. "He would play with GI Joe dolls in the dorm—and people still liked him." A cartoonist, Ethan later took a summer internship at Marvel comics in New York City.

Ethan grew up lower-middle-class in the rough-edged fishing village of Gloucester. His father was a social worker, his mother a nurse. He attended the University of Vermont on a partial scholarship, worked, and took out loans, which he promptly repaid by working as a marine biologist on the New England coast and an outdoor educator on California's Catalina Island.

Ethan was exuberant and goofy and passionate. He was nearly six feet tall, barrel-chested, with close-shorn and uncombed hair. He inspired his coworkers and students to dress in elaborate costumes and perform skits and songs. He transformed into SLOP Man (Stuff Left on Plates!) to persuade kids not to waste food. He invented contests. While traveling the world with his friend Brian Thomas, Ethan decreed that when in New Zealand they would neither drive a car nor travel on buses. Hitchhiking only. Why? More fun! Brian was Huck Finn to Ethan's Tom Sawyer. Brian began to juggle on the side of the road, and Ethan drew a cartoon sign that read, WILL TELL JOKES AND STORIES, and before long they were picked up. In Indonesia, Ethan concocted another challenge: the friends would travel only in the cheapest seats available—third-class ferries and local microbuses. They lived like the locals, even learned the language. These constraints—no matter how artificial—brought them closer to the local people and made the adventure all the grander.

Ethan's playfulness was tempered by a growing grief at the state of the world. In Ecuador he visited plantations and learned that the lovable, innocuous-seeming banana caused the death of hundreds of workers, who are exposed to noxious chemicals and grueling work conditions. He saw firsthand the devastation wreaked by spills at Texaco's oil fields in Lago Agrio, Ecuador—eighteen billion gallons of wastewater in open pits. The petrol was destined for the United States, and yet when Ethan recounted what he'd seen, his friends told him he was mistaken: if something that terrible had actually occurred, they would have seen it on the news.

"It was the first time I realized that the media twisted the world," Ethan told me. "Here I was witnessing an absolute nightmare, and yet nobody was hearing about it in the States." (After more than a decade of lawsuits, an Ecuadorian court ordered Texaco's parent company, Chevron, to pay $8 billion in damages, a judgment the company refused to pay and that a U.S. court refused to enforce.) In Kenya he visited a dump where scavengers picked through heaps of garbage for anything edible or usable. He saw pickers at a flower plantation corralled like prisoners by armed guards. In high school he had pinned a carnation on his prom date. Was this where it had come from?

While these losses of innocence are standard fare for a certain type of left-leaning college graduate, Ethan's response was singular. He determined that what enabled the system of pollution and exploitation, and even killing, was his own participation in it. Through the nineties, the decade of the booming stock market and gas-gulping sports trucks and behemoth mansions, Ethan began to simplify.

This moment in Ethan's life resonated with me. He and I had led similar lives to this point: leaving the office career path and working as low-paid outdoor educators during our twenties. But then we diverged sharply. I started publishing and found a college teaching job. Ethan, on the other hand, stopped using ski lifts and started climbing the slopes under his own power. He gave away his scuba tanks and began free-diving. He stopped eating bananas. He never had an email account, he stopped using a computer, and he ceased going to movies. He gave up alcohol and coffee. Having never been especially drawn to tobacco or illegal drugs, he quit those without issue.

In 1999 he and Brian Thomas moved to Cottage Grove, Oregon, where they began an apprenticeship at Aprovecho, a center for sustainable living skills. Here he found his people. Oregon was the hub of a loosely affiliated radical movement that included tree-sitters, anarchists, and members of Earth First! and the Earth Liberation Front. Here was a place where young malcontents might stay up all night around candlelight in fierce debate about the most ethical way to start a fire. Lighters, with their plastic cases and petro guts, were anathema. What about matches? Where did the sulfur come from? And the wood? Who was exploited to make them?

Ethan was inspired by Jerry Mander's 1991 polemic *In the Absence of the Sacred*, which argues that technologies like cars, computers, and genetic modification are not neutral—in the sense that they can be used for good or for ill. On the contrary, their very design necessarily centralizes authority, disempowers citizens, and destroys nature. "I would hate to think that my work as a writer could not be done without a direct dependence on strip-mined coal," wrote Wendell Berry in "Why I Am Not Going to Buy a Computer." "I do not see that computers are bringing us one step nearer to anything that does matter to me: peace, economic justice, ecological health, political honesty, family and community stability, good work."

Ethan developed an ethos that over the years he whittled to a one-line mantra: I don't want my freedom, comfort, and mobility to require killing, polluting, and exploiting.

Ethan dwelled in a tree house. He gave away binoculars and sleeping bags and a tent, sleeping under a tarp with a wool blanket. He bicycled. He pared down his possessions to what fit on his bike. He gave away his synthetic ski jackets to wear cotton and wool from the thrift store. Forsaking laundry machines, he hand-washed his clothes and hung them on a line. He ate only local organic food, and after years as a vegetarian, he began to occasionally eat roadkill animals. He never owned a cell phone. "I was going to try what the mystics said," he told me. "You have to give away everything to gain everything."

Even as he simplified, he was vexed by a single technology that seemed at once the most destructive and pervasive. How many radicals did he know who were fiercely vegan, primitivist anarchists who still drove around in cars? Automobiles were undeniably destroying the world. They were a chief cause of climate change, not to mention air pollution and early death in collisions. Keeping the oil flowing required a worldwide military empire. Cars congested our cities, transformed them with cacophonies of revving and honking, and were unsafe for pedestrians. Driving in autos made us lazy and obese. Freeways had hastened white flight from our cities, carving segregated ghettoes on one end while gobbling up farms for commuter subdivisions on the other. So much of what was wrong with America, as Ethan saw it, was the result of a single technology, and yet damn near everyone drove one.

His revulsion was not merely political. When he was thirteen years old, his father had been struck and killed by a drunk driver. After sixteen years of grieving and debating, Ethan reached a decision in 1999. While visiting his childhood friend Tony Remington, Ethan said, "There's something I have to tell you." Tony thought maybe he was going to say he was gay. Instead Ethan said, "I'm never going to set foot in a car again."

He rode trains and buses, but not in taxis. Although he would make exceptions for emergencies, even when a car-owning friend drove to the same destination, Ethan rode his bike, or walked, or stayed home. He quit airplanes, too.

Ethan grappled with another conundrum. On the death of his grandfather, he learned that he had inherited $100,000. It was a lot of money for any young man; for one living in a tree house it was mind-boggling. Ethan had not grown up poor, but neither had he been rich. After his father's death, his mother had supported both her sons on her nurse's salary.

Ethan didn't need the money—or want it. He deposited the funds in a bank and spent a few years debating the ethical use of money. Finally the choice was clear. Ethan launched a giving spree. He gave $6,000 to a nature preserve in New Zealand that he had visited. He gave to Aprovecho, to the Center for Appropriate Transport in Eugene, Oregon, and to Oregon Peaceworks. In all, he gave a third of his money to social justice groups like Wellspring House in Gloucester and the War Resisters League, and a third to ecological projects like an outdoor school on the Chesapeake Bay where he had worked and the World Carfree Network in the Czech Republic. He donated seed money to the Grenada Chocolate Company, a "tree to bar" fair-trade, carbon-neutral enterprise that shipped its goods by sailboat to Europe, where they were distributed by bicycle.

As for the final third, he gave it directly to friends and family in what he called the Dream Fund. He gave small gifts, a couple hundred dollars, with one stipulation: The recipients were not merely to bank the money; they were to spend it on something they had always wanted to do. One friend took his wife to ballroom dance lessons. Another bought an original painting from a local artist. His mother bought a sea kayak. His gifts were not need-based. He gave three hundred dollars to a friend who had just inherited three hundred thousand dollars. One friend pinned Ethan's check to his corkboard and looked at it every morning for six months until it expired. He called Ethan to say that he had realized, finally, that he didn't need the money and would rather Ethan give it to someone else. Ethan met a girl on a train who was making dolls to raise money to save endangered species. He handed her three hundred dollars in cash. He gave five hundred to a friend, Helena Marcus, to help the students she was teaching at an inner-city school start a garden. Tony Remington burst into tears of worry at his spree, and Ethan's cousin was convinced that he either had lost his mind or was dying of cancer.

"It felt so joyful," Ethan told me, "realizing that instead of having this money in the bank—and I could be dead tomorrow—I got to actually *use energy* to create the world I wanted to see."

At the same time, Ethan began taking action to end what he saw as injustice. In 1999 he and his friends from Aprovecho traveled by train to Seattle to join the protests against the World Trade Organization. For Ethan, the WTO symbolized the worst elements of globalization: an unelected international body with no legal jurisdiction that had nonetheless thwarted laws passed by sovereign nations. For instance, the Endangered Species Act prohibited Americans from importing shrimp harvested with nets that could kill sea turtles. Asian nations challenged the law before the WTO, which sided with the shrimpers. America was forced to back down.

Political as he was, Ethan was no sourpuss. The protests were a celebration of song, games, theater. Ethan donned the garb of Woodchuck the Gray Squirrel, an unfortunate mishap of laboratory splicing. He was accompanied by Genetically Modified Man and Obvious Man, whose superpower was to call out observations like "We're on a city bus!" Ethan was a clown-provocateur in the spirit of Abbie Hoffman and Allen Ginsberg. Brandishing a carrot, he announced to onlookers that by harnessing its power, he would levitate the policemen standing by. When one of his jokes got a laugh out of an officer, Ethan turned to the crowd and cried, "At least we have one human being!"

With his two-hundred-pound frame, Ethan was not cowed by Seattle cops in riot gear. He had been studying the nonviolent resistance of Gandhi and Martin Luther King Jr. He was a good pupil because he was not afraid of violence. As teenagers in Gloucester, he and his buddies had rumbled with other kids, and he gave and took plenty of punches. During one such melee, the police arrived. Ethan snuck into the squad car and emerged gleefully sporting an officer's hat and billy club. He was arrested for larceny and obstructing an officer in the line of duty and given two years' probation.

A decade later, striding directly into a Seattle barricade in his Woodchuck suit, he was pummeled with nightsticks. But even with the adrenaline rush he did not fight back. Instead he felt preternaturally calm.

"Concussion grenades being thrown!" shouted Obvious Man. Police battered protesters, who in turn threw rocks and smashed windows. Ethan and his fellow superheroes began to clean up the mess. Ethan scrubbed the word FUCK from the window of a McDonald's. Yet the good deeds of Woodchuck were not appreciated. Instead some black-clad anarchist shouted that the Gray Squirrel was a sellout and spat at him.

Ethan left Seattle overjoyed by the celebration and unity he'd felt in the streets, but also disillusioned with the results. For all the careful organizing, the movement needed more training in nonviolence. "People were singing for peace," he said. "But once the rubber bullets and concussion grenades started, they were hurling concrete at the police." The protests reinforced the chasm between citizens and cops, perpetuating the model of a police state. Reporters had deepened the divide, focusing on the masked vandals instead of the elderly Quaker women chained in place with bike locks, leading their arresting officers in a round of "Amazing Grace." "This is the manufactured division that keeps us separated," Ethan told me. "And separation is the source of how we're in this position." What if he could re-create the joy and song and theater of the protesters but without a demonstration?

Hence, a year later, the Haul of Justice. A revolving band of a few dozen superheroes pedaled eastward over the Rockies. In Wyoming they sang the Hokey Pokey with a Salvadoran family in both English and Spanish. A car stopped and gave them a watermelon. In Missouri they rescued hundreds of turtles that were on the road. They painted more than six hundred faces. Ethan stayed in costume—and in character—from dawn, when he emerged from his tarp, until nightfall, when he crawled back under it. "I always wanted to combine Gandhi with Silver Surfer," he told me. He was a Pied Piper, inspiring strangers to assemble costumes and join the ride. They sang in hospitals, told stories in nursing homes. In Judson, Indiana, some local boys led them to the swimming hole. In Chelmsford, Massachusetts, they sang and danced with a hundred adults with learning disabilities.

Ethan discovered a way of living that he had not dreamed possible: the gift economy. The superheroes often didn't know where their next meal would come from, and yet a household of high school dropouts donated a pantryful of Pop-Tarts and orange soda. They didn't know where they would spend the night, but often they were taken in by strangers. In Mattoon, Illinois, the local police put them up in a hotel.

In October sixteen superheroes, including the Desert Queen, Ethan's mother, who had pedaled the final four hundred miles, soared to the coast and dipped in the Atlantic. Ethan didn't want to shed his cape! He was ready to keep going, but the superheroes had other commitments.

Ethan was tortured. He believed that the small joys—a song, a chance encounter, a watermelon—should be adequate. At the end of the Haul, he wrote, "In every town we would make people smile and laugh with our bells, horns and silly costumes. That alone was enough."

Yet it wasn't enough. Ethan wanted his good deeds to spark other good deeds, a chain reaction of spontaneous joy that stripped life to its wonderful essence. He wanted to rid the planet of automobiles. A superhero did not just rescue a cat from a tree; he vanquished evil from the world. But Ethan could not even convert his girlfriend and his closest friends to his cause, much less the rest of humanity. They were pursuing conventional things like marriage and careers. And as much as he told himself not to keep track of how much others contributed to the common good, he couldn't help noticing. With the last of his inheritance he had created the Superhero Fund, a few thousand dollars that along the route they'd used for good causes—buying and building a handicap ramp for a women's shelter or renting a room for a month for a homeless family. And yet, the fund was apparently outfitted with a one-way valve. Halfway across the country the money was spent. "Give what you can to the Superhero Fund!" Ethan exhorted his fellow travelers. But nobody did.

He took the train to Michigan, where his girlfriend of four years, Kitty Kat Calamari—also a part-time superhero—had just begun medical school. But as Clark Kent knows, once the cape is removed, maintaining a relationship is tough. Kitty Kat felt the best way to serve humanity was through modern medicine, a path that seemed incompatible with Ethan's. And by the time he arrived in East Lansing, she had met someone else anyway. The heartbroken Blazing Echidna lugged his bike onto an Amtrak train heading for Oregon, hoping to move back in with Brian Thomas. Upon arriving at Cottage Grove, however, he discovered that Brian was setting up house with his new girlfriend—his future wife. Pity the superhero!

Ethan was alone. His superpowers seemed to have evaporated. Maybe, he thought, he would just wander off into the woods.

IN FEBRUARY 2001, Sarah Wilcox arrived in Oregon nursing a vision. She wanted to live close to nature, and she wanted life to be beautiful. She picked vegetables from the garden and flung them in the pan, never following recipes. She detested foods that suffocated in plastic wrappers. She preferred the glow of candles to the glare of lightbulbs. She hated the itch of polyester against her skin and adored smooth cotton, light linen, and soft wool. She collected secondhand fabrics and sewed her own clothes without a pattern, cutting and stitching by instinct. She loved the crackle and pine perfume of a woodstove, and she choked on the recirculated huff of gas furnaces and the metallic whiff of glowing electrical rods.

She had been this way as long as she could remember. On a family trip to Amish country she had seen a horse-drawn buggy and begged her father to buy it. Growing up in Houston, the daughter of teachers, she pored over back issues of *National Geographic* and *Sierra* magazine, enthralled by wild nature and indigenous tribes and heartbroken by their looming extinction. She devoured stories in *Greenpeace* about rebels who risked their lives to save dolphins and redwoods. In high school, while touring Europe with her father and his college history students, she swooned for French culture: the language and cheese, the poetry and art, the villages and rolling pastures of hand-piled haystacks. She sang opera. She sewed robes and costumes to don at Halloween and the Renaissance Faire. During a semester abroad in Cameroon she became fluent in French and drew an invitation to hunt forest rats with Bagyeli Pygmies. She enrolled in a permaculture course on the Navajo Nation and herded sheep for a summer, living happily without electricity or plumbing.

Sarah knew that she could never achieve her vision alone. It was too much work, too much isolation. Like so many utopians before her, she knew that only a community based on shared values could succeed. Arriving in Oregon, she began a nine-month apprenticeship at Lost Valley, a community for simple living. Their vision was less radical than hers—they used electricity—but they at least taught organic gardening. It was a start.

After college at Grinnell, in Iowa, where she majored in anthropology, she had forgone the competitive world of professional singing and instead worked as an au pair in Switzerland, then moved with a boyfriend to Japan to teach English and repay her college loans. When she revealed her desire to move to Lost Valley, her boyfriend was proud that she was following her dream, but he didn't want to live in an intentional community. After their seven years together she went to Oregon without him. She observed, seeping up from within her, a small prayer: *If there is someone out there who can help me manifest this vision, let him appear.*

A few weeks later, Sarah was invited to a May Day celebration. From an old sheet she sewed herself a white cotton dress. She feasted and danced around the maypole. Despite her Methodist upbringing, she didn't bat an eye at the pagan tropes. In high school she had become disillusioned when her minister had remained silent during the first Gulf War, as Sarah believed that the core of Christianity was peace. She'd started a recycling program at the church, only to see parishioners amble past her bins and toss their soda cans into the garbage. Around the same time, Sarah's mother announced that she would stay home on Sunday mornings and tend her vegetable garden; she felt closer to the spirit there. Mother and daughter dabbled in Zen meditation, and Sarah's parents eventually became Quakers. Repelled by the patriarchy of Christianity, Sarah studied earth-based spirituality. In Japan she and her friends had invented their own rituals, including eating eggs and seeds to celebrate spring.

As night arrived, the May Day revelers gathered around a heap of kindling and logs. Something stirred overhead in the tree limbs. With a snapping of branches a creature fell to earth, a silhouette brandishing a flaming baton. On closer inspection, they saw that it was a man, naked, his head shaved bald, bedecked with moss and garlands of leaves. "I am Spring!" the satyr bellowed, and between writhing in the mud and darting past the woodpile, he delivered a soliloquy about the renewal of life, the sap coursing through his blood. He commanded the revelers to remove their shoes and feel the earth between their toes. He thrust his torch into the pyre, and a giant bonfire crackled in the night.

That night as Sarah zipped up her sleeping bag in one of the group tents, she found herself beside this odd beast. He was certainly not her type: she imagined herself with an introvert, a lover of classical music and poetry. The druid—or whatever he was—offered to tell her a bedtime story. She consented. He recounted a Maori myth of a mist maiden, the story of how rainbows were born. Sarah was charmed, and freezing. So he suggested that they zip their sleeping bags together.

"No, thank you," she said, but in the morning when he asked to see her again she told him to ring the house at Lost Valley.

A few days later the creature called and asked her on a date. She resisted. He called again. She begged off, asked if he'd take a rain check.

"I'd take a thousand rain checks."

Sarah agreed to meet him at a party at Lost Valley. He would ride his bike the forty miles to get there. As she waited she realized she felt giddy. She had not dated much since high school. She'd had only the one boyfriend, and they had met the first day of college. She felt somehow betrothed already to this stranger. She fixed herself a whole quart of chamomile tea.

When he arrived, the two peeled away from the party and walked along the creek to a green pool. "I'm going to jump in," Ethan said, and asked if she wanted to join. Sarah just about choked. She'd been tempted by the creek, but the water was too cold! And besides, although she knew that skinny-dipping was normal in Oregon, she had never actually done it.

"A friend of mine just told me that anytime you want to jump in a body of water but don't," Ethan said, "you lose part of your life force."

Heart pounding, Sarah dropped her clothes in a heap on the fir needles and splashed into the cold. She felt alive.

THREE-PART HARMONY FOR HER, the Hokey Pokey for him. Despite the aesthetics gap, if there was one man in America capable of helping her create her vision, it was probably him. After all, she had prayed, and this answer had come. And they had this much in common: they both liked capes.

At the end of 2001, Sarah and Ethan moved into a cottage near Aprovecho, in a place called Echo Hollow. She worked as a French tutor and on an organic draft horse farm, while Ethan taught biology at a public Quaker high school. Sarah made tinctures and salves and candles. They kept one room in the house free of electricity. Although both had been vegetarians, they began to eat local meat, pulling roasted chickens apart with their fingers. When Sarah revealed that she had studied opera but given it up, Ethan said, "Put on a concert for us!" Ethan would not scoff at anybody's dream. He believed that life was short and precious. He cried freely. Sarah had never met anyone quite like him.

As Ethan plotted the next superhero ride, Sarah sang with the Eugene Symphony and landed a part in the chorus of *Carmen*. Singing made her feel a oneness with spirit, close to God, she said, "the richness and beauty of life and creation pulsing through me."

Even as they inspired each other, they realized just how out of touch they were with the rest of America. Their friends who lived simply tended to be isolated from politics. The ones deeply involved in social action were using cars and planes and computers. But Sarah and Ethan simply didn't want the things that others wanted—not even what their milieu of Oregon radicals wanted. "People thought we were crazy because we didn't want to go to Burning Man," Ethan recalled, "didn't want to go to Reggae Fest, and didn't want to go drive into Eugene for dessert at the vegan chocolatier."

As far as Sarah could tell, nobody in America was living the way she wanted to. Of course there were the Amish, Mennonite, and Hutterite colonies, but these folks were born into the tradition, taught the skills from birth, and often inherited the land. Sarah and Ethan were born and raised in Mammon; how could they escape it?

Their dilemma lies at the heart of why people choose to leave the mainstream and become homesteaders. The pleasures of rustic life—the clean living, the clear skies—are generally not enough to justify an existence of voluntary hardship. To stick with it, the motivations must also be economic and ethical. The grandparents of the back-to-the-land movement, Helen and Scott Nearing, did not flee the city to Vermont merely for pastoral bliss. Their goal was to be "independent from commodity and labor markets, not interfered by employers." The Nearings did only the minimal amount of "bread labor" to meet their material needs and spent the rest of their hours in leisure and study and activism. Their second goal was to improve their health by living closer to the earth and eating natural food. Finally, their ambition was ethical, to free themselves from the "cruder forms of exploitation: the plunder of the planet; the slavery of man and beast; the slaughter of men in war, and of animals for food."

Their book *Living the Good Life* remains as bracing as a faceful of ice water. It is one half revolutionary manifesto, of the type broadcast by human megaphone at New York City's Zuccotti Park sixty years later during Occupy Wall Street: salvos against the "gambling centers" of the finance world and the "domination by the wealthlords" and the "entire apparatus of a competitive, acquisitive, exploitative, coercive social order [that] is rigged and manipulated for the rich and the powerful and against the poor and the weak." The other half is a homesteader's how-to that prescribes the specifics of pouring concrete down to the fraction of an inch: "On the ends of the studs we nailed a piece 7/8 x 3 x 6 feet, thus making a shallow box, exactly 6 feet long, 18 inches wide, and 3 inches deep on the inside."

A teetotaling geezer born just two decades after the Civil War, Scott Nearing was an unlikely hero to libertine baby boomers who trusted no one over thirty. He was an ornery professor with a PhD in economics who had been fired from the University of Pennsylvania in 1915, after lambasting state-sanctioned child labor, and blacklisted from further college jobs for espousing antiwar socialism. He'd even gotten booted from the Communist Party because his tract on imperialism contradicted the Leninist orthodoxy. In reporting the excommunication, the *Daily Worker* sniffed, "Nearing's non-Marxian conceptions disable him from giving the self-sacrificing service which the hour demands."

The Nearings' critique of power resonated during the Vietnam and Watergate era, and they were inundated with pilgrims. "Keep out of the system's clutches and you have a chance of subsistence," exhorted the old couple, "even if the oligarchs disapprove of what you think and say and do." Yet Scott never warmed to the new ways. He railed against the "dances, gossip-bees and beer parties" of his new Vermont neighbors. "They were vacationers at heart," he snorted, "not workers."

Some seekers, perhaps expecting a sort of cozy country inn, did not survive the austerity of the alleged good life, least of all its breakfast. "Ah, there came the rub," wrote the Nearings. "No coffee, no cereal, no bacon, no eggs, no toast, no pancakes or maple syrup. Just apples, and sunflower seeds, and a black molasses drink. Such a fare sent many a traveller on his way soon enough. . . . They came to us all days of the week and we served them raw cauliflower and boiled wheat!"

Toward the end of his life Scott Nearing lamented, "This affluent, drugged, debauched, corrupted, polluted, deluded nation is a country I never envisioned in my youth." Decades later, when the Nearings were deceased but their books still in print, Sarah Wilcox was drawn to their ethos. Yet the Nearings had supported themselves through lecturing and publishing. Sarah wanted to wrest a living from the land, as her ancestors had done on the Iowa frontier. What's more, the Nearings had started their experiment late in life, when their children were already grown. Sarah hoped to raise a family while homesteading.

After a lifetime of believing in peace in the abstract, Ethan saw the United States rattling for war in Iraq. He registered as a war tax resister and vowed to earn less than the nine-thousand-dollar threshold that required paying federal income tax. In February 2003, he and Sarah marched in Eugene, part of a worldwide demonstration of eight million people in six hundred cities. It was the largest war protest in history, but the event hardly made the evening news.

Ethan was infuriated not just with the president and other war makers but with his own allies who could not seem to unite. The tree sitters accused the Buddhists of merely meditating and sipping green tea; the monks replied that the anarchists needed to seek inner peace. The activists accused the homesteaders of watching the world burn from their safe haven; the farmers retorted that flying on jets to rallies and eating fast food in the airport wasn't going to save anything.

Ethan delved deeper into the teachings of Gandhi and Jesus and the Buddha. Pounding away on a thrift-store typewriter, he composed a forty-page rant against the war. Then he scrapped it and started over. "The last few months I have been swept up in the fear," he wrote. "Yes, it got me out into the streets, but it also got me labeling other human beings. Ignorant, foolish, evil, and greedy are a few of the words that have been living in me."

Ethan concluded that the answer lay not in confrontation, but in faith. "I am stepping down from the debates and the facts. Instead I am standing with a simple verse from a remarkable soul who said 'Love one another . . . love your enemies, do good to those who hate you.'"

He announced that for the entire month of March he would leave work and sit in silent prayer. "What would happen if I started trying to love George W. Bush?" he asked. And meditate he did, straining to love George W. Bush, and Saddam Hussein, and the liberals who drove in cars to protest an oil war. Though over one hundred people joined him, Ethan's prayers were ignored; midway through his vigil, American forces roared into Baghdad.

That summer solstice, Ethan arrived at Sarah's place of work leading a steed and dressed as a prince. He wrapped her in a blue cloak and carried her off blindfolded on horseback to what he called the Enchanted Land of the Sun, which turned out to be a rose garden where he pulled away the blindfold and performed the dance of the blue-footed booby. Sarah accepted his proposal. That evening he led her through the woods to a clearing where he'd built a bed of fir round-wood. They listened to the twilight and dawn calls of the Swainson's thrush and gazed at stars while he told stories of the constellations. Ethan loved everything about Sarah: her ethics and aesthetics, and her glass-shattering laugh that sounded to him like the soul itself.

But it wasn't long before Ethan again told Sarah, this detail-oriented introvert who loved working with plants and animals, that his first commitment would always be to the world. Sarah's mother took Ethan to sit beneath an apple tree by the creek and dished out the tough advice of a Midwestern matriarch. Ethan should not be a husband or father, least of all with her daughter. He ought to join a monastery, and free Sarah to marry a carpenter, a homesteading type. Yet Ethan wanted to be a husband and father. What's more, Sarah wanted to marry him. Defying her mother's advice, the couple remained engaged.

In the fall of 2003, however, disheartened by the war, their path forward was unclear. Earlier Sarah had had something like an epiphany. "I smelled the smell of fall blow in the breeze, and I knew I had to go to France and learn about goats and goat cheese," she told me. French peasants had been raising goats and making cheese for centuries; surely some could teach the craft, and how to live without electricity. Ethan's first response was, "Fine. I'm not going." He was planning another superhero ride. But now Sarah persuaded him, and in the spring of 2004 the couple traveled by train and Greyhound to Montreal, where they boarded a freighter loaded with tons of peas. Thirteen days later, trailed across the Atlantic by a flock of birds pecking at the cargo, they disembarked in Spain and pedaled to the Pyrenees.

After a long climb by bicycle and a steep hike, they reached Mas de la Griffe, a rustic homestead amid stone ruins and flowing springs. No roads, no cars. Their hosts were former Parisians—he a bouncer, she a hairdresser—who had fled the city to herd goats in the mountains. Sarah and Ethan were assigned to milk forty animals morning and night. Sarah learned to make ricotta, *lactique*, *fromage blanc*, and *tomme*. "I'm in love with goats now, and I feel quite competent w/ cheese," she wrote to Brian Thomas, determining that no matter how badly she messed up, she always wound up with something edible. "We've had freak occurrences of emmental, camembert, oozy-drippy cheese, a botched batch of tomme that Ethan poured wrong so we had to bread and fry it—yum!" They set up house in a restored pigsty.

Meanwhile Ethan packed sixty-kilo loads onto a donkey named César for treacherous runs into the village. "How humanity ever turned in a donkey for the automobile I will never know," he wrote to Brian. And yet he was acutely aware of the ways in which the farm fell short of purity. At night, to watch movies, their hosts ran a gas generator that vibrated the stone ruin. Hay and feed were delivered by helicopter. They drove in a car to the border to buy organic vegetables. And the goatherds' dream of building a road up to their secluded valley broke their hearts.

After a month they set off by bicycle for Ramounat, an off-grid collective founded by French and German radicals in the sixties. There was no telephone. Two days of pedaling brought them to a trailhead, where a member of the community met them and led them half an hour on foot to a village of beautiful handmade structures and rebuilt stone ruins. "I was preparing to let go of my expectations of finding a truly petroleum-free farm," Ethan wrote, "when SHABAM, Sarah and I walked into the most incredible place we both have ever seen."

Like the hosts at Mas de la Griffe, the homesteaders at Ramounat were not traditional peasants. But when they had arrived decades before, they had learned their skills from the disappearing farmers and herders around them. Sarah and Ethan reveled in the abundance: 300 kilos of blueberries harvested, 60 kilos of sauerkraut fermented, 450 gallons of water hauled uphill to water the leeks. The community grew almost all they ate and were masters in the art of preserving food. In the cellar Ethan and Sarah nibbled the last of last year's beets; the next day they pulled and ate the first beets of the new season. The only items imported were butter, flour, cooking oil, medicine, and— this being France—coffee and cigarettes, which fueled their hosts through epic days of planting leeks, sunrise to almost midnight with no lunch, just a short break to gulp from a decanter of fizzy, fermented blueberry juice. They sneered at Ethan's battery-powered headlamp and called him "Las Vegas." Instead of phones they yoo-hooed across the valley. A frog colony outside the latrine gobbled up flies.

"How peaceful it is here with only the sound of the birds and the flies," Sarah wrote. "I'm outside now in the shade near the clothesline, looking out over the valley, a perfect breeze blowing toward me the smell of sun-drying hay, cut fresh this morning—just pure and simple tall grasses mixed with wildflowers."

What thrilled Ethan more than the simplicity was the ideological victory. "No cars, no power, total independence from this insane globalized world!" Herding goats and scything hay might appear quite ordinary, he mused, "not a threat at all to the industrial-global-war complex, but it is! In fact it is the greatest threat to it because these families do not depend on the system anymore." He determined that living outside the system "is dependent on one main factor: not skill, not knowledge, not circumstance, but choice. It is that simple. You make a choice. No excuses, no arguments for or against, no hypotheses, you just choose."

As Ethan waxed philosophical, Sarah cataloged the peasant ingenuity of spring-fed aqueducts: "The main channel runs through the upper gardens, down past a little seed-starting cloche, then curves around toward the house, where two smaller branches channel water." For her, the true test of an ideology was whether it delivered the dishwater, and she devoted a full page to the hydro-specs, in which one ditch poured "to a beautiful large rock and cement sink-basin built onto one of the walls of the house (where dishes and clothes and food are washed and drinking and cleaning water is collected for the house (no indoor plumbing))," while the second, "hoses water into a goose and duck pond."

Meanwhile Sarah and Ethan were falling more deeply in love, far from the causes and people that had absorbed him. "I was astonished to have so much time with him, and was enjoying it greatly," she wrote. "Now I think I'm spoiled."

Peering into the future, though, she didn't see quite how it would work. She was ready to get married and start a family; Ethan was waving the flag for revolution. "I'm in love with a wild man," she wrote, "and to him it feels like I'm restricting him with these timelines of having children, finding a place, etc."

And two crucial elements were missing at Ramounat: spirituality and activism. The couple left for yet a third community. They rode a train to a tiny mountain village, then followed a bent sign through the dilapidated stone walls of an eighteenth-century village. A pair of wolf dogs howled from behind a fence. The place seemed deserted. Sarah and Ethan pushed their bikes along a rocky wooded trail, arriving at what appeared to be a medieval convent. A turret of red brick rose from green hills. A woman welcomed them through the old wooden door.

The Ark had existed for more than sixty years, she explained, after being founded by an Italian disciple of Gandhi after World War II. Without electricity or tractors, its members plowed with horses to grow tons of wheat and potatoes, risked arrest to block nuclear power and GMO crops, and hosted refugees. Cows grazed in pasture. Sarah and Ethan were led to a cell in the hamlet, furnished with hand-crafted wooden chairs and oak candleholders. Sarah swooned. The Ark combined all that she found beautiful: artisan crafts, zero fossil fuels, and Francophilia.

That night they attended evening prayers in the courtyard. The dozen residents wore hand-woven woolen shawls. A bundle of boughs was lit and the flames licked at the underside of a shade tree, shadows dancing on the stone walls. In French they sang the prayer of Saint Francis, first the men, then the women, then together, four strands of braided harmony, the voices of angels resonating off the bricks. Sarah gazed at Ethan through tears and saw that he was weeping, too. They had found what seemed like home.

Three

I gathered with the group for another Experience Week session. Ethan put a question to us: "What would you attempt if you knew you had no chance of failure?"

A thought slithered into my mind, a thought so wrong and shameful that it walloped me with nausea. As the rest of the circle shared their dreams—virtuous plans to save the coral reefs, minister to refugees, start a nonprofit school—I concealed mine like a switchblade. I certainly wasn't going to reveal it to these exemplary youngsters. Indeed, it would be years before I ever spoke it aloud.

My turn to share was approaching quick, and I had to think of something acceptable to say. I blurted out, "If I knew I wouldn't fail, I'd write a book that could change the world, change people's hearts." This won me a few approving nods.

It wasn't until much later that the scope of my self-disgust sank in. Because here is the thought I'd had: If I had no chance of failure, I'd have a fling. Why not? Couldn't I have the love and commitment and respect of my marriage with a harmless dalliance on the side? But the idea filled me with shame, so I told myself it had just been a little joke. But was it? The mere existence of the thought suggested that it expressed my true desire. Or was it just a case of church giggles, my lifelong habit when pressured to access my heart to instead say the most glib thing I could think of? I didn't know. And what about my wife? Just weeks after our wedding I felt I'd already spoiled our vows, failed her, revealed my truest self as unworthy. Even writing this three years later I fear my privilege to admit these flaws comes at the expense of her humiliation. I felt sick and guilty.

What a fraud I was, presenting myself as some purveyor of the virtuous life when I didn't have a grip on my own longings. How was I any different from the hypocrites who preached that we shouldn't use fossil fuels while they flew around the globe on airplanes to tell more people they, too, shouldn't use oil and gas? Or the ones who preached against cheap industrial food while they bought gourmet grub with their trust fund or the wages from a job that, thanks to the same industrial forces, allowed food to be cheap? Or the guru who taught renunciation of earthly cravings as he satisfied his own with a harem of disciples? Here I was, writing a book about how domesticity might save the world, and I was struggling with its most basic premise: fidelity.

Did I really want what my mind claimed to want? Having the occasional fling sounded alluring; like, if I could smoke heroin for the rest of my life without overdosing or getting addicted or falling sick or going broke, would I do it? I'd love to! But that's not what heroin is. And I didn't think that a marriage failing was just a possible outcome of infidelity: I thought that infidelity was the definition of a marriage that had failed. I knew plenty out there disagreed, and some made compelling arguments in defense of open marriage and polyamory. But I didn't think it would work for me. Having girlfriends—or whatever they were called—around town would be like having a little stash of black tar in the pantry.

My inner house was out of order.

Ethan led an icebreaker called milling. Each of us picked another person from the group, and then the partners faced each other, clasped hands, and gazed into each other's eyes. And that was it. The point was to communicate without talking. To actually look at each other. Now, I know this sounds kind of bizarre. But having done similar things in my years at Outward Bound, I liked them: they made me feel quickly closer to strangers.

I found myself paired with one of the apprentices. Her legs were pocked and bloody from chigger bites. As we stared at each other, I felt her eyes pooling with emotion, some combination of sorrow and tenderness. My own chest swelled. And then time was called. We switched partners.

I paired with another woman, and we began. This time, we were allowed to say something to our partners if we were so moved. If one person spoke, the other was not to respond. Just to listen. So the two of us stood there, eyes locked, and I was growing skeptical of the efficacy of this exercise. I wanted to participate, but I was afraid to say something meaningful to someone whose name I didn't even know. Then I remembered my superhero mission and thought, Why the hell not. With a crack in my voice I said, "I just got married. And I'm terrified."

OUR WEDDING CEREMONY had been traditional, complete with singing of hymns and readings from scripture. At the moment when the priest bound our hands with a silver rosary, I felt like the ocean, that there was more to me than this body, and not only that my union with Cedar would outlast this lifetime but that it had preceded this life, that our souls had been bound together in some other realm ages before we had even been born.

Which was strange, because I was more or less an atheist. My parents are Christians of that increasingly rare variety: liberal mainline

Protestants. They met at a Presbyterian seminary—my mother a Southern Baptist, my dad a Presbyterian who got a badge on his Boy Scout uniform for not missing Sunday school for three years—where social justice trumped theology. They resolved to let us find our own way.

The church in which my brother and I were raised had retreated from dogma to the point where it was hardly religious. There was no talk of hellfire or damnation, and very little of Jesus. My parents sang in the chorus of the church productions of *The Sound of Music* and *Damn Yankees*. As teenagers we took ski trips. When I was twelve, I attended several weekends of confirmation camp, during which we were instructed to sit quietly for a long while and let the spirit enter us. I felt it, sort of, a humming in the room, in my head.

It didn't stick. What I remember most about confirmation—and what affected my path more immediately—was that I kissed a cute girl from our sister church in Palos Verdes. Shortly after I was confirmed and given my own Bible with my name embossed in gold on the cover, my parents allowed me to decide whether or not I wanted to continue going to church. I stopped.

Cedar's parents were Catholics who converted to Buddhism about the time she was born, then became lay ministers who held a weekly service in their home. Cedar took the Buddhist precepts as a girl and continued to practice as an adult. She struck me as an unusual combination of radical and conventional: on the one hand she didn't eat meat, rode a bike everywhere, and marched to block the World Trade Organization in Seattle; on the other hand, she regularly went to services with her parents.

I had begun to meditate and attend along with her family. Buddhism appealed to me in ways Christianity had not. Most important, I wasn't required to believe any of it in order to practice. And that's what you do in Buddhism: practice. That was something I could accept more readily than converting, or even praying. I could practice. Maybe one day I would get good enough to make the team.

IN THE MIDST of the independence movement in India, a young pilgrim in search of Gandhi was disappointed to find the Mahatma sitting half dressed in the dirt, spinning cotton thread with a wooden spindle.

"Is this the weapon with which you are going to drive out the English?" said the youth.

"I hope, my son, you do not take the English for our evil," said Gandhi. He predicted that the English would leave of their own accord as soon as Indians drove out the evils that had kept them enslaved. Serenely spinning his thread, Gandhi listed all he loved about the English: their open minds, appreciation for science, lack of superstition, respect for women, courage as sailors and explorers. "Finally, I love their love for the freedom they have been able to win so early and keep so long, the freedom they claim to be bringing us even while subjugating us and which they promise to grant us some day."

Gandhi insisted that India had not been conquered by Britain's might but seduced by its promises of leisure and comfort. "The English have degraded us, warped our nature and reduced us to dust. Not from wickedness, nor by force of arms, but by the quiet gnawing of trade and civilization. India's conquest was not an invasion by a people but the operation of a trading Company."

The solution, as Gandhi saw it, was to deprive these merchants of their profits by refusing their products. The greatest direct action of the Indian freedom movement, the Salt March, was not a call for revolution but an insistence that instead of being forced to buy salt from the British, Indians should be allowed to harvest it from the ocean, as they had for eons before the empire. As for Gandhi's incessant spinning, it, too, was an act of civil disobedience. India had grown its own cotton, linen, and wool for centuries, spun its own thread, and woven its own fabric. Colonialism changed that: now the raw materials were shipped to England, spun in mills, and returned to India as commodities. Indians now needed money to buy them, and the outsourcing of the weaving had left millions of Indians out of work. The preindustrial system—the spinning wheel—was for Gandhi not merely a superior technology but the seed of an economy of justice.

"You must make with your own hands whatever you need, and be satisfied with whatever your hand can make, or with its equivalent," Gandhi warned the young man. "But if you dispense with work for any other reason than illness, you should know that you are living by the labour of others, and you must ask yourself if you are not taking part in abuse."

This sort of thinking drove Westerners nuts. Among his imperial oppressors, Gandhi inspired as much rage with his couture as with his politics. Winston Churchill sneered that Gandhi was "posing as a fakir . . . striding half naked up the steps of the viceregal palace." Even Gandhi's admirer George Orwell belittled his "home-spun cloth, 'soul forces' and vegetarianism," adding that "his medievalist program was obviously not viable in a backward, starving, over-populated country."

Westerners inspired to replicate Gandhi's political victories still tended to shy away from his peculiar austerity of raw and unspiced food, third-class trains, homemade loincloths, and celibacy. But for Ethan and Sarah, the spinning wheel was the piece that unified their two visions. Simplicity was both an aesthetic and an act of dissent. A wicked means, such as colonialism, never justified a desirable end, such as inexpensive fabric. If one wanted to live nonviolently, he could not use products that were produced through the violence of coercion and exploitation. To wear cotton garments produced by slaves was no different from owning and abusing a slave. The person filling his tank with gasoline was in the same ethical position as the corporation clear-cutting the Amazon and displacing Indians.

Gandhi articulated what Ethan and Sarah had felt all along. Riding a bike was not just riding a bike; it was a boycott of the fuel industry that waged wars and destroyed indigenous people. Milking your own cow—and then butchering it—was resistance against feedlots, subsidized genetically modified corn, slaughterhouses, plastic packaging, and supermarkets. Singing on the porch was a boycott of Hollywood and the electricity cartels.

When their visas expired, Ethan and Sarah returned from France ready to overhaul the United States. "This culture is lost and a revolution does indeed need to happen now," he wrote. "A revolution that is recreating how we move, eat, laugh, entertain, and love each other and ourselves." Ethan conceded that technology was serving some purpose other than destruction, but said, "We can have an even higher level of inspiration, sharing and connecting . . . without having to oppress other human beings, ecosystems and lifeforms."

They had given up on reform. "Reform has got us where we are now," Ethan told me. "All the wonderful liberal politicians—there's more corporate power in the government than ever. All the reform of the environmental policies—there's more species going extinct per day than ever. So I was never a reformist."

Yet they could not spark a revolution by themselves. They planned an open forum to discuss forming a new community. Eighty friends came to their slide show (solar-powered, of course), and dozens signed up to help. At their wedding in 2005, Ethan and Sarah asked their friends, in lieu of gifts, to donate to their project. They collected $10,000. But as the meetings continued, enthusiasm dwindled. Faced with the prospect of actually forsaking computers and cars, friends were noncommittal.

In the spring of 2006 the newlyweds returned to France, this time determined to spend three years at the Ark and to have a child there.

But once Sarah became pregnant, the thought of starting a family far from their own families and friends was daunting for Ethan. What's more, the Ark had fallen into factions of modernists and traditionalists, as a slim majority voted to bring electricity within its stone walls. The couple could not wait for others; they would simply act and hope others joined them.

One friend had already stepped forward two years earlier with a firm commitment. Helena Marcus had known Ethan for years, ever since they'd taught outdoor education together. She'd ridden with the superheroes under the alias Love Ninja. Helena had been shocked and inspired when Ethan had given her the five hundred dollars from his inheritance that she'd used to start a garden for her class. "I had never witnessed someone really living their convictions like that," she told me. Years later, she systematically gave away the $200,000 she'd netted in the sale of a house during the real estate bubble. She considered the windfall a gift. "I didn't want to just let it go on buying stupid stuff."

Helena visited Ethan and Sarah at the Ark and had pledged $100,000 to their project. Together they wrote up a charter for "A Movement for the Upliftment of All Beings," a translation of the Sanskrit word *sarvodaya* that Gandhi had invoked. It would be based on "complete non-cooperation with any and all systems of violence, abuse, oppression and inequality. Thus, our land will be a sanctuary, free from the industrial paradigm, which by its belief in growth, profit and convenience can only add to the suffering for all living beings."

In long discussions, Ethan and Sarah articulated the twenty criteria that would allow them to create a Gandhian village:

To allow them to be car-free, yet not isolated, the place would be
- Within five miles of public transportation, preferably Amtrak
- Within biking distance to a college town
- Within biking distance to an existing intentional community

To allow them to grow sufficient food, the place would have
- A year-round water source
- Plentiful rainfall and a long growing season
- Preexisting food systems such as orchards or fish ponds
- A diverse ecosystem for foraging

So that they could be electro– and petro-free, it would
- Have preexisting off-grid buildings
- Have no building codes, which would allow them to build inexpensively and use natural materials
- Be near the Amish, from whom they might learn skills

To allow them to perform service, as opposed to just escape industrial problems, it would
- Be within two hours of a big city
- Have damaged land that could be restored

To let them live in beauty, it would have
- Close proximity to nature
- A swimming hole in a pond or a creek
- A designated wilderness or national/state park within ten miles

For their community to grow, it would have
- Affordable land
- Adjacent land and houses for sale
- Zoning that allowed for multiple families to dwell on the property

Last were their two personal preferences:
- An opera
- An ocean

Ethan and Sarah held hands and prayed for help in finding such land. And then, before they had spread word of the plan to friends in America, they got the call from the friend who had found the Amish farm in La Plata, Missouri, that met eighteen of their twenty requirements. Ethan and Sarah leapt at it. After Ethan had drained what was left of his inheritance, they had been gifted $10,000 at their wedding, and there was Helena's $100,000. They needed another $50,000. They were opposed on ethical grounds to paying interest on a mortgage, and in any case a bank probably would not have financed a house that lacked electricity, gas, and indoor plumbing. They sent word to their friends in Echo Hollow and the Superhero Alliance: they needed to raise the rest of the money in three weeks. And the money arrived, in dozens of small donations: the gift economy at work. By the end of January 2007, they had secured the funding, and their offer was accepted—Ethan, Sarah, and Helena were owners of a Missouri farm.

NO SOONER HAD THEY ARRIVED in La Plata than Ethan was flung into doubt. "Overwhelmed," he wrote in his journal. "Kicking through piles of plastic and rusted steel. Confusion: things break, important information ends up in the fire, books are lost in the mail and the plumbing leaks." Like others before him who felt they had been called to create a better society, he wondered if he had gotten the wrong message. "The universe seems more interested in having me surrender than actually install[ing] any infrastructure for living simply."

Ethan slipped into depression. His doubts about Missouri intensified the stress of becoming a father. He suffered yet another relapse of the Lyme disease he had contracted a decade earlier, and some days as his pregnant wife planted trees and hoed the garden, Ethan lay miserably in bed. Helena had not yet arrived, and the community still had only one other resident, twenty-year-old Katrina Gimbel, who was dazzlingly competent at gardening, planting, and cooking, but who was nonetheless just one person. A late frost killed most of the fruit blossoms. They had committed three years to this experiment, and Ethan was already counting the days. He told Sarah they should admit defeat and start searching for something else.

It was not the first time Sarah's fierce vision for a simple life conflicted with her love for a man. And her easy smile and lovely singing voice belied a will as steely as that of her pioneer forebears.

"If you need to go, then go," she told her husband. "But I'm staying here."

She told him that if he found someplace he liked more, he should spend a few months there alone to be sure it suited him. She wasn't willing to follow him on some quest. Forced to decide, Ethan chose Sarah.

The birth of the baby, just four months after their arrival, put his commitment to an even harsher test. After three days of home labor, the midwife sent Sarah to the hospital. For the first time in years, Ethan rode in a car, racing with his wife in his mother's sedan to Kirksville, the closest major town, fourteen miles away. A healthy girl, Etta, was delivered, but days later Ethan rushed with Sarah back to the hospital; she had a life-threatening blood clot. She was bedridden and medicated for nine months. The family had no health insurance. The hospital bill topped $17,000. Since they had no income, it was paid by Medicaid. Accepting aid violated Ethan's goal to live independent of the government, but while they were willing to forsake lightbulbs and cars for their beliefs, and though they were willing to risk their lives for some of those beliefs, this was not one of them.

Caring for a sick wife and a newborn proved too difficult on the farm. The family spent three weeks with Sarah's parents, who had rented a house in La Plata to be near them. As they and Ethan cared for Sarah and Etta, Katrina ran the farm the best she could. Chores went undone. Ethan had always known that he and Sarah could not go it alone, but now they urgently needed additional able bodies. Dire times required dire measures. Using his mother-in-law's email account, Ethan sent his first—and only—email: a plea to the superheroes for help.

But nobody showed up. The revolution had stumbled at the gate. Ethan itemized his grievances in his journal:

- Poison oak everywhere, impossible to walk in woods in the summer.
- Many skilled visitors planning to come for a month or longer did not actually ever come, none of them.
- Another donor offered funds and then reconsidered.
- Someone w/ no skills, a bad back and a small motion disorder is the only help so far from nearby ecovillage. Ha!

He railed against the spiritual teachings that had led him this far. "I have been following your god damn eight-fold path for years now. I am not smiling. I want to kill somebody. . . So kiss my ass Buddha."

One day, he pedaled fourteen miles along the highway to Kirksville to pick up an order of bulk food with the bike trailer. On the way home a thunderstorm burst, soaking the rice and flour. Then his tire popped. He huddled on the shoulder, patching the flat, as semis blasted by. "I've never been suicidal," he told me, "but at that moment I wouldn't have minded if one of the trucks just did me in."

The family returned to the homestead. Finally a lone superhero answered Ethan's call. CompashMan, a.k.a. Christian Shearer, flew in from Korea, where he had been teaching a permaculture course. He stayed six weeks and alongside Katrina and Ethan whipped the place into shape. They survived through the fall and winter largely on turnips.

Ethan began to see that landing in Missouri was not bad luck but the logical destination of his life's path. He had set out to reverse the damage done by global capitalism. But globalization's victims were not in the places he loved: the Massachusetts beaches and California islands, the Vermont mountains and Oregon forests. Those places prospered in the consumer economy. They had that intangible thing that Americans seemed to value above all: lifestyle. They had ski hills and seashores and national parks. They had universities that attracted start-ups and wine bars and indie bookstores. It was admirable that Americans had come to appreciate natural beauty, and were willing to pass laws to preserve it and pay a premium to live near it. But these places were becoming as exclusive as New York and San Francisco: to live there you had to work in some thriving industry like finance, tech, or entertainment, which were the ones that benefited most from globalization. People who worked in "old industries" like farming and manufacturing could not afford to live in these scenic, vibrant places.

One advantage of the Midwest for Ethan was that land was cheap, which was a result of economic stagnation, which was a result of global economic forces. While coastal cities and college towns thrived, the heartland declined, both its factory hubs like Detroit, Cleveland, Gary, and St. Louis, and its thousands of farm towns like La Plata. Family farmers had been pressured during the Nixon years to compete on the international market, lured deep into debt by low interest rates to buy big machinery and more land. With fewer humans required to cultivate larger tracts and with profit margins thinning, farm towns declined. When the Fed raised interest rates to stop inflation, farmers who had relied on easy credit suffered. President Jimmy Carter's grain embargo had the unintended result of dropping the bottom out from under wheat prices. More small farms failed and were gobbled up by big farms that required fewer farmers. The population of farm towns dwindled.

The survivors, to remain competitive, bought the latest petro-fertilizers, pesticides, and GMO seeds. The romanticized American version of a farmer milking cows and picking crops beneath blue skies was increasingly being replaced by that of a farmer doing something like factory work: applying toxins with gigantic machines.

Meanwhile, in the towns, the mom-and-pop hardware stores and grocers tried to compete with Walmart and Home Depot, which set up outposts twenty miles away. These big-box stores were the true geniuses of globalization, having figured out how to bring products from China to the Midwest to sell more cheaply than the goods actually manufactured in the Midwest. Free-trade agreements allowed factories and farms in Mexico to undersell those in America. Local jobs on farms and in factories were replaced by those in sales and customer service, most of which paid minimum wage and lacked the benefits of union factory jobs or the self-determination and equity of owning a farm. As economic security dwindled, the one thing that remained relatively inexpensive was gasoline, allowing Midwesterners to drive from shuttered villages like La Plata to the nearest big-box stores in Kirksville. La Plata, much more than Eugene, was the kind of place where Ethan's vision of a neo-agrarian revolution could do the most good.

What's more, Ethan was learning that he had more in common with his conservative Christian neighbors than he did with the radical activists back in Oregon. On the night of his and Sarah's arrival, their neighbors Don and Dana Miller had stuffed the stove with wood to welcome them. They lent them a card table and folding chairs and invited them to dinner the first week. Ethan cringed at their framed, autographed portrait of George W. Bush, but the fried chicken was tasty. (Isn't it always?)

He saw that their neighbors shared so many of his values: a commitment to physical labor, frugality, and doing things yourself rather than paying someone else to do it or make it. While buying supplies at the hardware store, he told the clerk about how his Oregon friends had been forced to demolish a cob house because it wasn't up to code. "If the county tried to tear down a house here," said the man, "we'd meet them at the gate, and it wouldn't happen. And if it did happen it would be over my dead body." Nobody in La Plata was bragging that their coffee from Guatemala was fair-trade or that their coconut ice cream from Thailand was organic. Don and Dana Miller ate their own cows. Both families had moral qualms about supporting the federal government with tax dollars. And though they might use different vocabulary to describe it, both families tried to live an ethical life based largely on the teachings of Jesus.

By year's end, Ethan's exuberance had returned. "This is an update from the only petroleum-free, electricity-free, and car-free center of its kind in all of North America," he gushed in a letter to donors. "We are a sanctuary and educational center committed to outward service, political and cultural change, simple and sustainable living, inner work (prayer, meditation and present moment awareness), and hospitality."

Despite the setbacks, they had planted more than 250 native fruit and nut trees and created four vegetable gardens. "Our flock of chickens is up to 35, and two pregnant goats have joined us and will be kidding in February, which means milk, yogurt and cheese!" He noted that his family and Helena were "still living under the poverty line, which enables us to be war tax resisters and socially and economically stand by our vow to 'love our enemies.'" He specifically thanked the "amazing neighbors, Don and Dana Miller, who have supported us in so many ways, from lending us their wheelbarrow for 9 months, supplying rides to the hospital and hosting our families when they visit." Ethan and Sarah had hosted a hundred visitors, started a bike co-op in Kirksville, and joined local farmers in blocking corporate pig farms from colonizing the county. And they had come up with a name for their experiment: the Possibility Alliance. The revolution was under way.

E. F. SCHUMACHER SUGGESTED that small groups would better steward the land than gigantic companies and governments, and that solutions to large-scale problems lay in "intermediate technology"— later known as appropriate technology—that didn't rely on constant inputs of oil and electricity. One such appropriate technology, of course, was the type of small-scale farming advocated by Wendell Berry: free from chemicals, pesticides, and oil. One area in which the PA had most intentionally utilized appropriate technology was building. The old cottage had just two bedrooms, and as the community grew, they needed more structures. After five years in the front bedroom of the cottage, the family built and moved into a tiny home nicknamed the Honey House. Just as a homegrown tomato tastes better than one picked two weeks before ripening, coated with wax and dyes, and shipped from California on a truck, a naturally built house simply *felt better* than new, conventional homes. The Honey House was solid, earthy, and comfortable. The walls were constructed with straw bale and plaster, and were nearly two feet thick. Rapping against them with a knuckle produced a solid thud instead of a hollow tap. They smelled good.

The size of the structure alone expressed dissent with the American norm, where the average house is 2,600 square feet. The Honey House, where Ethan and Sarah and two children now lived, was just three hundred square feet. There was a nook for a bedroom, and a little kitchen with a sink and a small wood-burning stove. The house was lit only by sunlight and candles instead of glaring electric bulbs. Wood and direct sunlight through the windows provided heat, which the thick walls were extraordinarily efficient at conserving.

Equally important as the end result was the amount of energy expended during the house's construction. At each step they tried to avoid industries that prioritized speed and efficiency over pollution. The modern American home was a potpourri of off-gassing synthetics like fiberglass, plastic, resin, vinyl, glue, petroleum, latex, and foam, all of which were regulated as toxic during the manufacturing process yet decreed safe once transformed into habitat. The Honey House contained virtually none of these concoctions. What's more, the house required much less "embodied energy" than it would have with conventional materials. Embodied energy is the amount of carbon required to manufacture a product. For example, a conventional wall is made of wooden boards, gypsum Sheetrock, fiberglass insulation, and paint, all of whose raw materials are derived from logging, mining, and drilling, then shipped to a factory or mill to be processed, then shipped once again—using gasoline—across the country to your local Home Depot. Although the price of these items and the time required to install them might be quite low, the embodied energy is high.

The materials for the Honey House walls—straw, mud, sand, Amish lumber—used no high-impact industrial processes and were procured locally. A nearby farmer grew the wheat for the straw bales. Unlike fir and pine, which take decades to regrow, wheat regenerates every year. The bales had traveled only a dozen miles or so. True, the farmer had used industrial machinery such as a tractor and truck to harvest and deliver them, but the embodied energy was tiny compared with that of conventional materials. Amish sawyers who felled the trees and milled the boards didn't clear-cut the way timber companies did. The plaster came from clay dug twenty feet from their home. It was dug by shovel and transported by pail and wheelbarrow into tubs, where it was mixed with water and sand and straw the old-fashioned way, with a dozen visitors—including me—marching in place, pants rolled to thighs, kneading the adobe with bare feet. The embodied energy of that process was zero. Windows and doors were purchased secondhand, thus not only preventing further manufacture but also pulling from the waste stream, avoiding participation in the mainstream economy, and saving money. The house was built without power tools.

The parts of a home requiring constant industrial inputs were eliminated altogether. No wiring or sockets or light fixtures or appliances. No gas line connecting to the power grid. No water heater or furnace or air conditioner. No pipes draining to a septic tank or county sewer. An outhouse stood fifty feet behind the house, to be moved to a new site every year, when the hole beneath it reached capacity.

The alliance did make several concessions to modernity. "All the screws and bolts added up in cost and industrial impact," Sarah told me. PVC pipes delivered water from the catchment to the kitchen faucet, then drained the gray water into the soil. The roof was tin. They decided that the industrial products they used would conserve far more energy over the course of decades than less efficient alternatives. And in the future they would try to learn to make alternatives, such as cedar shingles and mortise-and-tenon joints.

Perhaps the best example of appropriate technology was the implementation of passive solar design. While solar panels require massive and expensive industrial inputs in their manufacture—from the mining of minerals to the electricity of the factories to the gasoline used in transporting them—passive solar required no such inputs. Simply put, passive solar meant orienting the house toward the south and installing windows on that face. In winter, when the sun was low in the sky, it burned through the windows most of the day, heating the thick walls, which in turn retained the warmth even after dusk. In summer, when the sun rose high in the sky, an awning over the windows blocked the sun, cooling the home. (Well, the awning was *supposed* to block the sun, but due to a trigonometry error in the design, it needed to be rebuilt.) This system avoided the loss of power caused by transforming sun into electricity and then back into heat, as required by solar panels.

The Possibility Alliance implemented other appropriate technologies to perform life's basic work. They washed laundry the pioneer way: with a washboard and wringer. All year round they hung it on an outside line to dry. During the hot summer they reduced the need for baths by jumping in the pond every few hours. In winter they heated water, which they poured over themselves in a claw-foot bathtub. "I love the sound of the water trickling on the tub," Sarah told me. "It's like music."

Transportation presented other challenges. At first the alliance had aspired to learn horse-and-buggy skills from their Amish neighbors, but Ethan nearly toppled the cart on his first test drive. Then they learned that, outside of the Amish, modern Americans with the necessary level of equestrian experience tend to be the extremely wealthy, and the extremely wealthy were not arriving to apprentice at the alliance to share their skills. So except for the occasional successful foray to the train station with their buggy to pick up guests, for the time being they relied on bicycles. Not only did they have the fleet of bikes I saw hanging in the warehouse, but they had a fully equipped bike shop. They regularly rode the six miles to La Plata and the fourteen to Kirksville.

Once a year Ethan and Sarah loaded the girls into bike trailers and hauled them to La Plata to board the train for the two-day ride to visit family in New England. The footprint of trains and buses was far smaller than that of cars and airplanes, was their thinking. One of Ethan's mantras was that in limitations we find abundance, and this was certainly true for train travel. He and Sarah did not miss the anxiety of traffic jams on the way to the airport, or the invasive checkpoints on the way to boarding, or the cattle-car conditions on the plane itself. The standard Amtrak seat was as big as a first-class seat on an airplane. Passengers roamed at will. There were no seat belts. Ethan made friends in the lounge car, joined late-night sing-alongs in the canteen with his guitar.

The problem with Amtrak, however, was that no matter the destination, the journey took approximately forever. Delays and missed connections were standard. Riding Amtrak took longer than driving a car—and cost more than filling the tank. And pity the traveler whose destination did not lie on one of Amtrak's dozen or so lines; that pilgrim was cast into the darkest ring of the public transport inferno: Greyhound. Here the charming eccentrics of the Southwest Chief and the California Zephyr were replaced by migrant laborers, the recently paroled, and those who carried their possessions in cardboard boxes rather than in suitcases.

For Sarah and Ethan, these circumstances, too, were in the Gandhian tradition; even at the height of his influence, the mahatma traveled only by India's third-class trains. "Greyhound is the fast track to enlightenment," Sarah told me with a laugh. "You have no rights. No respect. You might lose your luggage at any moment." She and Ethan often observed some frazzled passenger at the ticket window on the verge of tears, shouting about the barbaric conditions or some outrage that had just transpired. *Must be her first time,* they would think.

The primary upshot of living without a car was that Ethan and Sarah rarely left the Possibility Alliance. Vacationing required huge swaths of time and quite a bit of money. While La Plata was a short bike ride away, there wasn't much to do. Ethan might ride to Kirksville once a week for a political meeting, which usually required spending the night so he wouldn't have to bike home after dark. Sarah and another resident went to Kirksville periodically to sing in the choir.

This isolation required—or inspired—residents to create their own entertainment. Fridays was porch night, in which they gathered to tell stories, perform skits, and sing songs. They played piano as well as fiddle, guitar, banjo, and flute. Residents were uncommonly musical, and in addition to loose sing-alongs of "This Little Light of Mine," they improvised three-part harmony to traditional hymns. When *The Hobbit* arrived in movie theaters, the PA staged its own live-action version. Still, if there was one element of pop culture that Ethan missed, it was the blockbuster sci-fi flicks that he and his brother had loved as kids. After Ethan quit watching movies, both brothers missed the tradition. So when Sean asked him to go see a movie together once a year, Ethan agreed. One Christmas, while in La Plata, they went to see *Avatar* in Kirksville. The temperature was five degrees. An hour before Sean and their stepdad loaded into the car, Ethan bundled himself in sweaters and coats and boots and set out on his bike to meet them at the theater.

Finding so much satisfaction in this life made Ethan all the more evangelical. And he was not shy to press visitors on their choices. Talking to the Experience Week group while sitting beneath the walnut tree, he took aim at our most beloved consumer good: the computer, which he insisted had become a more destructive technology than the automobile. The smartphone resulted from a global industry of mining, toxic manufacturing, grim factory conditions, and the dams and coal plants that supplied the electricity—none of which its users ever had to see. "Would you be willing to have a rhino-sized load of toxic chemicals in your home? And twenty-five hundred gallons of wastewater?" Ethan asked. "Because that's what it takes to produce a single computer." What's more, the Internet—the whole network of servers running 24/7 to store cat photos—burned more fossil fuels than the entire airline industry. Ethan had no tolerance for cyberutopianism. "People say computers are democratic, but ninety-three percent of the world does not own a computer," he said. "One billion don't have access. And if seven billion had a computer, we'd all be dead."

Ethan disputed the accepted belief that high technology is more efficient than low. Of course a man could cut down trees faster with a chainsaw than a handsaw. It was more efficient *for him.* But you had to consider the total output of energy used in building and running the chainsaw, from the minerals mined to the factory workers, the transportation from China, and the gas and oil drilled to keep the thing running. By that rubric, he said, the handsaw was the more efficient tool.

Ethan was hypnotic, disturbing, prophetic, inspiring. He challenged us to make a vow, then and there, to stop using a single piece of technology. "I want to invite you to look at all your beliefs deeply and see if any are limiting you in any way," he said.

As a rule I resist this sort of proselytizing. And yet I considered the amount of time I spent online, my inability to quit. When it came my turn to speak, I dropped the pretense of objective journalist. I was not willing to quit the Internet, but I thought up a compromise. "I'm going to stop bringing my laptop home at night. I'll leave it in the office," I burst out. I looked around the circle anxiously, waiting for someone to giggle at my milquetoast promise. Nobody did.

That week I participated in the PA's version of conflict resolution, when a married couple who were visitors bravely volunteered to bring to the group what appeared a minor dispute. I was amazed by the intimacy and effectiveness of opening up to near strangers. Within an hour the couple discovered that the "minor" matter represented deep changes in their life about parenthood and mortality that they had yet to articulate. And the fact of confronting this publicly, with supportive friends, made the problems seem entirely manageable. Cedar and I had gone to premarital counseling once in Missoula, and found it helpful, but at $200 per hour, we never went back.

After a few days at the Possibility Alliance, my skepticism evaporated. I was ready to move in. I liked Ethan and Sarah and everyone else I met. More than that, I was inspired. I wanted my life to be more like theirs, this combination of handmade simplicity, inward examination, and outward engagement. And I wasn't alone: the rest of the visitors were having similar flashes of epiphany and hope, and calls to action, and we talked a lot about things we would do differently when we got home. I walked down the country road to reach a hilltop with a decent signal and called Cedar.

"This place has it all," I gushed. "The simple-living part, but also the activism and the spiritual side. We should really come spend some time here."

I heard the far-off rumble of someone's tractor.

Finally Cedar said, "I already have a spiritual community."

By the time I stumbled back to the kitchen, I must have looked rattled, because Ethan took one look and said, "Is everything all right?" I had known him only a few days but I already trusted him enough to reveal my fears. In that, too, I was not alone, as Ethan over the years has served as counselor and confidant for hundreds of friends and visitors. I told him that I felt that, because she had been religious her whole life, my wife didn't take me seriously when it came to matters of the spirit. In that realm, I'd never be more than her follower.

Ethan chewed on this information. "What do you think is going on for her?"

I blinked. I had forgotten to ask her that question.

BOYCOTTING INDUSTRIAL FOOD AND FUEL was more straightforward for Ethan and Sarah than excising themselves from the financial system. They did not believe that money per se was evil, but there were elements of the finance system that they chose not to support. They believed that the most destructive elements of civilization—the plunder of rainforests and the genocide of indigenous people for oil exploration—were funded by international banks. When you deposited your life savings in the bank, as Ethan had done before giving away his inheritance, the dollar bills didn't just collect dust in a vault. The bank invested your money as it chose, and you had no control if what it chose resulted in deforestation or fracking. When opening a checking account for the Possibility Alliance, Ethan and Sarah researched until they found one—ShoreBank Pacific—without ties to military and fossil fuel industries.

But that wasn't quite enough. They simply did not believe that money was to be saved. Money embodied energy and action, and they wanted it put to good use. As a result, one requirement of joining the PA was that full-time members give away all their savings and investments. To be clear, they were encouraged to give that money to someone else, not to the community (or its founders). The other full-time member, Dan Truesdale, who had worked as a chemical engineer before joining, split his savings between donating to outside causes and investing in infrastructure for the community, buying, for example, a dairy cow and a log arch, a preindustrial forestry tool. The idea was to not keep anything in storage but to have full faith in the land, the community, nonviolence, and God. It was a vow of poverty, similar to that taken by monastics throughout the ages—and more recently at the Farm.

Having two children had raised the threshold under which Ethan and Sarah could continue, thanks to poverty, to be war tax resisters, to about $20,000 (it varies year to year with changes in the tax code). At the level they earned, they would have qualified for a yearly earned income credit, but they opted not to file at all.

In order to open their programs to people of all incomes, they devoted their energy to creating alternatives to the money economy. The first of these was what Ethan calls the "reduction economy," which, simply put, meant that by reducing their dependence on purchased goods, they increased their actual wealth. By eliminating utilities, Internet, cars, and insurance, the Possibility Alliance survived on a yearly operating budget of $9,000, consisting of just four expenses:

property tax, bulk food, city water, and telephone service. Of these, the $300 tax bill was the only essential. "If we don't raise nine thousand dollars, we can cancel the phone," said Ethan. "Then we can cancel the water and boil from the pond and collect rainwater. Then we can stop buying food and eat only what we grow."

This might not fit everyone's definition of wealth. But it freed them from earning income. Members and apprentices were not required to pay rent or dues. Instead, everyone performed six hours a day of "bread labor" that directly contributed to the community's survival: gardening, building, chopping wood, cleaning, milking. Each day one person served as cook, providing three meals for the others. In the words of Gandhi disciple Lanza del Vasto, who founded the Ark in France, the goal was to "find the shortest, simplest way between the earth, the hands and the mouth." The thirty hours per week of bread labor were far less than the hours the average American worked, and it left plenty of time free for activism, music, prayer, and play. So the wealth created by the reduction economy was not one of material things but of time.

The second alternative was the "creation economy." This encompassed any effort to mimic the ways that nature creates abundance without the input of money. It could be something as simple as harvesting seeds to plant, turning one squash into many squashes. The PA planted peach pits and gave the seedlings away, in order to bring more peaches into the neighborhood. "Two tractors, no matter how hard they try, no matter what position, can never reproduce," said Ethan. "But two draft horses can reproduce."

Neither of these two economies, however, would raise the annual $9,000 that the PA currently spent. They employed a third alternative: the gift economy, in which people give what they have—money, labor, goods—without the expectation of receiving anything in return. The hope is that all the gifts will eventually distribute themselves more or less evenly. The two-week permaculture design course, complete with room (tent) and board, cost nothing, to remove the economic barrier that has made permaculture largely a movement of privilege. Comparable courses offered elsewhere cost upward of $2,000. There was a two-year waiting list to enroll. Some participants made big financial contributions; others gave nothing. A superhero named SuperStretch took the course one year, then returned the next to volunteer as cook for the entire course.

I found the gift economy deeply appealing, and also perplexing. After nine days at the Possibility Alliance I wanted to make a donation, but had only thirty dollars in my wallet and no checkbook. My credit card was useless. I offered to drive to Kirksville and fill my car with bulk food. But Ethan said they didn't need food at the moment. And besides, I felt that car-delivered, store-bought food would affront their low-carbon bioregional diet.

"If you want to make a gift, pay it forward," Ethan said. "Give to someone in your own community."

I had a long drive to Montana to contemplate this proposition. I didn't donate much money to charity. I never gave to panhandlers. In Bozeman, I stopped at a market where a man in camo fatigues and a rucksack held a sign asking for money. Rightly or wrongly, I took him for a veteran of Iraq or Afghanistan. I asked where he was headed.

"Boston," he said.

I gave him my thirty dollars. Later that fall I gave five hundred dollars to the temple where my wife and I were married and three hundred to a nonprofit that recycled bike parts so anybody could build their own bike for free.

Other visitors to the alliance gave money directly. A young philanthropist named Aron Heintz wrote a check for ten thousand dollars after spending a few hours walking the property with Ethan. After mostly paying off its initial debts, each year the PA received enough in donations to cover its operating budget. They tithed 20 percent of every gift given, to other causes. Ethan and Sarah were also repaying the $17,000 that Medicaid had paid for her earlier hospitalizations, giving it directly to neighbors with medical bills.

"I hope that through our contributions we are making it up," Sarah said. "I don't want to abuse the system."

PARADOXICALLY, Ethan and Sarah's escape from dependence on industrial civilization relied in part on civilization's discontents, on the physical labor of members and apprentices and the financial contributions of visitors and guests. Their donor Aron Heintz was a Yale graduate who made a fortune in computers in the nineties, then quit the business to search for a more meaningful life. In 2004 his quest landed him at Dancing Rabbit Ecovillage, forty miles from La Plata. Techy Stanford grads had founded the place after an exhaustive search based on criteria similar to those used by Ethan and Sarah. They'd concluded that with its affordable farmland, plentiful water, and lax building code, northeast Missouri was the ideal place for radical simplicity. By the time Heintz arrived, Dancing Rabbit was thriving, with dozens of members. Another nearby intentional community, Sandhill, had existed for decades, and a third, Red Earth Farms, split off from Dancing Rabbit in the early 2000s. (These communities were one factor that brought Ethan and Sarah here.) These three experiments, along with the Possibility Alliance, had bestowed on northeastern Missouri—NEMo for short—a red territory in a red state, the unlikely mantle of current national proving ground for radical utopias.

Heintz had been drawn to Dancing Rabbit by his conviction that modern civilization was on a disaster course. Studying the history of empire, he concluded that America had overreached its resources, which was why it now had to extract them from other nations. "I was looking for structures that will be the next phase of humanity," he told me. "Now in the United States there's not much chance to rewrite the economic system. We're stuck in the 1700s with what the British left us."

Convinced that an actual revolution would not occur, Heintz wanted to help design a model that would spread virally. "What happened in the American Revolution was that a new idea spread around the planet, kings and queens were overthrown by parliamentary systems, which in turn improved our own democracy." He found the replicable model he was seeking in intentional communities: their sharing of resources, village intimacy, consensus governing, and small carbon footprint. In Ethan Hughes he recognized the requisite vision and charisma. "He's a maven," Heintz told me, "and it takes a connector." What's more, Ethan and Sarah weren't just talking radical simplicity; they were living it—as much as anyone who's not part of an indigenous culture can.

And the model was already spreading. One family from Nevada with two small children lived for a season at the PA and then launched a similar project in urban Reno, buying a foreclosed fixer-upper for $49,000 and living without electricity, petroleum, or a car. A PA apprentice started an off-grid farm in California called Loving Earth Sanctuary. A group started an urban farm in Kansas City called the Shade Tree Collective. On an adjacent thirty-acre parcel, a former apprentice named Adam Campbell launched the Peace and Permaculture Center. All these projects were partially funded by Aron Heintz, who estimates that he contributed about $20,000 to the Possibility Alliance, $45,000 to its offshoots, and lent another $30,000 at zero interest to Loving Earth.

He also lent $120,000 interest-free to acquire the eighty acres adjacent. Ethan and Sarah's close friends Brian Thomas and his wife, Teri Page, in partnership with another couple and a single woman, formed a land trust and built off-grid homesteads.

"I wanted to find something at the cutting edge," Heintz told me, "that can become a movement."

IF SUCH A MOVEMENT has a name, then perhaps it is permaculture, the philosophy I'd often heard invoked on my travels but whose essence proved maddeningly difficult to pin down. The word was coined in the 1978 manifesto of Tasmanian farmer-scientist Bill Mollison and his student David Holmgren, who defined "permanent agriculture" as "an integrated, evolving system of perennial or self-perpetuating plant and animal species useful to man." Estimates of their scope of influence were modest: the system had "caught the imagination of hundreds of people in Australia where [they had] given verbal descriptions and short resumes." Yet between the discussions of humusphere, protein inefficiencies, symbiotic interaction, and blackbirds as table meat, in a subchapter innocuously titled "2.2 Modern Agriculture Refs. 1, 6, 27, 29, 3," the authors dropped an intellectual grenade: "The energy now needed to produce these crops far exceeds the calorific return from them."

For eons, humans had transformed sunlight into food, through the growing of edible plants and animal feed. In recent decades all that changed. Modern industrial farming relied not on the sun but on fossil fuels, refined into pesticides, fertilizers, hormones, antibiotics, and the oil and gas needed to transport food hundreds of miles to market. Our farming system represented a *net loss* of energy. Whereas sunshine was infinite, oil would one day run out. In the meantime, the damage of industrial farming to the world's soil might be irreversible.

Permaculture originated in a movement to cure our addiction to oil, but over the years it had metastasized into a culture of its own, a secular framework for a quasi-religious attempt at purpose and meaning, and a set of beliefs that permeate all elements of life, from science and technology to finance and spirituality. It was hard to resist its utopian appeal. What if we could clean up Superfund sites with mushrooms? Could we replace New Orleans levees with swales and food forests that would not only prevent flooding but also provide sustenance? I was captivated by the idea that permaculture could heal the world, and luckily its most full-throated advocate lived in Missoula. I looked him up.

Paul Wheaton, a former code writer, ran the world's most popular permaculture online forum, Permies.com. Wheaton was large, in charge, and unabashedly evangelical. "I quit my career because I found this information and I needed to get it out there," he told me over dinner at a farm-to-table café in Missoula. "These people aren't going to hear about this unless I tell them." A bear of a man in denim overalls, with shaggy hair and an unruly beard, he told me that Permies.com had received 1.3 million visitors in the last month. "Permaculture is taking off because I'm making it take off."

Unlike at most clearinghouses of ecological information, at Permies there was little hand-wringing to be found. You weren't asked to sign petitions or call your congressman. That government had failed us was an accepted fact in these forums, which nurtured a carnival of anarchist grassroots self-empowerment through action, with Wheaton as ring-master, heckler, and cheerleader. In one of his more popular videos, Wheaton upended the assumption that compact-fluorescent lightbulbs conserved energy and claimed that the industry that produced them was a publically subsidized greenwashing boondoggle that deluded citizens while enriching the bulb manufacturers. But his performances were not dour. He drew a stick figure that he referred to as "Mr. Stinkypants" to represent the CFL industry. Indeed, the video parodied the scientific seriousness of environmentalists: a hip woman in a white lab coat, with a clipboard and a stopwatch, was seen repeatedly calculating how long an electric light must be on in order to perform basic household tasks like pulling a coat from the closet (8 seconds) or peeing (28 seconds). Wheaton concluded that more energy could be saved—along with billions of dollars—if instead of distributing high-tech lightbulbs, the power companies simply gave away clotheslines.

Permies is fun and funny. Through it, thousands of users report and discuss their experiments with everything from backyard chickens to hugelkultur, a method of burying logs in earthen mounds as the basis for gardens, a nifty function-stacking that stores nutrients and moisture in the soil while sequestering the carbon of waste wood that might otherwise be burned. The folks on Permies tended to be hands-on, less theoretical and philosophical. Even the neophyte could grasp such articles as "Using a Cast Iron Skillet Ain't So Hard," "How to Render Lard," and "Bug Killer You Can Eat!" Although permaculturists shunned some technology, most were not Luddites; they shared with cyber-utopians a belief that in the free exchange of ideas lay our salvation. Wheaton's prescription for lowering heating bills: dial back the thermostat and place a cheap electric heating pad on your chair and another under your feet. I've tried this. It works.

In so much of the climate change movement, the attitude is that the problems are insurmountable and the only solution is electoral politics. Whether or not this is true, it breeds a sense of hopeless paralysis. At Permies, however, the attitude is that in the best-case scenario, the wisdom of permaculture would spread to the masses (and the elected officials) before it was too late, averting a climate catastrophe; while in the worst-case scenario, those of us with kick-ass food forests would be prepared for doom and post-carbon living.

With this kind of innovation and enthusiasm, you'd think that permaculture would by now be a household word, something taught in schools. Yet for complicated reasons, permaculture remains stuck on the margins. Most techniques have not been rigorously studied and there-fore have never been proved or repudiated, giving rise to accusations of pseudoscience. One farmer I met compared permaculture courses to selling Avon products on the pyramid model: after paying for the class, the only thing one was qualified for was teaching it to others.

But the true believers harbor no doubts. "What would you do if you knew the way to end all wars?" Wheaton asked as I bit into a locally sourced beet burger. "Would you sit on it? Or would you spread the word?"

I asked how permaculture was going to end all wars.

"Because today's wars tend to be energy-based," he said, adding that every American paid about $8,000 in taxes for the war in Iraq. "And you really don't have any say in it. So you can go and get your protest sign and be angry about whatever war we happen to be in. On the other hand, if you do this, we can eliminate the number-one reason we go to war."

His nominee for the innovation that would bring peace for our time? The rocket mass heater, a homemade furnace so efficient that you can hold your open palm over the chimney. There's no heat or smoke or pollution because everything gets burned. Whereas conventional furnaces gobble valuable resources like wood or gas, only to create waste in the form of smoke and escaped carbon, these devices transform waste into a valuable resource: heat. "There was a guy who heated his house one winter with nothing but junk mail," Wheaton told me, his voice rising. "There are a lot of people heating their homes with nothing but the branches that naturally fall off of the trees in their yard. For home energy use for the average American, seventy-five percent is for heat, so if half of Americans heated their homes with something like this, that would put such a massive dent in our energy needs that it would eliminate eighty percent of war."

When I pressed him on these numbers, Wheaton conceded that rocket mass heaters alone might not actually end war—just one of the main justifications for war. "If nothing else, we've killed many birds with one stone." Yet the stoves could be difficult to perfect, and I met at least one couple who, even after following online instructions and investing hundreds of dollars, had never gotten theirs to work properly.

Nonetheless, for advocates, permaculture transcended farming and presented a cure for a world drunk on fossil fuels. To a degree it resembled Alcoholics Anonymous, with its twelve steps to end addiction. Some of permaculture's twelve principles were truisms that might appear in a self-help tract: "Integrate rather than segregate," "Use and value diversity." Indeed, number four, "Apply self-regulation and accept feedback," was uncannily similar to AA's number ten, "Continue to take personal inventory, and when we are wrong, promptly admit it."

As with all recovery programs, at the heart of permaculture lay a gorgeously empathetic view of human nature: people aren't inherently wasteful and greedy, but fall into those patterns because of the temptations of the modern world. We have slipped from grace—fallen into depression, addiction, boredom, and drudgery—because we live in homes that don't face the sun and because we eat from gardens that require either toxic poisons or bone-aching labor. But through discipline and restraint—and with the help of good design, permaculture's version of a higher power—we shall be redeemed. And no myth is more alluring than alchemy, the elusive magical process through which we might transform our most wretched waste—junk mail— into our most precious element: world peace.

Four

Back in Missoula, I told friends about my inspiring visits. I proposed we all set up some sort of meeting in which we offered one another supportive and free counseling, but when nobody leapt at the idea, I got embarrassed and dropped it. When I told them about this community that practiced Gandhian nonviolence, I was often met with a smirk. "And these people are white?" they said. I felt a flash of humiliation, so I kind of smirked along with them. What did a bunch of middle-class white people know about Gandhi anyway? I held the same opinion of most Westerners—myself included—who dabbled in yoga or meditation or Buddhism. In fact, while Eastern teachings on peace and selflessness resonated with me more strongly than those of my Christian upbringing, I had to acknowledge that the messages were virtually the same. Sometimes I felt like a mere snob, forging some exotic path toward enlightenment while dismissing the religion of my heritage as fodder for the gullible and obedient. True, I couldn't find much to admire in most expressions of American Christianity, which had once condoned slavery and segregation and the killing of Native Americans and which continued to endorse war and lethal injection, to persecute gay people, and to sit passively as we devoured the planet. As a kid I had boycotted hymns because I found the lyrics stupid. But was it such a badge of wisdom that I now sang a Sanskrit mantra, my ignorance of its meaning allowing actual bliss? It seemed I was willing to praise the Lord only in a foreign language.

I maintained my pledge to cut down on the Internet. I canceled service at my office. Twice a day I carried my laptop down the alley to the laundromat, where I poached WiFi and checked email. I left the computer at the office at the end of the day. I spent less time seeking evidence of my failures, more time outside, more time reading actual books, more time cooking and sitting at the dinner table with Cedar. We argued less at bedtime about whose turn it was to wash the dishes. Ethan's challenge actually worked. I spent less time with the Committee. Aside from whatever trees and rivers I was saving by using less electricity, I found that I was happier.

WHEN I RETURNED to La Plata a year later, I rode public transportation. The trip required four buses and an overnight train and lasted twenty-eight hours. I could have driven it in eleven, spending half as much on gas as the price of the ticket. Traversing flyover country by public ground transportation revealed a side of America I'd rarely glimpsed in its metro airports. I did not see dot-commers buzzing from Silicon Valley to MIT, or Hollywood execs rushing to a Manhattan meeting. The seats were filled with segments of the population becoming more invisible: the poor, elderly, infirm, obese. The per-capita rate of cigarette smoking was high. Mennonite clans with beards and bonnets chatted in German, occasionally emitting some incongruous phrase like "Amtrak rewards card." A mother asked the conductor if she would be charged extra for a Hefty bag stuffed with pillows and blankets.

Despite all that, or maybe *because* of it, riding the train was fun. After dark the conductor announced through the intercom that all musicians should report to the canteen. I found myself with a professional jazz trombonist from San Francisco en route to his daughter's wedding, a long-haired banjo player, two skate punks from Bulgaria toting a guitar, and an old folksinger in a fisherman's cap. Tuned to the trombone over the clicking of the rails, something like a gypsy Dixieland ensemble emerged, and we sang songs and swapped leads and drank beer all the way across Nebraska.

When I disembarked in La Plata, two hours late on a cold October night, Ethan greeted me with a big smile. He had ridden a bike to the station, towing a second bike behind him. He heaved my suitcase into his small trailer and we rode the six miles to his home.

The next morning, a crisp autumn chill in the air, I found Sarah and their daughters playing in the sorghum patch. They knocked down a cane and snapped off sections and chewed them, offering me one. It was as sweet as pure sugar. The dog yapped and danced in circles. The girls wore whimsical capes that Sarah had sewed on an antique pedal Singer. (Gandhi himself had approved of treadle sewing machines, she told me.)

Sarah wore corduroy jeans and ditch boots and a vintage navy wool peacoat. With a handknit cap and scarf and fingerless gloves, she appeared to have stepped out of the Sundance catalog or some shabby-chic mommy blog.

"*Tu veux nourrir les chèvres?*" she asked her daughters.

Isla toddled toward the fence, offering a seed head at the end of a sorghum cane. The goat on the other side nabbed it. The girls squealed with laughter. From here no roads were visible, and the ridges of oak and hickory had burst into red. Linens fluttered on the line and a trace of woodsmoke hung in the air. Later Ethan would watch Isla as he split firewood, and Sarah would teach Etta from the Waldorf homeschooling curriculum. Ethan would bundle Etta in a wool blanket in the wheelbarrow and bounce her across the land, inventing an elaborate game in which she played the princess lost in the woods and he, with a pair of raspy Cockney accents, portrayed both the ogre stalking her for a snack and the knight defending her with his life. Etta squealed in utter delight. It was a Monday.

Ethan and Sarah seemed immune to the anxieties that plagued most parents I knew. They worked—at home—between six and eight hours a day, much of it outdoors, much in the company of their daughters. As for the headaches of modern life—bills, smartphones buzzing at dinner time, children throwing tantrums about wanting the gadgets their friends had, the need to chauffeur them in rush-hour traffic to and from school and lessons—Ethan and Sarah had simply eliminated them.

After nine years without modern conveniences, Sarah didn't miss them. "When you have a garden and a root cellar and a milking animal, there's no reason to have electricity, in my opinion," she said. She had not veered from her original belief that the preindustrial life was more beautiful. "Man, I abhor electric lighting." She had crafted kitchen shelves using hand tools, without screws or nails or bolts, slotting the pieces together with mortise and tenon.

"When people built things out of natural materials using their own hands and simple tools, they managed to craft them with more beauty than with the labor-saving devices and industrial tools of today," she said. "What is the gain? People are caught in a trap of making or buying more ugly stuff they're not connected to and they're less likely to take care of. When I get to make something myself with natural materials and simple tools, of course it's hard work and it takes time, but the crafting itself becomes a spiritual experience, and it makes a finished object of delight and reverence, as well as utility. You take care of it and pass it along to the next generation."

Or in the words of Lanza del Vasto: "The machine enslaves, the hand sets free."

Sarah had shielded her daughters, thus far, from the things that children demand: junk food, television, electronic toys. Her mother had bought a house in La Plata and lived there six months of the year. She was something like a part-time member of the PA herself, offering her expertise on gardening and canning and preserving food. But she also occasionally drove Sarah and the girls on errands or to visit family—Sarah having suspended her efforts to be utterly car-free after her hospitalization. And the grandparents were allowed to give gifts, although Sarah requested that they limit themselves to secondhand items made of natural materials. "Sometimes someone gives us a plastic toy or a polyester coat," she told me, "and I just quietly slip it into the Goodwill bag. My senses are offended by synthetics." Sarah and two neighbors had recently hired a Waldorf teacher to conduct class for their children one day a week. She remained opposed to sending her girls to the public school, where "they sell M&M's and Snickers to the captive kids."

Sarah was aware that all her careful shielding could backfire, and her girls might one day binge on commercial culture like famished people at a buffet. She took them regularly to live theater and music at the university in Kirksville, and wherever they traveled, as an alternative to watching television or movies. But once, while visiting family, she'd sat with Etta in front of a television and showed her *The Sound of Music*, and later, *Mary Poppins*. "It's like giving her homeopathic doses of pop culture," she said. "So she has something to judge against." Nonetheless, she didn't think her children lacked for material comforts. Among other treasures, Etta had her own pair of cross-country skis, a gift from her grandmother.

To some people, all this sewing and gardening and child rearing might sound like pure drudgery. But many Americans fantasize about the rustic life, as evidenced by the millions of readers of the Pioneer Woman blog and books, and a flood of back-to-the-land titles like *The Dirty Life* and *Rurally Screwed* and *Made from Scratch*. Gazing at soft-focus shots of sun-dappled mason jars and fresh-picked pears from the confines of a cubicle is one of the defining conundrums of our age, along with wolfing a sack of potato chips while watching *Top Chef.* Often what keeps the dream out of reach is not lack of will but lack of time, which might stem from a lack of money. Something as simple as a weekday in the garden with the kids is a luxury many feel they can't afford. Planting a garden is expensive, as is taking a day or even a morning off from work.

As any homesteader can attest, a single task—say, growing food or homeschooling kids—can swallow all the hours in a day. So how did Ethan and Sarah manage it all: grow food without tractors, raise children without daycare or schools, build a home without power tools, wash the laundry without a machine, march into the barricades expecting arrest, and still find time for singing songs and goofing around?

Their first "secret" was as simple as it was frightening: poverty. Their bucolic life was not merely a consumer choice, like buying a Prius instead of a Yukon or a wool sweater from Patagonia instead of its acrylic twin from Old Navy. Rather, they had renounced nearly every benefit of being born into the world's largest economy. Their voluntary poverty had a long history in nearly all world cultures— from Buddha to Jesus to Mohammed to Saint Francis—yet was generally practiced only by monastics, who combine vows of poverty with vows of celibacy. The Protestant United States never had a monastic class, and perhaps as a result, the tradition is rare. "The love of poverty," declared John Adams, "is a fictitious virtue that never existed."

The modern secular equivalents are people living in radical simplicity, with or without partners but without children. For some of them, childlessness is part of their belief system: the world is already overpopulated, and their efforts will be better spent trying to improve the quality of life for those already here, the thinking goes. But Gary Snyder contended that historically monastics had been left alone by the state precisely in exchange for their promise to not reproduce.

"If they gave birth to their own children, they would become a tribe," Snyder wrote. "As a tribe they would have a deeper investment in the transformation of society and would *really* be a thorn in the flesh . . . an alternative to society that might be too threatening."

What would happen if people as radical as Saint Francis and Mother Theresa and Thoreau were to have reproduced? Raising children in voluntary poverty—in the manner of Stephen and Ina May Gaskin and the Farm, or of Sarah and Ethan at the Possibility Alliance—is a practice with little historical precedent. In capitalist economies that require continuous increase in consumption, voluntary poverty constitutes a threat to power. What keeps the gears spinning is income that is both taxable and disposable.

Snyder was describing precisely what the Possibility Alliance was attempting: to learn to live as a tribe. The flip side of the fear of living without a social safety net—of fearing, as I did, that I would end up destitute, sick, homeless, or worse—was the joy Sarah and Ethan had found in embracing the parts of poverty that they liked: simplicity, domesticity, freedom from underwriting war and corporate malfeasance. This required alternative means of creating the security that most of us derive from money, savings, and insurance. And that required renouncing the most distinctive aspect of the American character: individuality. Instead of relying on themselves, they placed their security in the hands of others.

"There are hundreds of people who would joyfully take Sarah and me into their homes," Ethan told me. "Instead of insurance we have relationships, beautiful interdependence. And others know we would do the same for them."

As much as they resemble homesteaders, Sarah and Ethan's goal was more than tending a piece of land. They were building a community devoted to nonviolent social change, which is why they trace their lineage less to so-called utopians than to Gandhi, abolitionists, and the Catholic Workers. Indeed, the newest project adjacent to the PA is a family running a Catholic Worker farm.

"Ethan would be content in a monastery the same way I would be content homesteading," Sarah told me, which is to say: not quite content. His superhero cape was his monk's robe, she said: it indicated to the world that he was in service. With two children, a dozen cohabitants, and thousands of guests, they had little privacy, solitude, or autonomy. Purchases over $100 had to be approved by all three members. If they wanted so much as swimming lessons for their girls, they might use money the girls had saved up from birthday gifts, or ask for it as a present from grandparents.

But they also had the tribe they had built. Someone was usually available to babysit the girls for an hour when needed. The rotation of labor meant that nobody was trapped in the kitchen day after day. As a result, the primary source of stress in Ethan's and Sarah's lives—rather than the bills and cars and jobs through which the rest of us try to gain independence—was managing the community and submitting to its will.

Most intentional communities fail not because of the hardship involved but because their members ultimately can't get along. As nearly everyone who has ever tried to live in one has learned, a commitment to strong ideals does not always make for an easygoing personality. Moreover, living as a tribe requires an entire set of skills that most Americans, with the value we place on individuality, have not honed. That the Possibility Alliance had lasted—and grown—for almost a decade was no happy accident, nor the mere luck of choosing good friends. Rather, they had structured the community to accommodate and resolve the inevitable infighting. They held weekly well-being meetings, where residents and visitors could express their joys and challenges. To address acute grievances, a system called "restorative justice" was in place, in which any resident could schedule a voluntary meeting, and the day's bread labor might be suspended until the conflict was resolved. If you're trying to build a roof before rain falls, such delays could be maddening; the PA's second new structure, a two-story straw-bale duplex, meant to be Ethan and Sarah's new home, had been under construction for three years.

There were also consensus meetings, which made residents feel empowered, but could also be difficult and petty. The founders didn't always get their way. At one meeting that Sarah missed, members determined that the tolling grandfather clock should be removed from the living room, where its middle-of-the-night chimes woke guests in the adjacent guestroom. When Sarah arrived to find the family heirloom exiled to the pantry, mounted haphazardly with a screw, beside five-gallon buckets of flour, she promptly returned it to its original place, and told Dan Truesdale she'd done so. A small war nevertheless ensued, not because anybody cared all that much where the clock hung but because Sarah had vetoed consensus, and the rules were clear: If you miss the meeting, decisions can be made without you (then re-addressed at later meetings). But Sarah was the only mother in the community, the only one capable of breast-feeding her daughter, and the regularly planned meetings did not accommodate her baby's nap time. A consultant who donated her services to the PA cited this as an example of the place's institutional sexism. The clock stayed in the living room.

Sarah and Ethan were in a different phase in life from the part-time residents with whom they had to achieve consensus. The others were young and single, most of them still undecided about whether to commit to this life, some of them spending half the year back in civilization. This schism in lifestyle sometimes flummoxed Ethan and Sarah. On one occasion an admirer wrote to request permission to scan their handwritten newsletter and post it online. Ethan and Sarah consented. But other residents—who use email and the Internet when not at the PA—opposed it. Other times, residents wanted to give away the last bit of money in the common account—the only funds that Sarah and Ethan had for their family's basic needs. The irony was infuriating. Those people still had savings to fall back on. "It's easier to radicalize an institution than it is to radicalize yourself," Ethan told me, again. Eventually, Sarah, Ethan, and Dan determined that the consensus process would be open only to permanent members.

And let's face it: some people, no matter how many meetings they attend, are just a pain in the ass to live with. Actually, all of us are. The PA was running up against the problem that plagues all experiments in community living: getting everyone to agree. This is partly why the nineteenth-century utopias of Fruitlands and Brook Farm had folded. The communes that blossomed in the 1960s suffered from the same dynamics. The short life and quick failure of the Sunrise Commune in Virginia was characterized by a visitor: "One half of the group was seriously interested in making the thing work, but the other half were lying on their backs and saying, 'Hey, hand me a cigarette.'" And as an ex-member of the defunct Massachusetts co-op Morningside House put it, "We found, once we were living together, that we really didn't like each other as much as we thought we would."

Gender roles often add to the conflict. While men at Fruitlands liberated themselves from toil and spent their afternoons debating ideas, they left the heavy lifting to their wives and daughters. "There was only one slave at Fruitlands," recalled Abigail Alcott, wife of the founder, "and that was a woman." Many of the 1960s communes devoted to upending patriarchal institutions like capitalism and marriage were strictly traditional when it came to gender roles, with men building and farming and women cooking, cleaning, and taking care of children.

The PA had built into its mission statement an effort to address this. Simplicity was just one of its five pillars; another was self-transformation, which the PA described as the "hardest work, removing the greed, hatred, anger, jealousy and selfishness from ourselves."

So, what exactly did self-transformation look like? Since voluntary poverty precluded expensive therapy, Prozac, and yoga retreats, the PA applies the do-it-yourself ethos to mental and spiritual well-being. Each morning began with an hour of spiritual practice, which might consist of prayer, meditation, yoga. Ethan and Sarah had become Quakers and held a meeting Sunday mornings that Sarah's mother often joined. (She also served as self-appointed "cult buster," reassuring worried parents whose offspring had arrived in La Plata with plans to renounce their possessions and privilege.) The alliance hosted workshops on conflict resolution, nonviolent communication, and, in the wake of Ferguson, undoing white supremacy. Sarah and Ethan worked through marriage conflicts by enlisting Dan Truesdale or another friend as a facilitator. I, of course, had participated in some of this self-transformation, and found that it worked wonders.

Superhero rides had involved a tradition dubbed the Supernova of Limitless Love, in which each departing hero was encircled by the others, who revealed something they loved or appreciated about him or her. It was the sort of structured intimacy that gave some outsiders the heebie-jeebies but deepened the friendships of the participants. The PA had adopted the Supernova tradition, but when some members expressed more interest in hearing what about themselves they could improve, a complementary tradition was invented: the Black Hole of Limitless Learning, in which everyone offered suggestions for a person's growth.

Too much processing might feel a bit solemn, or tedious. Indeed, many intentional communities have suffered from dour seriousness or excessive obedience to a leader, as when Farmies were required to recognize Stephen Gaskin as their "spiritual teacher." The PA made a concerted institutional effort to avoid such pitfalls. "This is an

experiment, and we strive not to take ourselves or our ideas too seriously," read their mission statement. Thus the third pillar: "Silliness,
Celebration, Gratitude and Joy." There was time for pond olympics,
puppet shows, miniature golf croquet, and music; whether by default
or design, a lot of the apprentices had fine singing voices. Friday sup-
pers began with each person recalling a "moment of joy" from the
week. Residents rotated at the helm of the Department of Homeland
Spontaneity. Notably absent, however, was our era's signature attitude:
irony. Where did the brand of organized G-rated fun leave those who
preferred to express their joy in their own way, in private, in spontaneity, or not at all? And which was more fun, after all: to watch *The
Hobbit* in a theater or to dress up as Gandalf and perform it yourself,
by candlelight, in the living room? I didn't know the answer to that.

IN ADDITION TO THE POSSIBILITY ALLIANCE'S three "inward"
goals of simplicity, self-transformation, and celebration, it pursued the
"outward" goals of service and nonviolent activism. Much of the service was local: helping their neighbor Don Miller round up his cattle,
throwing a roof on Brian and Teri's home after Brian sprained his
ankle, helping to raise an Amish barn, singing songs at the nursing
home. But members were encouraged to spend twenty days per year
outside the sanctuary working on causes. Some protested and risked
arrest. Many embarked on superhero rides; after Hurricane Katrina,
forty-five heroes rode into the Ninth Ward and spent as long as three
months rebuilding.

In the fifteen years since the WTO protests in Seattle, Ethan had
been expecting a movement to blossom. There were moments when it
looked like one might: the worldwide demonstrations against the Iraq
War, Occupy Wall Street, the battle against climate change as it was
waged against the proposed Keystone pipeline, the Black Lives Matter

marches and die-ins. But none of these had swelled into a sustained national movement. Part of the problem was that it seemed unclear exactly what united these various causes. Was this a movement about war? Economic inequality? Destruction of the planet? Entrenched racism?

All of the above, according to Ethan. As he saw it, we were at a point in history similar to that in the mid–nineteenth century when we were enmeshed in, and dependent on, an unjust system. Then it was slavery and colonialism; now it was global capitalism, the industrial economy, commercial civilization—whatever you want to call it. In slavery's day, even those who opposed it were de facto supporters; their basic necessities—from cotton to rice to sugar to tobacco—were produced by slaves. Meanwhile those who benefited most from the slave trade—the plantation owners and mercantilists—had bankrolled generations of politicians, professors, and clergy to argue that slavery was ethical and necessary. The forced complicity created a soul sickness, which perhaps explained the blossoming in that era of spiritual revivals: Transcendentalists, Mormons, utopian colonies. Only a few committed sects—the Quakers and Amish—were able to renounce the products of slavery. The abolition movement took decades.

And so it is today. Virtually every product we touch comes from the industrial economy. Rail as we might against fracking and wars that protect our oil supply, we support those things with our gas furnaces, cars, and taxes. Grieve as we might over the clear-cutting of the Amazon and the extinction of the polar bear, we are complicit, governed by appetites for beef and electricity heretofore undreamed of in the history of mankind. Grumble as we might about Wall Street felons, we keep the banks in business by lending them our money, paying their interest on mortgages and credit cards, and amassing our savings in their IRAs and money-market accounts. Protest as we might about police killing unarmed black teenagers, white people have created segregated ghettoes by fleeing to "safe neighborhoods" where the public schools are good. As with other radical experiments, the PA tried to find a balance between building a new world and helping to save the existing one.

One of the apprentices spent months attending the hearing of Chelsea (formerly Bradley) Manning, the soldier accused of passing secret files to WikiLeaks. An artist, she drew courtroom sketches that she provided to the media for free. She said that she was the only activist there who packed her own lunch. The rest ate the cheapest kinds of fast food, from mini-marts and drive-thrus. Which led to a discussion: How do we fight the Man if we continue to buy his cheeseburgers? Ethan pointed out that when he protested fracking and pipelines, he was often the only one who did not use natural gas. I found him oddly aligned with Rush Limbaugh and Sean Hannity when they tell liberals, If you're opposed to drilling, then stop driving.

What had become clear to me was that while the Possibility Alliance resembled secular utopias of America's past, it sat more firmly in a parallel tradition of religious activism. The ashram that served as its model was the haven Gandhi had founded in 1915 to grow food and spin cloth. "Our ambition was to live the life of the poorest people," he wrote. "I decided to live on a pure fruit diet, and that too composed of the cheapest fruit possible." This regimen precluded the need for cooking, as members subsisted on raw nuts, bananas, dates, lemons, and olive oil.

The ashram expanded on the experiments of Tolstoy Farm, which Gandhi had led in South Africa for three years. He considered Tolstoy "the greatest apostle of non-violence that the present age has produced" and was deeply influenced by *The Kingdom of God Is Within You*. When I cracked it, 125 years after publication, it was still a blistering rant. Here was a landed aristocrat who instead of pickling in privilege tried to smash the system, and literally took to walking the countryside, Jesus-like, in robes. He savaged the well-intentioned liberal: "I sit on a man's back, choking him, and making him carry me, and yet assure myself and others that I am very sorry for him and wish to ease his lot by any means possible, except getting off his back."

The count called for widespread "non-resistance to evil by force" and applauded the elites who "prefer the condition of the oppressed and try to resemble them in the simplicity of their life." Creating these conditions was Gandhi's goal at Tolstoy Farm and Sabarmati Ashram. Only after two decades of simple living were Gandhi and his followers prepared to topple the empire. During that incubation, Gandhi determined that passivity in the face of oppression was mere cowardice. What was required to actually win was defiance simultaneously courageous and peaceful. He recast Tolstoy's slippery term "non-resistance to evil by force" as nonviolent resistance, and in 1930 he and seventy-eight followers began a 240-mile walk to the ocean to illegally harvest salt. By the time they reached the sea, their numbers had swelled to tens of thousands. Although independence for India took another seventeen years, the movement was born, and in it a model for the black freedom struggle in America, as well as liberation movements in South Africa, Poland, the Philippines, and elsewhere. "First they ignore you," Gandhi said, "then they laugh at you, then they fight you, then you win."

But where had Tolstoy gotten the idea for nonresistance? It surprised me, who had associated such radicalism with places like India and Russia, to discover that the idea sprang from America. A belief in ethical withdrawal from corrupt society was a premise on which the nation was founded. The Puritans had imagined a city of plain Christian rectitude, safe from not only England's persecution but also its freewheeling commerce that gratified only the body. The Quakers envisioned a utopia of faith and work free from luxury and usury, and wove their own clothing rather than support the slave-powered cotton industry. John Adams and Thomas Jefferson urged Americans to resist overseas taxation and forgo the goods—tea, for instance—that bolstered empire. (While meeting with the British viceroy, Gandhi reportedly produced a satchel of illegally gained granules and said, "I will put a little of this salt into my tea to remind us of the famous Boston Tea Party.")

As America became an industrial power, the Founders' doctrine of "simplicity as dissent" was pushed to the margins. But Tolstoy did not forget them. He was inspired by the Quakers for their nonviolence and their refusal to rely on the fruits of slavery. He was also influenced by the abolitionist William Lloyd Garrison, who founded the New England Non-Resistance Society to oppose war and capital punishment. "We believe that the penal code of the old covenant—an eye for and eye, and a tooth for a tooth—has been abrogated by Jesus Christ," wrote Garrison. As a result, he and his nonresisters would "voluntarily exclude [them]selves from every legislative and judicial body, and repudiate all human politics." He publically burned a copy of the constitution, calling it "a Covenant with Death, an agreement with Hell." (Garrison eventually disavowed pacifism, supporting the Civil War as a means of ending slavery.)

Tolstoy and Gandhi (and Martin Luther King) owed a specific debt to another nineteenth-century American, Henry David Thoreau, whose "Civil Disobedience" declares, "Under a government which imprisons any unjustly, the true place for a just man is also prison." Upping the ante on Adams and Jefferson, Thoreau insisted that "the government is best which governs not at all."

All of which raises the question: If anarchist Christian radicalism was birthed in the United States, what became of it? Why did it take a full century—and a detour through Europe and Asia—to return to our shores with Martin Luther King and the Student Nonviolent

Coordinating Committee? Even a homegrown radical like Scott Nearing paid little debt to his American forebears, instead hailing Tolstoy as his teacher.

While the roots of American radicalism are deep, its branches have been few. The Quakers still exist, of course, but their numbers plummeted after colonial times. During World War I they used their remaining influence to form the American Friends Service Committee to oppose the draft. These days Quakers account for fewer than 100,000 of America's 260 million Christians. They are more scarce than Jews, Buddhists, Amish, Muslims, Hindus, or Mormons. The historical peace churches—the Amish, Mennonites, and Hutterites—withdrew from politics and military service and worldly wealth, and as a result, their views all but disappeared from the public conversation. In 1933, Dorothy Day and Peter Maurin founded the Catholic Worker Movement, embracing poverty and pacifism to "live in accordance with the justice and charity of Jesus Christ," yet the movement has never represented more than an infinitesimal fraction of Catholics.

As mainline denominations continued to decline—their liberal members drawn to secular causes and Eastern religions—American Christianity became more conservative than ever. Churches founded on the teachings of Jesus regularly advocated war and capital punishment, seemed to equate material wealth with divine providence, and fell mute about the suffering of workers who contribute to that wealth. Of course there were still Christians who ministered to the poor and the outcast, and who condemned war and violence. But very few took seriously Jesus' embrace of poverty. The Catholic Workers were a notable exception.

Another was the Highlander Folk School, founded in Tennessee in the 1930s. "The job of Highlander was to multiply leadership for radical social change," said its founder, Myles Horton. He was raised in turn-of-the-century Appalachia in a poor Christian family that believed "God is love, and therefore you love your neighbors." In 1928, just out of college and decades before the civil rights movement, Horton organized an integrated YMCA meeting in a segregated Tennessee hotel. "I took the gamble of doing something about a moral problem instead of simply talking about it." After two years at a seminary in New York, he returned to Tennessee and founded a school without classrooms, teachers, curriculum, or tuition. It was to be a forum to address labor exploitation, poverty, and racism. The founders planted a vegetable garden and subsisted with "less than two hundred dollars, a sack of beans, some flour and books." Among Highlander's students were Martin Luther King and Rosa Parks. "At Highlander, I found out for the first time in my adult life that this could be a unified society," Parks later said, "that there was such a thing as people of different races and backgrounds meeting together in workshops, and living together in peace and harmony." Just weeks after attending a workshop at Highlander, she refused to give up her seat on a Montgomery bus. The point is not that white people like Myles Horton deserve part of the credit for the civil rights movement. It's rather that its leaders were consciously acting in a long tradition of radical Christianity.

Ethan worked with Adam Campbell to launch the Peace and Permaculture Center, modeled in part on Myles Horton's Highlander Folk School. A native of Branson, Campbell was drawn to permaculture after doubting the value of what he'd been taught at the University of Missouri. "After graduation, I realized that I didn't know how to do anything," he told me. "I knew how to write a really good paper but couldn't do anything, with regard to Maslow's hierarchy of needs, to take care of myself." He set out to learn a way to live within limits that actually created abundance, which was how he had arrived at the Possibility Alliance. He saw his classes there as "a course in mature ethical action." He began with the assumption that as a species, humans were living beyond their ecological limits. "People are trying to live their lives in the best way they know how," he told me, "and they keep

unintentionally creating a wake of devastation around the world."
After two generations of access to cheap energy, we've been taught an
immature way of living, and since we are so far removed from the
effects of our consumption, we don't see our impact—and don't want
to see it. *I'm a good person,* went the reasoning, *so don't tell me the way
I'm living is causing village culture and ecological systems to collapse.*

In Campbell's view, the heart of permaculture is not ecological but
economic. "What we need is a giant reframe," he told me. "Because
economics is driving this whole culture of immature unethical action
that is laying waste to the world." Pulling a small thread—asking
where your tomatoes or your drinking water come from—causes the
whole system to unravel, leading some to conclude that what's needed
is cultural revolution. What Campbell aspired to—and what he felt
Sarah and Ethan had achieved—is "practicing right livelihood in the
belly of empire."

Peter Scott is a superhero once known as Genetically Modified
Man and HugMan who went on to partner with the Department of
Energy to design and build low-cost, high-efficiency woodstoves to
reduce deforestation in Africa. "He's a force of nature," he said of
Ethan. "He has the real belief that he can manifest his vision. He
wants a core band of revolutionaries to be a vanguard of global love
and simplicity."

"The greatest conspiracy on the planet is that we need to oppress,
kill, and pollute in order to get our needs met," Ethan told me. "And
it's not true. I look at the trees and the birds and I know it's not true.
I'm not yet sure how to do it, but I'm going to learn."

Five

By many measures the experiment was succeeding. The Possibility Alliance hosted far more visitors than they ever expected to. Without a website or any major press coverage—indeed, without intentional effort—the place had attained a certain mythic status, as a Lost City that pilgrims found only at the end of a long quest. Seekers sometimes arrived unannounced, in the middle of the night, in search of an alternative. Like me, hundreds of visitors left each year feeling transformed and energized. And certainly the PA had succeeded in creating a broader family, with like-minded projects and homesteaders nearby, and the handful of offshoots across the country.

And yet by one rubric, Ethan and Sarah had failed. The founders had hoped that by now there would be dozens of full-time members in the PA itself, some their own age, also raising children. But after eight years, they had recruited only one other full-time member. By contrast, nearby Dancing Rabbit Ecovillage, with its WiFi, solar panels, and beer, had seventy-five.

Helena Marcus, the founder whose original investment had provided the bulk of the funding for the La Plata farm, stayed at the Possibility Alliance for less than a year. She suffered the typical conflicts of living in a community, and her French husband longed for his native Brittany coast. During my second visit, I learned that the three residents who'd been on the verge of joining full-time had decided against it. Why didn't more people want to join? Most people cited the same reasons Ethan and Sarah had given when they left the Ark: They wanted to be in a different location, closer to family and friends. They wanted to start their own project, along the lines of their own ideals, not merely implement someone else's plan. Adam Campbell, for example, though he decided not to become a member, moved just a stone's throw away, to the Peace and Permaculture Center. Ethan thought the main reason people did not join was the difficulty of hosting 1,500 visitors per year. And yet some who left had suggested that Ethan and Sarah ruled by personal preferences.

I asked Ethan if he took it personally. "Sometimes," he said. "But the vast majority of them—it's not like they're going and living this way somewhere else, without electricity, petrol, or cars. So I think they're just not ready to live this way."

Sarah and Ethan had no intention of compromising their ideals just to attract members. In the years when the consensus process was still open to short-term residents, the founders were not really amenable to suggestions like getting Internet service or buying a car. "It would be like someone going to a Zen center," Ethan said, "and saying, 'Oh, I don't want to do the Eightfold Path, I want to try a Sevenfold Path, or a Sixfold Path.' Integral nonviolence is wholistic. You can't drop one aspect of it."

For Sarah, certainly, the hardest part about her life at the Possibility Alliance turned out to be the feelings of isolation and loneliness. If we are doing the right thing, she reasoned, then why don't more people do it with us? And that led to peeking over the fence at a different life they might have chosen, longing for the things they had sacrificed by moving to Missouri. Ethan dreamed of the ocean. When he read Etta a story about the sea, he found himself weeping. Sarah longed for classical music, the kind that was simply hard to come by here.

"There's a tension between loving the fine arts and being a Gandhian," she told me. "If the whole world were living like this, I would definitely go sing. But the world isn't living anything like this, and I feel this vision is my calling."

She joined a chorus in Kirksville. The twenty-eight-mile round-trip by bicycle was prohibitive, so she took a public van or hitched a ride with her mother. The musical theater in Macon, thirty miles away, was simply too far. "I've embraced poverty and I have to accept certain limits," she told me. "If I want to take private voice lessons or enroll at the college for a master's in music, I need to go do some fundraising. But do I want to fundraise for a team of horses, or a building, or voice lessons? When you have voluntary poverty, you really realize the value of things."

The more she longed for something that was not available in La Plata, the more she banged up against rural America's design flaw: things are spread out. With scant public transportation and no car, the isolation was formidable. The like-minded ecovillages were forty miles away. Her neighbors zipped into Kirksville in cars. "Even those people don't understand the philosophy about cars, and nonviolence, and why we're doing this. If we believe this, we have to do it this way. Otherwise, who will do it this way?" For her and Ethan, the means and the ends were the same thing.

"The only sadness," she said, "is that it would be so much more rich if more people were doing this, and we had more networks, and things weren't so far apart. There's not the local village that used to be here, that you could walk to."

It was a chicken-and-egg conundrum. Life in the rural Midwest was isolating because there weren't many people; what prevented more people from moving there was the isolation. The Kansas agrarian Wes Jackson had wrestled with this dilemma for decades. "From Oklahoma to Saskatchewan, from east of Denver deep into the Midwest, thousands of small towns and rural communities are dying," he wrote. "The unsettling of these towns with the migration of people to urban areas has led to an unsettling of the culture at large with its rising crime rate, increasing national debt, increase in soil erosion, and increase in chemical contamination of the countryside."

Jackson lamented that rural America had become unpopulated, with less than 2 percent of Americans living on farms. He pointed out that today's universities had only one true major—upward mobility, which tended to reward the same exploitation with which the prairie was settled. What if we taught instead the practice of homecoming? he asked. "It would educate people to go back to a place and dig in. We need a new generation of settlers, people who could go into these places with a fundamentally different mind-set, with the skills for what we might call 'ecological community accounting.'"

This might be a case of two problems that contained the ability to solve each other. Near cities where there was a market for natural foods, places like Portland and Brooklyn and Missoula, thousands of young people wanted to become farmers and homesteaders but were deterred by the exorbitant cost of land. Meanwhile, the Midwest had ample and affordable farmland but lacked the critical mass of population to sustain farmers' markets and community-supported agriculture (CSA) and farm-to-table cafés. What would happen if instead of mortgaging themselves to the throat in Santa Cruz or Vermont, these young farmers repopulated the ghost towns of Missouri, Kansas, Nebraska, and the Dakotas?

I asked Sarah what types of businesses she would like to see in La Plata. After all, she and Ethan didn't really spend money. They didn't eat in restaurants or buy clothes or even many groceries. A few years back, a coffeehouse had opened on the town square but had soon failed. The only La Plata stores she patronized were the Amish fabric shop and variety store. ("It breaks my heart," she said. "The Amish wear polyester.") She was stumped. She wasn't quite sure what business she'd be able to support.

I left Missouri without an answer. On the Greyhound from Kirksville to Ottumwa, I sat across the aisle from an old man in the telltale straw hat, suspenders, and an Abe Lincoln beard. Either Amish or Mennonite. While he was looking out the window I craned my neck and inspected his black trousers.

The synthetic fibers glistened in the sun.

I felt a twinge of grief. If even the Amish must wear clothes spun from petroleum products, hadn't America truly lost its way?

The man got off at the next stop, a gas station where a horse and buggy was lashed to a post. A nearly identical-looking man in a straw hat and suspenders greeted my seatmate. I was eager to watch them ride off together in the buggy. The two men entered the gas station and emerged licking soft-serve ice cream cones. And instead of climbing aboard the buggy, they slipped into a sedan and drove away.

Two months later Sarah Wilcox called me. She had been mulling over my question, about which businesses she'd patronize, and had finally arrived at an answer.

"Oh," I said, reaching for pen and paper.

"An organic grain co-op," she announced. "And a theater."

ETHAN'S STRUGGLES WERE THOSE that most founders of radical communities and movements had faced. He was pulled between his ethical views, on which there could be no compromise, and the religious teachings that instructed him to love everyone. He continued to meditate every morning. After years of atheism, in which he was once nearly thrown out of the Vatican for refusing to remove his hat, he had returned to Christianity, though the Quaker meeting is a far cry from the Catholicism of his upbringing. But nonjudgment was a challenge:

How could he not judge people when their behavior was so obviously destructive? For all his inspiring, Ethan could inadvertently compel people to act by making them feel guilty. When I followed along on a tour he led, he praised his off-grid neighbors—who included some of his closest friends—but also referred to them as "just homesteaders." In regard to mainstream America, he said, "It's fine if some people think they need to live in two-thousand-square-foot homes, but if we keep doing it the planet will be dead."

He was disappointed when others didn't follow his steps. He stopped describing the PA as "car-free," and now said it's "moving toward car-free," because strictly speaking he is the only one who doesn't ride in cars. While I was there, a group commandeered Brian's pickup to gather apples from an orchard fifty miles away. Ethan would have preferred to bike the hundred miles pulling a trailer but was otherwise occupied. He is also the only one getting thrown in jail. "Why aren't all these young single people getting arrested?" he asked me.

When he'd first arrived in Missouri, he dedicated pages in his journal to this sort of thinking. He lambasted warmongering conservatives "going to bible study 3 times a week . . . blessing the bombs we drop on women and children . . . and cursing the godlessness of this culture." He aimed his fiercest words at fellow liberals "going to their summer festivals in their cars eating organic fair trade chocolate while the bombs fall for their right to consume and casually talking about why the mainstream American can not embrace peace. 'How could people be so ignorant,' they say while dancing to the sound systems made by the sweat shops in China."

I loved these polemics, filled with the sort of moral outrage that has fueled prophets though the ages. Yet what makes for prophecy doesn't always make for leadership. Over the years, he tried to transform his anger, and by all accounts, he partly succeeded. Still, he could be overbearing at times, conflating his agenda with concern for another's well-being. In one instance, Christian Schearer, aka CompashMan, who homesteaded the land next door for a year, had a road bulldozed through the woods to access his property. Instead of commending the progress, Ethan suggested ways in which it could have been done more sustainably. "I judge myself when I'm around him," said Schearer. "I feel inadequate or I'm making bad choices, because I know he wouldn't make those choices. He doesn't tell me what I should do, but he will inquire into my choices, and ask, Is it really serving you? He has such a good heart, such good intentions for himself and the whole world, even if it might come out in a way that makes people feel judged, or drives them away."

As I spoke to his closest friends, a complicated picture emerged. They were awed with love and respect, and also hurt by his judgment. Helena Marcus said she sometimes felt bullied. "When he pointed fingers at my lifestyle, it made me bristle," she said. "The closer you get to Ethan," another friend told me, "the less you want to live with him." Chris Moore-Backman, an activist who spent a month at the PA with his wife and daughter, felt judged. "After that I decided I would love and respect him from afar. It took a couple of years before I wanted to be back in touch."

Nonetheless, these friends continued to admire him and implement elements of his vision into their own lives. His long friendship with Helena Marcus foundered after she left the alliance, and her parents, convinced that she had been brainwashed, pressured her to demand her seed money back. Ethan offered to raise the funds to repay it, but she was resolved to leave her capital in place, and years later, living her own version of the simple life with a husband and two children and very little income, she harbored no regrets. "I believe in this vision beyond anything else, and I believe in Ethan and Sarah and their hearts' intention," she told me. "The money was supporting a dream of how we can possibly live on this planet."

Chris Moore-Backman, after leaving the PA, produced a radio series on the mass incarceration of African Americans. He lived without a car, computer, cell phone, or refrigerator. He told me, "When the rubber hits the road with the movement, and I reach out to Ethan and say come and help, I know he'll be there."

"At times I wish he wasn't so adamant about saving the world," Ethan's mother, Francine Hughes, told me. "After his father's death, he had to deal with his own mortality much earlier than most people. He put things in perspective. We only have one life, so we should do what we want. I know now that success is defined wrongly. It's all how much money we make, and all that bullshit."

I asked Aron Heintz, who funded the Possibility Alliance and its offshoots, if he was disappointed that after all these years it had attracted only one full-time member. After all, what drew Heintz to the PA was his belief that its vision would spread. "I finally realized that creating a replicable model is not Ethan's primary dream," Heintz told me. "It's more an allegiance to how things should be." He himself lived in an intentional community—but one that was wired to the rest of the world. "I don't think that handwriting newsletters to sixty other people is the wave of the future," he said. "Returning to living in villages while having an Internet connection—that's the wave of the future. That's what they want in India and Nicaragua," he said, referring to places where he had spearheaded philanthropic efforts. Yet he still found the Possibility Alliance transformational. "It's more like Cirque du Soleil," he said with a laugh. "It's a bit of a performance to impress people and send them off inspired by what humans are capable of. It's not to teach them to be in the circus. The relevance is that people are inspired and take that back to their community."

"I've never met anyone besides Ethan who has the whole picture," said Kyle Chandler-Isacksen, who, along with his wife, Katy, and two sons, lived at the PA for a year before launching a similar, petrol-free project in Reno called Be the Change. "The philosophical base, the practical skills, the charisma to share it, the attention to joy. He's flawed, and that's fine." Kyle considered Ethan "a clown, like Crazy Horse, who takes things to the extreme just to show it can be done."

And living by example was not the same thing as leading, as Katy Chandler-Isacksen pointed out. "When Gandhi was starting his ashram," she wrote me in a hand-penned letter, "there was a culture of having a guru: someone who has come upon a body of wisdom. In our culture that's hard to follow. Ethan and Sarah don't want that position, but that's really who they are. People go to the Possibility Alliance because these two people are holding this incredible wisdom and knowledge."

She gets to the heart of it, I think. Were Ethan willing to declare himself a guru along the lines of Stephen Gaskin, and to rule the community by his will, he might spend less time trying to soften the delivery of his strong opinions. And yet he's committed to consensus, which when coupled with such uncompromising standards results in a lot of efforts to persuade, some of which backfire.

"They didn't 'give it up' just so they could do laundry by hand, can food all fall, and poop in a composting toilet," Katy continued. "They didn't give it up at all. They redirected and reformatted their incredible talents and education to be of service to their vision of a world that honors and supports all of creation."

I had to agree with his friends. I had found in Ethan a model of how one might live the good life as a husband, a father, and an activist.

WITH ALL THE COMING AND GOING of residents over the years, some of Ethan and Sarah's closest friends these days were not fellow activists, but rather their conservative neighbors, Don and Dana Miller. The two couples agreed not to broach certain subjects: abortion, war, gay marriage, global warming. "If we looked at our differences, we could not have a relationship," Dana told me. "We love them for who they are, and not for how they live." Before Ethan and Sarah arrived, the Millers were considering selling the farm and moving to town. They were getting too old to take care of it. But the PA offered help. When Don was diagnosed with cancer, Dan Truesdale ran his tractor, and instead of lecturing him about organic ranching, fed the cattle their genetically modified grains.

"They've been a real blessing for us," said Don. "We've got so much more from them than they have gotten from us." He and Dana hosted the PA for regular craft nights. And when people from church would fish for gossip about "the bike people," Don Miller assured them that while his neighbors might be unconventional, they were of exceptional integrity.

And for all that they could not discuss, there was a great deal that they did discuss. After a lifetime of searching for mentors in political leaders, monks, and radical activists, Ethan had found something like a father in his Republican neighbor. They had long conversations about values, parenting, God, and the never-ending effort to live according to one's values.

When I asked Ethan about the criticisms of him, he conceded that they were mostly right. "I lose my way," he said. "We are always failing at our ideals." One of Ethan's great traits, I thought, was his willingness to accept feedback—indeed to have built it into the structure of the PA. And so it was that in the spring of his forty-fourth year, Ethan called for a Black Hole of Limitless Learning, inviting his community to help him see his blind spots. He found himself sitting in the middle of a circle that included his wife, Brian Thomas, Adam Campbell, Dan Truesdale, a half-dozen residents, and a handful of neighbors.

After a long silence, Truesdale began.

"When you use people as examples for ways you don't want to be," he said, "it sounds like throwing them under the bus. It creates a sense of competition. And it makes people wonder if you're talking behind our back."

"Why are you thinking in this competitive way?" asked someone else.

"Your way of loving looks like pushing," said a third. "So I have to cut myself off."

Brian Thomas spoke. "You think your world is the only way, yet there are so many worlds. The PA is not *the* solution. It's one experiment that you are called to try."

"White men created most of the world's problems by trying to control it," said someone else. "To think a white man can control the solution is erroneous."

"Is there a way to invite people to take you less seriously?"

"You have an attachment to being alone in your fight. It brings you pain and gain. But you are not alone. What if you believed in your faith that you could count on others, that their way is helping the cause?"

"Your goal is to save the world, and you know you can't do that alone," said Adam Campbell. "You have to enlist others for the great awakening, the worldwide nonviolent revolution. And your strategy for changing their hearts is to be a vessel of love. But you can't be a vessel of love if that is merely a strategy. That's not how love works. You will always be blocked from living an authentic life."

Ethan wept before his friends. Everyone was quiet.

"But the hammer is coming down on the earth!" His voice cracked. "I have to stop it."

"What if the hammer is already down?" asked Campbell. "What if it's too late to save the world?"

"I guess I'd just go get a cabin in Maine. Sit by the sea. Watch the world die and try to honor it."

Sarah understood that her husband had just crossed some threshold. Part of their calling was radical simplicity, but another part was to follow their hearts. Ethan had revealed the longings in his true heart. In the months that followed, he and Sarah began to consider leaving Missouri, and launching a sister project. Maybe they would start a new life, a similar one, out on the coast of Maine, closer to the sea, closer to the music.

PART TWO

Detroit

Six

In the rental car lot, I debated between two econo-boxes. The first was a Chevrolet with a dashboard and seats that appeared to be cardboard. Had I been asked to guess the vehicle's country of manufacture, I would have said Walmart. Instead I wedged my cowboy boots into the tomato-red Fiat with shimmering gadgets and neon purple dials like the cockpit of a spaceship. I revved toward the exit, knees folded against the steering wheel, and presented my papers to the man in the booth, who burst out laughing.

"I just can't get used to seeing a *dude* in the Fiat 500," he said, wiping his eyes. "I mean, it's really a *chick car.*"

The man in the booth invited me to swap cars.

"This is Detroit, dude. Get a Chevy."

I thanked him for his concern but forged ahead in my Italian sportster, defiant as the violet tachometer spun.

DESPITE MY TWENTY YEARS in the hinterland, I am a city boy. My roots in Los Angeles run deep: my great-grandparents arrived in 1924 to open a grocery store in the Crenshaw District. My grandfather graduated from Hollywood High School, and my dad recalls as a teenager seeing Harry Belafonte play the Greek Theatre. So the first thing I felt flying over Detroit's freeways was homesickness. I had expected the place to resemble New York or Philadelphia, but its wide streets of bungalows made it feel more like L.A., and the vacant lots and ramshackle houses around the razed site of Tiger Stadium in Corktown filled me with nostalgia for my youth.

My dad held season tickets for the University of Southern California at the Coliseum, and one Saturday each autumn I donned maroon and gold for a game. The football and the bedecked Trojan atop a white stallion were only half the adventure. A native Angeleno, my dad was too savvy—or too cheap—to pay for parking, so he'd find some empty lot or curb east of the Harbor Freeway, where old men reclined on porches in undershirts and charged five bucks to park on their lawn. Dad would lead me through a dark tunnel that reeked of piss, while cars rumbled overhead.

Which is to say that, although I'm no prepper, when I moved to Montana and inventoried its ample rivers and snowpack and sparse population, I recognized a good place to survive whatever hellfire might come. When others were rioting at empty supermarkets, I would have well water and a root cellar.

Yet I was starting to see that Cedar and I could not sustain our own version of the good life. As much as we wanted to commit to a piece of land, Missoula was too expensive for our homesteading idyll. When we had discussed what she wanted to do in the coming years, she said, "Write and travel." Which is what I had been doing for twenty years. It appeared that we were gravitating toward each other's background. I came from a family of academics who told me that they would find a way to pay for college, no matter how much it cost. I proceeded to get straight A's and followed my dad to Stanford. Now I wanted something simpler. Having been raised back-to-the-land, Cedar now felt the pull of opportunity and ambition. When I suggested we not drive and fly so much, she said, "I'm from Montana.

We don't have public transportation. If you want to go anywhere you have to fly or drive. And I'm not willing to just stay home."

So we did as she proposed: wrote and traveled. She published her first book of poems. We spent two winters in Nepal and one living in our car on the beaches and mountains of Mexico. It was an excellent arrangement. Both self-employed, we basked in Montana's summers and escaped its winters, when our idyllic cottage became a dark, drafty, mouse-ridden shack at the end of a long, icy lane.

Our simple life depended on the complicated grid of economy and technology. Cell phones and the Internet freed us from having to work in someone else's office. I taught creative writing online from a palapa in Mexico and from a studio in Kathmandu. As a journalist, I could live in Montana because I could fly around the country on assignment. Cheap flights also allowed us to winter overseas, which is what allowed us to tolerate our affordable, uninsulated shack. Our lovely life was enabled by cheap oil and cheap tech.

Leading a semi-pastoral life like mine—or even living fully off the grid—had come to seem less like a gesture of dissent and more like merely fleeing the problems wrought by consumption, a new iteration of privilege. Living on some mountain in comfort made possible by solar power, propane stove and fridge, satellite modem and cable, all paid for by work dependent on telecommuting or car commuting, really meant enjoying all the wealth and security of the industrial economy without having to look at its costs, like pollution or poverty or racial inequity. The off-grid commuter was just a suburbanite with a longer driveway.

Self-reliance is a mirage (sorry, Emerson), and chasing it might exacerbate the problems it purports to address. It is not efficient for everyone to build and maintain their own house, tools, and car. "Living close to nature" usually means encroaching on nature, especially the big animals that require large habitat. And the flipside of not having to see or hear neighbors is isolation, both social and economic, remedied usually by commutes into town for company and provisions. Wouldn't it be better if we pooled supplies, shared labor, and lived within easy reach of one another?

Such radical communitarian experiments already exist. They are called cities. By this measure, as David Owen points out in *Green Metropolis*, New York is the most sustainable city in America.

Indeed, one glimmer of hope in my lifetime has been the rediscovery of the wonders of cities. A generation raised in suburbs flocked to the neighborhoods that their parents and grandparents had fled for the suburbs, and learned the satisfactions of walking, public transportation, great food from a range of ethnic backgrounds, and the vibrant cultural life that only a dense population can sustain.

Historically, the city has been dependent on the countryside for sustenance, but parallel to the resurgence in homesteading, in some urban centers—parts of Brooklyn, Oakland, Portland, and even my hometown sprawl of Los Angeles—a movement toward urban simplicity was flourishing. With shared gardens, rooftop beehives, farm-to-table cafés, time banks, and free boxes, residents were seeking a practical balance between doing it yourself and taking advantage of urban density, as outlined by Kelly Coyne and Erik Knutzen in their book *The Urban Homestead*.

"We don't call ourselves farmers, we're just gardeners," Knutzen told me. "We don't grow all our own food. We live in communities with other people." Instead of self-sufficiency, he thinks in terms of "stacking functions." Take something as basic as riding a bike. "In the same way the interconnected relationships of the 'three sisters' benefit your garden," he says—referring to the practice of growing corn, squash, and beans together, which provides a climbing structure, soil fertility, and complete nutrition—"a bike not only provides transportation but also provides you with exercise, and at the same time helps you develop relationships with your community that you could not initiate while locked inside your car."

The mantra of urban homesteaders was to look for solutions within the problem itself. In New York the problem was limited green space because of tightly clustered high-rises; the solution was rooftop gardens. In Los Angeles the problem was low-density sprawl that caused dependence on cars; the solution was backyard produce distributed to neighbors by bicycle.

But the chosen cities—tech and finance boomtowns like New York, Seattle, and San Francisco—have become so desirable that the only people who can afford them anymore are college-educated professionals. When I moved to what I'd thought of as a gritty city—Brooklyn—I found myself surrounded by the same type of white middle-class people I'd grown up with. Neighborhoods once known for a mix of race and class—Brooklyn's Williamsburg, San Francisco's Mission District, Seattle's Capitol Hill, Los Angeles's Silver Lake—have become enclaves for the privileged. High rents and property values forced others out, especially the people of color who had preceded them.

Meanwhile, cities not graced by the magic wand of NASDAQ continue to decline. Detroit, Cleveland, Baltimore, and St. Louis have not recovered from last century's white flight. Staying in crumbling urban centers turned out to be overwhelmingly the fate of the poor and the nonwhite. And many of them were already living some version of the apocalypse the preppers on their mountaintops were fleeing: The failure of basic services, like garbage collection and ambulances. Neglect of the infrastructure—transportation, public buildings, power supply. Financial collapse leading to mass layoffs and shuttered businesses. Pollution and blight. Rising crime. Governmental paralysis and indifference. At just the moment when a movement of white people was preparing for a coming collapse, millions of people of color were already being pulled into its spiral.

I wanted to see what it was like not merely to predict and prepare for our country's deepest failures but to truly engage with them. Detroit had become the poster child for urban failure, as a city that no longer had the distinct characteristics—and advantages—of a city. Even in its heyday, it had a car-dependent layout similar to that of Los Angeles, sprawling over an area the size of San Francisco, Manhattan, and Boston combined. Now it had grown dysfunctional in nearly every way. The experts had thrown up their hands. And yet I'd heard about resilience flowering amid the vacant lots of Detroit—a movement spearheaded not by the well-publicized white newcomers but largely by the longtime black residents, working outside the purview of government or nonprofits. It appeared that some sort of civil society was forming from the ground up.

So I went.

OTHER OUTSIDERS, OF COURSE, had been to Detroit before me. I'd read their journalism and seen their photographs of the splendid architecture crumbling, a metaphor for America's undoing that required little explanation. A new breed of tourist had materialized in the city, mostly northern Europeans, who had come specifically to view the blight, or, as it has been dubbed, ruin porn.

But nothing can prepare the uninitiated. Once I got off the freeway and cruised the blocks of waist-high grass and boarded-up bungalows, as a person who had himself come to believe that America's industrial and economic models were doomed, I had a giddy feeling of "I told you so." Here was my evidence that perpetual growth that exploits people and nature does not end well.

My triumph lasted about ten minutes. A few more miles of devastation and I felt nauseated, tears in my eyes. I idled the car in front of a collapsing cottage, tree limbs protruding from the roof, and imagined the people who had lived there, grown up there. I imagined them returning to see their former home. I was sick with grief, a grief at the failure of America—not just its economic and ecological failures but specifically its failure to redress the wrongs of slavery, even 150 years after emancipation. Here the descendants of slaves—first sharecroppers, then factory workers—had become something like permanent refugees, prisoners of crime-ridden slums, trapped amid the iron-grated windows and abandoned lots. "I made a prediction a long time ago, and it's come to pass," the white county executive of adjacent Oakland County told *The New Yorker* in 2014. "I said, what we're gonna do is turn Detroit into an Indian reservation, where we herd all the Indians into the city, build a fence around it, and then throw in the blankets and corn."

I took refuge in a museum, the Detroit Institute of the Arts, and marveled at the Diego Rivera frescoes depicting the human devolution from radiant simplicity to murderous industrialism. I found myself chatting with a security guard, a gray-haired woman who told me she'd lived in Detroit her entire life. I told her why I was visiting, and no sooner had the words *urban farm* slipped my lips than she let out a hoot.

"Farms?" she cried. "That's the last thing we need around here."

BUT SOMEWHERE BETWEEN THE NEON SWIRLS of MotorCity Casino and the looted husk of Michigan Central Station, amid the vacant lots and boarded-up houses, it was a farm I found at last. I drove past a clapboard house toward rows of crops and a greenhouse, where I saw a tractor in the driveway and a black woman of indeterminate age bent over a tray of basil starts. In a white cotton dress, a floppy straw hat, and sandals, she looked vintage cool, as if she had been outfitted for a production of *Porgy and Bess*.

I had read about this farm online, but my phone calls and emails had gone unanswered. And just the night before, at an anarchist collective elsewhere in Detroit, someone had cited it as a good place to exchange labor for vegetables. And yet as I stood there, with a shudder of professional embarrassment I realized that I had forgotten the name of the farm and its owners. The woman regarded me without enthusiasm as I launched into an explanation of what I was doing in Detroit. She remained stoic as I rambled on about the journey that had brought me there.

It was Ina May Gaskin who came to my rescue.

I mentioned the Farm and meeting Ina May. It was as if I'd said that I'd just had breakfast with Jesus. "*Spiritual Midwifery?*" the woman sang out, a dazzling smile spreading. "I read that!"

She relented. She told me her name, Olivia, and the name of the farm, Brother Nature Produce, and she let me know that she and her husband were its proprietors. The farm spread out over a block of vacant lots in North Corktown, a neighborhood adjacent to downtown and so devastated for decades that only a handful of rickety wooden homes remained on each block. Olivia was twenty-eight years old, spoke with a lilt that was more Mississippi than Michigan, and presented as more blunt than sweet. The topic turned to preppers filling their basement with packaged foods and generators from big-box stores.

"Their preparing for the collapse is what's leading to the collapse," she said, "because they're not doing anything to stop it."

Olivia Hubert spoke with an authority unique among the homesteaders I had met, because the world in which she'd been raised was one that had already collapsed.

Seven

Some fool at the mission was handing out apples to the homeless. For proper nutrition. And so some crook carried a bag of fruit down Mack Avenue and hid in the thicket. When a car rolled to a stop at the corner, the crook beaned it with an apple. The driver was dumb enough to get out and inspect the damage. The crook emerged from the brush with a pistol, scared off the chump, and stole the car.

Mack Avenue cut through the factories on the east side of Detroit. The building where Olivia and her parents lived had once been a nut-processing plant. When they bought it in 1999, about the time Olivia entered high school, it was just a brick shell. Her mother's dream, moving from a leafy lane to a busy avenue, was to open a resale shop for vintage clothing and furniture. In the garage her stepfather would start a car wash. That the family owned their own home and businesses placed them in what remained of Detroit's black middle class. After the white flight of the sixties and seventies, well-off blacks also fled to the suburbs in the nineties, leaving the city more impoverished than ever.

Olivia and her mother and stepfather were not deterred. They worked a whole year hauling drifts of trash off the yard, exhuming debris, then erecting walls inside the husk. They found an old conveyor belt and heaps of Brazil nuts. Behind the building was a park where neighbors said that an old Negro League baseball team used to play. Rising beside the diamond was the most magnificent symmetrical elm tree Olivia had ever seen.

They scoured the curbs, loading furniture into the sedan. Her mom had an eye for treasures, like a genuine white horsehair couch. Olivia's mother stripped the paint from the frame and had the cushions restuffed and Scotchgarded—she was the type of woman who memorized her upholsterer's phone number—and you could not sit on the thing unless it was a special occasion. They transformed the factory into a two-bedroom loft with sun pouring through the windows onto a cognac leather armchair. The leather crackled when you sat down, and it smelled like an oiled baseball mitt, like quality, and after a few seconds it was warm and just right.

Just right, except for the dope dealers stashing product in the park. From her bedroom window Olivia heard prostitutes fighting with knives. She and her mom gave them names. Lil Stank, for one. A few months after her mother opened the shop, Lil Stank rushed in, bare naked, and grabbed a coat from the rack. After that, Olivia's mother ditched the clothing and stuck to furniture.

Traffic was steady on Mack Avenue, and the home was enclosed by an iron fence. Driving westbound, you could nose onto the sidewalk, check for lurkers, hurry to unlock the gate, swing it open, then rush back to the driver's seat and dart inside. Going eastbound was trickier—you had to pass the house, then turn around in the driveway of a vacant house. Not long after the apple-jackings, Olivia's stepfather turned around in that driveway, and just as he straightened the car on Mack Avenue, a man emerged from the brush and tapped on the window with a pistol. Olivia's stepfather had driven a cab in Detroit for decades. He was no sucker. He punched the gas and escaped.

They never knew if this perpetrator was the same as the apple-thrower. The next time he struck, in the same driveway, the driver was not as fortunate—or as quick. He was shot dead behind the wheel of his car.

One day Olivia and her mother came home to find the gate flattened and a shimmering new SUV, mostly unscathed, parked atop it. If the rightful owner of the car had crashed here, they figured, he most likely would have called the police, or a tow truck. The car must be stolen. They called the police.

But the police didn't come.

In an hour they called again.

Still no police.

The next time they poked their head out the window, the vehicle was gone. There seemed to be only one explanation. The car thieves had crashed into the gate, fled the scene, monitored the car, and after a few hours had passed with no response from the law, returned to their prize and made a clean getaway.

Olivia was not allowed to walk anywhere. Not that there were many places to stroll to, between the abandoned factories and the boarded-up homes. You needed a car, or an escort, even to go to Green's Deep South Barbeque down the block, whose lone Yelp reviewer asked, "Would you like some bulletproof glass to go along with your take-out barbeque?" Her family wanted to support the local black grocer, but he took so long to ring up purchases that they often drove to the Kroger in Grosse Pointe instead. Olivia was not allowed to catch the bus that lumbered at irregular intervals down Mack Avenue. Riding the bus was not particularly dangerous. It was waiting at the curb that made you a target. Detroit was twenty miles across but had no rail or subway. Her parents drove her to Martin Luther King High School in the morning and picked her up in the afternoon. "When you get growed up," said her mother, who was born in Mississippi and still sounded like it, "you can do whatever you want."

Little Olivia—she was petite and pretty and even as a high school

senior could pass for a child—didn't actually *want* to walk down Mack
Avenue and ride the Detroit buses. She was afraid. Over the years she
had pored over enough *National Geographic*s to know that not everyone lived like this, that elsewhere in the world kids played in the street
and slept with the window open. She wanted that world so badly, a
home that was safe and secure.

OLIVIA'S GRANDMOTHER FRANCES POWE had been raised on a
farm near De Kalb, Mississippi, but country life never suited her.
When her marriage ended in divorce, she headed north on the City of
New Orleans with her five children, making every stop from Cairo to
Kankakee. "It was just toddlin' along," Powe told me decades later. "It
was in no hurry." Olivia's family was not alone in this journey. They
caught the tail of the Great Migration. In the largest relocation in
American history, between 1910 and 1970, six million African Americans had fled the segregation and lynching of the South for the hope
of freedom and jobs in the North. The shift was not only geographic;
it altered the structure and livelihoods of black communities. While
most of the migrants came from small towns and farms, nearly all
landed in big, crowded cities: New York, Philadelphia, Chicago, St.
Louis, Los Angeles, and Oakland. Nearly every family had worked
the soil, whether as slaves or sharecroppers or field hands or landowners, but in the North they took industrial jobs. Centuries of farm skills
disappeared in a generation.

The family disembarked at Michigan Central Station in 1967.
They hauled suitcases past the marble pillars and the brick walls of
the concourse, beneath the gaping copper skylights. As they descended
the granite stairway, Detroit sprawled to the horizon: freeways and
factories and smokestacks and skyscrapers. And blowing across it all
was something Frances Powe had never seen: litter.

With its booming auto plants that hired across racial lines, Detroit was the Great Migration's fourth-largest magnet after New York, Chicago, and Philadelphia. Between 1910 and 1940, its black population soared from 5,000 to 150,000. That number doubled in the next decade, as blacks replaced white workers drafted into World War II. By 1960, 480,000 African Americans lived in Detroit. They constituted 40 percent of the workforce at Ford's River Rouge plant, and a similar portion across the industry.

Despite their advances, blacks did not join the middle class at the rate of their white counterparts. Even as the Big Three automakers integrated, small shops that manufactured tools and parts remained almost all white. Blacks were often relegated to the dirtiest, most dangerous, and lowest-paying jobs, as janitors or in the steel foundry. "Some jobs white folks will not do," said an auto company official, according to Thomas Sugrue's *The Origins of the Urban Crisis*. "So they have to take niggers in, particularly the duce work, spraying paint on car bodies. This soon kills a white man." It killed black men, too: "It shortens their lives, it cuts them down, but they're just niggers," said the same official.

In the thriving postwar years, when Detroit unemployment sank to 7 percent, the black unemployment rate was 18 percent. Black men gathered on street corners looking for day labor. White commuters driving past saw in them confirmation of a stereotype of black men as shiftless loafers. Meanwhile, black people's attempts to flee the slums were blocked. In the 1940s, more than 80 percent of Detroit property held racial covenants stipulating, for example, that land "shall not be used or occupied by any person or persons except those of the Caucasian race." Even after these codes were struck down by the Supreme Court in 1948, they remained de facto law, as white real estate agents refused to show black clients properties in white neighborhoods.

The urban underclass was born. Blacks were confined largely to clusters of dilapidated homes owned by absentee whites. These landlords, realizing that black tenants had few options, raised rents far higher than what white families in white neighborhoods paid. In a catch-22, if a black family attempted to buy one of these rental properties, the Federal Housing Authority, the New Deal program that subsidized mortgages for low- and middle-income buyers, often refused to finance the purchase, deeming a slum home too risky. If some enterprising black family scraped together the cash to buy without a federal loan, the landlord might finance the house at an interest rate far higher than the rates available to whites in outlying subdivisions. In the event that the family lost its source of income and missed a few payments (a frequent scenario because, in the auto factories, blacks were often the "last hired, first fired"), the landlord simply evicted them and rented or sold to someone else.

Slum houses were subdivided into cramped apartments to maximize revenue. Meanwhile more and more blacks arrived from the South looking for work. As demand and revenue increased, landlords had little incentive to improve their properties, and the ghetto became more crowded, more dilapidated, and more expensive. At the same time, the construction of freeways razed fledgling black business districts in Detroit neighborhoods like Black Bottom and Paradise Valley. This taxpayer-funded construction benefited white suburban commuters while destroying black urban neighborhoods.

By the late 1950s, many whites had moved out of the city. Some streets were transformed from all-white to all-black in a few years, or even months. "Much to their chagrin," wrote Sugrue, "many new black suburbanites found that integration was just a phase between when the first blacks moved in and the last whites took their children out of the public schools."

Just months after they arrived, Frances Powe and her family witnessed the consequences of this discrimination and the resulting resentment. In the summer of 1967, police raided an unlicensed black nightclub where a party was under way for returning Vietnam veterans. A battle erupted against the police. After five days, forty-three people were dead, more than seven thousand had been arrested, 2,500 stores had been looted, and 412 buildings had burned.

The racial tension shocked the Powe family. In the South they had managed to insulate themselves from the worst of Jim Crow. The family had owned several hundred acres of farmland there, and the children had attended all-black schools. They had little contact with whites.

"I didn't realize I was black until I came to Detroit," said Vicky Powe Ransom, Olivia's mother, of being placed in an integrated Catholic school. "I had never seen that many white people at one time in my life. I didn't really face prejudice until I got to this city."

The riots split Detroit. Many whites consider them to be the end of the city's heyday—the last gasp of safe streets and shopping at Hudson's department store and a short commute to a good job—and the beginning of racialized politics, drug epidemics, and rampant crime. But for many black Detroiters, 1967 was the beginning of the heyday. They had finally overthrown the white regime. Access to every neighborhood had been won, with whites either accepting black neighbors or fleeing to the suburbs. "My uncles talked about how they stood on the border waving at the white people leaving, then bought their homes!" recalled University of Michigan professor Angela Dillard. "It wasn't such a terrible thing when these people who had been terrorizing us for decades left." A roster of black luminaries chose Detroit as their home: Marvin Gaye, Smokey Robinson, Diana Ross, even Rosa Parks. As for the glory days of Hudson's—the store had never exactly been for black people in the first place. Its flagship store closed in 1983. The city had its problems, but at least one of them wasn't apartheid.

In the early seventies, Detroit became the first major American city with a black majority. Voters elected its first black mayor, Coleman

Young. Seeing that many city employees—especially white police and firefighters and paramedics—were taking advantage of the good pay and benefits of municipal jobs but living and paying property tax in the suburbs, Young decreed that all city workers must live in the city. To desegregate public schools, he had kids bused from white enclaves into the ghetto, and from the ghetto into the enclaves. More whites fled beyond the city limits, and the black majority increased. Between 1950 and 1980, while the population of Detroit dropped from its high of 1.8 million to 1.2 million, the black population jumped from 300,000 to 759,000. Meanwhile the number of whites plummeted from 1.5 million to 400,000. (By 2010, the number of non-Hispanic whites was 55,000.)

For Frances Powe, these shifts were largely happy. When she began shopping for a home, she could freely move her family to any part of the city, and she used her savings to buy a small brick bungalow on the east side, a neighborhood that had until recently been all white. Her white neighbors in the stone house across the street were friendly and welcoming. Powe enrolled her five children in Catholic schools, and the church helped her find a car and a job in a hospital. "We had so much fun," Powe told me one afternoon, when Olivia took me to the modest bungalow where Powe had lived for decades. The children rode bikes and played in the streets, put on talent shows with the neighbor kids. They took the bus downtown to shop. Vicky recalls that on July 3, her mother would deposit her and her siblings on Belle Isle, an island in the Detroit river just across from downtown, and let them spend the night unattended, to secure a good place to view the next day's fireworks. At a time when Detroit schools were failing and the youth crime rate was soaring, all the Powe children—including Olivia's mother—graduated from East Catholic High School.

The oldest boy, Russy, joined the Marine Corps, and while home on leave he introduced his Marine buddy Angelo Hubert to his kid sister. Angelo and Vicky were soon married. Angelo took a job at the post office in Ann Arbor, and Vicky began training to be an X-ray technician.

And yet, the heyday of black Detroit didn't last. The fleeing whites took most of the jobs, tax base, and community organizations with them. By the time Olivia was born, in 1985, the city was gripped by its worst epidemic yet: crack. The drug flooded the streets for as little as $2.50 a rock. An addict broke into the home of eighty-one-year-old Rosa Parks and, even after recognizing the hero, stole fifty-three dollars and punched her in the face. Olivia's father began using. In his family an entire generation of men—six of them—succumbed to the drug trade, whether by overdose or gunshot. Olivia was still a toddler when her dad lost his job. Soon he moved out, and eventually he disappeared.

After her divorce, Olivia's mother remarried and bought a house on the far east side of Detroit, a relatively safe neighborhood shoe-horned between the stately homes of Grosse Pointe and the bleak party stores along Warren Avenue. The brick homes were neither large nor fancy, but they weren't boarded up or burned. They were neatly kept, with mowed grass, swept driveways, and beds of flowers. This was one of the rare neighborhoods that instead of flipping black had actually integrated. There were black, white, and mixed-race families. There were gay couples and single retirees. Through years of hard work, Vicky Ransom had been able to achieve the dream: she owned her home and was providing a better opportunity for her daughter than she herself had had.

SOME PEOPLE GROW UP around rough things and become rough themselves. Not Olivia. She vowed that she would never be the single mom she saw fighting with her baby daddy at the bus stop. Scared by the addiction she'd seen, she never even sampled alcohol or drugs. "I don't play that shit," she told me. In high school, she never had a boy-friend. "Who you gonna date in the hood?" she said. *"Please!"*

Olivia seemed immune to the temptations of modern adolescence. Her grandmother recalled the time she gave Olivia her Macy's charge card and sent her shopping: "Now you go get some of that stuff the other girls be wearing, with the name on the butt." Olivia dutifully plodded off to the mall, returning not with two-hundred-dollar bedazzled jeans but a plain wool sweater. "She's a tightwad," her mother said. "She do not like to spend money. If I take her shopping, even if it ain't her money, she don't want to spend it. I have to *force* her to take stuff."

Perhaps Olivia owed her frugality to the paradox of growing up sheltered in Detroit. When Olivia reached school age, her mother enrolled her at St. Clare Catholic school on the Grosse Pointe side of Jefferson Boulevard, just a few blocks from the house. Their block was safe enough that some Detroit police officers lived on it, but close enough to the sketchy Warren Avenue that those cops' homes were sometimes burglarized. Vicky forbade Olivia to walk or bicycle to school, and instead drove her each morning. Olivia was allowed to venture three houses to the north and three houses to the south. There were few young children in the neighborhood, and fewer still within her roaming radius.

As a result, Olivia was an isolated child and a fearful one, imagining disaster around every corner. She devoured books, which let her dream about places other than Detroit. "That way I could go anywhere," she told me. "I could go to the past, the future. It exposed you to new points of view. It made you really imagine what the world would look like, and reimagine, because the first way you imagined didn't really make any sense." She read romances and fantasy and science fiction. She read books about girls; *Little Women* was a favorite. She had a double bed, and mornings her mother found her sleeping straight as a pencil on one half of the mattress, the other half covered with books.

As she entered junior high school, Olivia did well in the classroom but showed little interest in other activities. She was encouraged to try out for the track team. "They always think black people have potential to be athletes," Olivia told me. "I didn't give a damn about no damn track." At recess and lunch the other kids just sat around gossiping. Bored, Olivia wandered to the front of the campus, where unsightly weeds sprouted from flower beds. She knelt to pull them.

The faculty noted the child's odd hobby. One day a teacher asked Olivia if she would like to meet someone who could teach her about plants. Vicky gave her blessing, and after school she delivered Olivia to a quaint cottage a few blocks from their home. An old-fashioned red mailbox stood by the curb. In the windows, bits of colored glass caught the sunshine. Tidy rows of vegetables grew where the lawn had once been. Little Olivia recognized the place for what it was: a perfect home.

Inside was Catherine Mack, a white parishioner at St. Clare who had retired after a career teaching biology at Wayne State University. Mack lived alone. She had no television. A turntable was reserved for classical music. She slept on a tiny wooden bed, the mattress supported by ropes of jute, like something that belonged out on the prairie. Miss Mack did not reveal her age, but told Olivia that she'd begun teaching when the pay was twenty-five cents an hour. She had grown up in this perfect little house, the only child of parents who had themselves been orphans. The reverential way she treated it gave Olivia the idea that Miss Mack's parents had built it themselves.

Olivia Hubert and Catherine Mack made fast friends. "She taught me all kinds of stuff," Olivia says. The basic biology of insects and plants and plant parts and natural systems. Handicrafts: knitting, weaving, cooking, and canning. How to spin wool with just a hook, like a piece of hanger, and how to prepare the spun wool and how to dye it using natural dyes. Miss Mack was so expert at spinning wool

147

that in her retirement she'd taken a weekend job at Greenfield Village, a historical theme park, demonstrating a wheel and loom.

Miss Mack owned a complete run of yellow-spine *National Geographics*, some so old that their interiors were in black-and-white. Olivia dived through this portal and into strange and exotic worlds. "She had all those Lavinia Derwent books, the little girl who grew up in the Scottish Highlands. And Lavinia used to wander around all day by herself, because they let kids do that kind of stuff back then. She was fearless. Playing in the ruins of castles."

One day, at thirteen, Olivia came home from Miss Mack's and said, "Ma, I know what I want to do."

What? her mother asked.

"Horticulture."

"Horti-what?"

Her mother had little idea how to prepare her daughter for such a career. "Here in Detroit?" Vicky told me later. *"Please."* Maybe it was just a phase that would pass. And besides, Vicky had more pressing concerns. She and her husband were selling their house and moving to the factory on Mack Avenue, a few miles west toward downtown, in a much rougher neighborhood, where she would open her resale shop. She enrolled Olivia for ninth grade at East Catholic.

Even without Miss Mack, Olivia adjusted well to the move. She was accustomed to confinement, so the exact location of her home mattered little. She discovered the main branch of the Detroit Public Library, and Vicky permitted her to spend the days there. "You know librarians," said Olivia. "They're serious about them fucking library rules. Like you ain't supposed to eat in here. They hear the wrapper and kick you out. They would kick other people out for eating, but they wouldn't kick me out because they were like, Wow, this teenager is in here reading books, for real! So then I would take a lunch and start hanging there all day."

One day a neighbor stopped by the iron gate on Mack Avenue while Vicky and Olivia were tending the garden. "I been watching you from the first day you got here," he said. He was impressed—amazed, actually—by how they had transformed the industrial husk into an attractive home. Vicky thanked him. She bragged about her daughter's green thumb.

The man's face lit up. He worked for the Detroit public schools, at the vo-tech center. Did she know, he asked, that there was an agri-science program, with a specialty in horticulture, right here in Detroit?

To qualify for the vo-tech program, Olivia transferred to Martin Luther King, the local public high school. She awoke well before dawn. The house was quiet. She made her own breakfast and packed her own lunch. From the school, Olivia took a bus to the vo-tech center on Jefferson Boulevard, and then, as the sun was emerging behind the empty factories, she boarded another bus. This one ferried her across the Detroit River, halfway to Canada, and deposited her at the Anna Scripps Whitcomb Conservatory on Belle Isle, where her mother and aunts and uncles had camped out on the Fourth of July decades before.

Technically within city limits, Belle Isle appeared to Olivia another world. It was considered Detroit's jewel, a relic from a gilded era long past. The old gray globe of the arboretum and its resplendent fountains were vaguely European. Chiming bells filled the air. Couples said their vows on infinite green lawns spread between towering elms. Women in swimsuits lay on sandy beaches along the banks of the river. The unfamiliar skyline on the far side was an actual foreign country.

The conservatory itself was founded in 1904. In its formal gardens were rows of manicured hedges and a round fountain with sculptures at each point of the compass: rabbit, hawk, eagle, and seal. Engraved at the base was an exhortation: *A continual hint to my fellow citizens to devote themselves to the benefit and pleasure of the public.* Wandering between the flowering willows and blue spruce, Olivia could shield herself from freeways and blight and pretend she was in another epoch, when citizens flocked in waistcoats and silk gowns to see with their own eyes some new species of tropical orchid.

While the outside was grand, the inside was magical. In the great glass atrium blossomed flora from the world over: Manila palm and cabbage palm and majesty palm and slender-lady palm. The great dome opened onto the hot dry Cactus House, with its South African ox tongue and Kenyan cow's horn and Mexican jellybeans. The old-man cactus peered down on the silver-dollar cactus, while the queen of the night floated overhead as if riding a thermal along the steel ribs of the sky. Lush vines cascaded off the tufa rock walls. In the court-yard, beside a lily pond, a stone turtle spurted water from its lips. A crab apple tree bore tiny red fruits.

Best of all was the Tropical House. As Olivia ducked under the oldest canary palm in America, a cloud of fragrant steam wafted over her. She danced past the exotic fruits: calamondin orange and blood-leaf banana, Surinam cherry and fiddle-leaf fig. She sampled the sweet-est grapefruit she had ever tasted. Moisture dripped along the inside of the glass walls. Wet leaves embraced her, drew her deeper into the jun-gle of hibiscus spider plant and white bird-of-paradise. The pink pow-der puff was an airy explosion of gold-dipped fuchsia tracers. There was peace lily and rainbow tree, heavenly bamboo and angel-wing begonia.

In the deepest recess of the Tropical House hid the orchids. Their perfume made Olivia dizzy. Supple pink petals peeled open to the sun-light to expose magenta capillaries. She didn't yet know their names. One was a princess in a scarlet gown with a gilded cape, a glittering jewel at her throat. Another was a bowl of fresh cream floating a strawberry. A white-feathered creature with a pair of yellow eyes wanted to flap its wings and fly. Climbing vines exploded gold and crimson like strings of firecrackers. These weren't just pictures in a book. Olivia could breathe their pollen and lay a finger directly on the stamens and petals.

While many of her classmates had come to Belle Isle merely to dodge geometry class, Olivia threw herself into study. "I was the only one who liked it there," she said. And the people who ran the place liked Olivia, too, as she was so different from the parade of listless students who didn't want mud on their Reeboks.

"They would have a geranium show," said Olivia, "and you needed to have thousands and thousands of geraniums of different sizes ready on such and such date or all hell was gonna break loose, because those old ladies have to have their geranium show. They taught me specifics of how to propagate plants for a show."

The schooling lasted two years, and at the end Olivia took her practicum exam and scored the first-ever A in the program's history. She didn't want to return to King for her senior year, and the staff didn't want to lose her, so they created a position just for her, student greenhouse manager. Olivia was paid minimum wage for her final year of high school to water plants, organize seedlings, and direct other students.

The conservatory not only felt like a fairy-tale castle, but seemed to have been designed in medieval times. Byzantine tangles of water pipes and gas lines and electrical cords that would have mystified a contractor somehow managed to pump the atrium with warm air and fresh water, insulating it from the Detroit winter. Down in musty stone dungeons, antique boilers were kept in service only through the tinkering of cagey custodians who had worked there for decades. A staff of seven ran the entire place. Most were lifers with the city, for which they got a living wage, health insurance, and a pension.

"They were crotchety and set in their ways, but I liked them," said Olivia. "They were willing to share their knowledge with me. They told stories about the glory days, with twenty full-time workers." The conservatory was absolutely immaculate back then. "In its heyday they had plant hunters going to Florida and stealing orchids from the

Everglades." They had even had a night watchman to check on the plants, in case of a power outage. Now all they had were memories of better days—and Olivia to hear them.

Olivia won a scholarship to Michigan State, in East Lansing, to study horticulture. She loved campus life. She marveled at the walking trails snaking through wooded areas. People were running, but they weren't running from anything or to anything. "They were just running for fun! And nobody got jumped. And there wasn't glass broken everywhere. And you could walk places by yourself. And your bike wasn't automatically going to disappear. I was like, Wow!"

Olivia loved the safety of her dormitory, the locked bedroom, the cafeteria that prepared three meals a day, and the janitors who scrubbed the toilets and showers. Students of agriculture, science, and engineering were housed together, and Olivia was the only black woman in the dorm. She got a work-study job cleaning the dorms, to supplement her scholarship and her loans. White people she took as one more exotic, if preponderant species. She observed how her white classmates left their expensive laptops on sofas and dining hall tables. Amazingly, they didn't get stolen, but some behavior she considered just plain dumb. A toothy girl from the north country had a habit of napping on her bed with her door wide open in the middle of the day, when dorm entrances were unlocked. Olivia pulled her aside. "Look, girlfriend. You can't do this. It's not safe." But the next afternoon, there was her friend, slumbering in peace, her hair a golden pool of silk. Olivia reached around the door, locked it, and gently pulled it shut.

Other behaviors of white teenagers were simply appalling. One morning while Olivia's parents were visiting, they came across a band of drunk students stumbling across campus to a football game. One of the girls was particularly smashed. "And she bent over and flipped her dress over her head and showed my parents her ass," Olivia said. "I was embarrassed. Because even though people think in Detroit you can do whatever you'd like, I had never seen anything like that in all my life in Detroit."

While there were plenty of black students in East Lansing, Olivia didn't quite fit in with them, either. "When they were in the hood, they did what they were supposed to do as far as education and showing up. But they had to prove something when they got to Michigan State. A lot of them thought they were too cool to go to class, so they stopped going. It was just a lot of fronting and bullshit. Come on! You know your family is dependent on you."

Olivia had worked all her life to get out of Detroit, to get to college. And her mother had worked her whole life to give her that chance. Her grandmother had worked her whole life to give chances to her children. As Olivia looked at her fellow students, she was struck by their ingratitude. She wondered what their parents thought. "They took a second mortgage out on their house to send their kids to school, and if they knew what their kids were doing, they would bring their asses home. A lot of parents tell their kids, 'Oh, y'know, have the time of your life, have fun.' Well, did you know that 'the time of your life' means snorting coke off some girl who's passed out's stomach?"

Though Olivia never quite fit in with any group, she had friends of all races. During high school she had attended summer programs for minority scholars, where she had met some Ojibway kids who had invited her to powwows, and she continued to attend them through college. Her great-aunts had told her that their grandmother had come from a reservation, and Olivia was intrigued by this part of her heritage. She loved the drums and learned some of the fancy dances and practiced them at home, but generally during the powwows she felt too self-conscious to dance. During her sophomore year she met an Ojibway guy at a powwow and dated him for two years.

Olivia spent the summer after her freshman year studying horticulture in England through a program at Michigan State. She and her fellow students learned preindustrial farming techniques, like harvesting hay the peasant way, by hand, with neither tractor nor baler. "It was the hottest days of the year," she told me. "I felt sorry for them in their pink faces." She visited Wisley, the flagship garden of the Royal Horticultural Society in the county of Surrey, southwest of London. With its majestic Glasshouse and vast rose collections and stone terraces, it was grander even than Belle Isle.

The Royal Horticultural Society offered a paid internship, and after graduation Olivia returned to London, this time alone. She discovered the joys of living in a safe and thriving city with functional public transportation. With an income of twelve pounds per hour she had plenty of cash to make the payments on her student loans and still eat out and buy new clothes. She discovered one corner of London that reminded her of Detroit, with black men opening their coats to hawk what they claimed were Rolexes. But in London, she could hop on the Tube and quickly be back in safety. "There's different degrees of danger," she said, reflecting on her experiences of London and Detroit. "There's you-might-get-knocked-off-your-bike danger, and there's someone-might-rob-you-when-you-get-knocked-off-your-bike danger."

Nonetheless, after a year in London, Olivia felt homesick. Despite her drive and means, Vicky Ransom hadn't wanted to leave her mother, and at heart Olivia was the same. She returned to Detroit. She still believed she could make a career there.

THE AUTUMN OF 2008 may have been the worst time in history to find a job in Michigan. Just weeks after Olivia's homecoming, Lehman Brothers failed, triggering a global recession. The Big Three carpooled to Washington begging for loans, then laid off more than ten thousand workers. Detroit's mayor pleaded guilty to obstruction of justice, resigned, and was sent to jail.

And the east side had only gotten worse. Powerboats were capsized on sidewalks, as if beached by a tsunami—apparently dumped by thieves who wanted the trailers on which they had been stored at a nearby marina. Vicky shuttered the shop. Green's Deep South Barbeque and the mom-and-pop grocer went under. The only businesses now were party stores, a Detroit institution in which cash was passed under bulletproof panes from a black to an Arab in exchange for liquor, cigarettes, and potato chips. In 2007, Farmer Jack closed, making Detroit America's largest city without a national grocery chain. Actual food was sold in the suburbs and at a handful of city markets, but with the meager bus system and the high cost of car insurance, most Detroiters had no means to get it. With many people depending on party stores for groceries, the city gained the ignominious title of "food desert."

In a decade the city had shed another 240,000 people, leaving its population at just over 700,000, roughly a third of its 1950 peak, and its residential property values had declined by 97 percent. It had the nation's highest poverty rate (34 percent) and highest unemployment rate (23 percent). In 2012 the city's rates of murder and aggravated assault were the highest in the nation, with the murder rate ten times that of New York City's. Olivia heard gunshots in the middle of the day.

Many of the abandoned homes and shops in Olivia's neighborhood had burned down. Now, as balloon payments on mortgages came due, hundreds of still-occupied houses went into foreclosure. Owners were evicted, windows and doors boarded up, w/cut spray-painted on the plywood to indicate that the water had been disconnected. Broken water mains bubbled up for months, flooding entire streets. And then, inevitably, the houses caught fire. Sometimes the fire trucks arrived, sometimes not. Detroiters spoke with certainty that the arsonists were on the banks' payrolls. The houses were not rescued. Some of the charred hulks were razed, while others just collected snow in the winter and sprouted weeds in the summer. Banks received insurance settlements at the original purchase price, not the market value; often there was no price at which these houses could sell. Homes that had sold for forty thousand a few years earlier were now listed under ten thousand. And still nobody bought. Hovering above the city on seemingly every billboard and bus wrap and transit bench was the milky apparition of an attorney named Joumana Kayrouz, bubble-gum lips and uptick eyebrows and corn-silk hair parted in the center like a witch's. INJURED? her ads screamed to the downtrodden. 1-866-YOUR-RIGHTS.

Gazing out at the ruins of Mack Avenue, Olivia saw that the marketability of her proudly acquired skills was dubious. She had borrowed $10,000 from the government to complete her degree and was paying it back at $150 per month. Her student health plan had expired, and her mom was hounding her to get coverage. She searched all winter across the nation for conservatory jobs, but she wasn't landing so much as an interview.

Meanwhile the jobs advertised in Detroit were the same minimum-wage grinds she remembered from high school: Long John Silver's, security guard, Family Dollar. And her classmates from King were still working them, or having babies and collecting food stamps. Or going to prison. One girl from school had been choked to death by her boyfriend. The other available jobs were dealing blackjack and making beds and cleaning floors at one of the three gigantic Vegas-style casinos that now shimmered in neon above the freeways, yet another of the city fathers' plots to save Detroit.

Stuck at home, Olivia wondered if going to college had been worth the trouble and money. What good was upward mobility if you were afraid to walk out the door of your house? She considered going back to her Paw-Paw's place in Mississippi and trying to make it as a farmer. It was as if Olivia had never left Detroit—and might never escape.

Eight

A few months after my first visit to Detroit, I returned, this time driving from Montana. Whenever I caught a good AM signal I tuned into *The Dave Ramsey Show*, the nation's most popular personal finance program. What struck me about Ramsey was that he did not encourage his listeners to get rich quick. Instead, in a honey-sweet Tennessee drawl, he preached frugality, savings, and, most important, getting out of debt. Ramsey was empathetic, folksy, and blunt. "Dude, it is *insane* for you to be driving a thirty-thousand-dollar car," he told a caller. "Sell it and buy a beater for a thousand bucks." He advised those who couldn't afford a car to ride a bike, and those who couldn't afford restaurants to stay home and eat beans and rice. Often a call about an outstanding credit card bill quickly exposed the fragility of the caller's marriage. Ramsey counseled that the first step toward getting your accounts in order was to get your inner house in order.

Deeply Christian, Ramsey sat firmly in the Calvinist tradition and was an advocate of the Protestant work ethic. He didn't shame people for being poor; he didn't tell them they needed a higher income. Instead he shamed them for living beyond their means, and exhorted them to simplify and reduce until they balanced their budget. The new status symbol, he said, was not a Mercedes-Benz but a paid-off mortgage. It was an antidote to what Americans often heard: Earn more so that you can spend more. Ramsey said to spend less. He claimed that the car companies hated him. He encouraged listeners to spend more time at home with our families. But first: we needed to pay our debts.

The culmination of the show was the "debt-free scream," when Ramsey invited a young couple to the studio to outline all they had renounced—an anniversary trip to Ireland, a new car, weekends out at bars with their friends—in order to pay off $40,000 in two years. Then they counted down from three and shattered the airwaves with a barbaric yawp. The thrill I absorbed from those cathartic screams was considerable.

Listening to Ramsey for a couple of hours would convince you that just about everyone in America was shackled by debt. And it was largely true. In 1999 the average savings rate of Americans dropped to negative territory for the first time in history: as a people we owed more than our net worth. Leading the way was consumer debt such as credit cards and financing for cars, which, unlike homes, depreciate, so those expenditures generally cannot be recouped. Americans were also taking on student loan debt in unprecedented numbers. In 2013, 70 percent of college graduates—Olivia included—were in debt, owing an average of $28,000. In a sense we are born in hock: with the national debt hovering around $18 trillion, each new baby delivered in America takes her first breath owing approximately $57,000.

Although this state of affairs may be startling, it's not a historical anomaly. America has long been a nation of debtors. We know that the frontier was settled largely by people willing to forgo the comforts of civilization for the freedom of being their own boss, but here's the fine print: they took these risks partly because they were fleeing from debt. "Two out of every three Europeans who came to the colonies were debtors on arrival," Jill Lepore wrote of the legions of indentured servants who gave seven years of service to someone willing to pay their passage to the new land. Georgia began as a debtors' colony, and roughing it in the New World was preferable to rotting in some European debtors' prison. Debt wasn't limited to the poor. Jefferson and Washington and many other founders owed large sums to creditors in Britain.

In the modern era, with debt increasing and real wages declining, what vocations would allow Americans to do their debt-free scream? And with her degree in horticulture and mountain of debt amid a global recession, what was available to Olivia Hubert?

EVERYONE IN THE FAMILY was thrilled when, in the midst of Olivia's job search, her grandmother called to report what she'd seen on TV: The Henry Ford was hiring. On the morning of the job fair, Olivia rose early and dressed in a white blouse, black slacks, and black shoes. She brushed her hair neatly. In the driveway she climbed into her stepfather's taxi as her mother unlocked the gate, and he shot down Mack Avenue toward the Edsel Ford Expressway. As it happens, it's quicker to get to the suburbs than to get across Detroit.

Twenty minutes later they arrived in Dearborn, birthplace of Henry Ford, headquarters of the Ford Motor Company, and home of River Rouge, the world's first vertically integrated auto plant. Beginning in 1927, loads of iron ore, coal, limestone, and raw rubber arrived by barge and within days rolled off the line as Model As, and later Thunderbirds and Mustangs, and now F-150 pickups. Molten iron smelted in the blast furnaces was poured from giant ladles into the foundry, where it was cast into engine blocks. The Rouge produced its own electricity, steel, and glass. Ninety miles of rail and 120 miles of conveyor belt delivered materials between buildings. Even Henry Ford's detractors could not help marveling at the scope, innovation, and efficiency. People referred to it as the first wonder of the industrial world.

But the jobs Ford was offering that chilly spring morning to Olivia

Hubert and hundreds of others did not involve forging engine blocks or stamping fenders or even attaching plastic cup holders to dashboards. Those jobs still paid well, but there were fewer of them every year. That very month the Ford Motor Company had announced a loss of $14 billion. The entity sponsoring the job fair, the Henry Ford, was not an automobile plant but a museum and amusement park. Here, on the few pastoral acres of Dearborn not paved over by his twentieth-century industrial masterpiece, Henry Ford had created a monument to the nineteenth century. His sanctuary was called Greenfield Village, and for the twenty-four-dollar admission ticket, visitors could peruse Thomas Edison's laboratory, the Wright Brothers' bicycle shop, and Ford's own childhood home. These were not mere reproductions, but actual buildings purchased by Ford and meticulously deconstructed, each board and plank cataloged and numbered, then shipped to Dearborn and reassembled. A coal-fired locomotive chugged around the perimeter. In the shops, tradesmen plied obsolete arts like glass blowing and yarn spinning, weaving and potting.

Also on the premises stood the humble Ohio farm of Harvey Firestone, the tire king who was Ford's friend, collaborator, and in-law. (Ford's grandson married Firestone's granddaughter. The son of that union, Bill Ford, is the executive chairman of the Ford Motor Company.) The Firestone farm was not some static museum piece. Historic reenactors, flesh-and-blood humans in woolen britches and felt hats, bonnets and long cotton dresses, performed the daily chores of a nineteenth-century farm. They even did some actual farming—planting and harvesting corn and tomatoes, milking cows and tending geese and slopping pigs, which they butchered for hams and hung from the basement rafters to cure. Each day the Firestoners ate a wholesome lunch, some of it grown on the premises and cooked over a wood-burning stove. There were cheese biscuits and crocks of sauerkraut and chicken potpies. "But we don't call it *lunch*," "Pa" told me when Olivia took me there. "Here on the farm it's called *dinner*. We need a big meal for all our afternoon chores. And then we have what you might call *dinner*. But we call it *supper*." As if through miraculous time travel, the verdant Michigan of Henry Ford's youth blossomed just twenty minutes from the derelict Michigan of Olivia Hubert's youth.

A hand-tooled sign relayed the words of Daniel Webster: "When tillage begins, other arts follow. The farmers, therefore, are the founders of human civilization." The job of reenacting the very founding of civilization, at seven dollars an hour, was that for which Olivia had come to apply. The irony did not escape her that here in the shadow of the world's most famous factory, the industry was not production but leisure. A theme park whose theme was work.

At Greenfield Village, the only historically accurate roles for a black woman were at the sharecroppers' quarters or the Susquehanna Plantation, portraying a slave. Which is not to say Olivia found the work beneath her. Olivia liked Greenfield Village. She had visited as a kid and had always loved the old-timey stuff: knitting and spinning yarn and dipping candles. And having been raised in a vintage clothing shop, she liked to dress up.

Hundreds showed up for the job fair. The park was hiring not just reenactors but ticket takers, janitors, cooks, and food servers. Olivia aced the interview. If college hadn't yielded a career, it had at least taught her to play the game. She knew when to stand, when to sit, when to smile, how firmly to shake a hand. A battery of psych tests was administered, with multiple-choice questions to indicate likeliness to steal from the till and to report others who stole from the till. Olivia sailed through. The human resources guy, a fellow alumnus of Michigan State, took a shine to her. Aware that she was overqualified, he offered her a job as an actual gardener on the landscaping crew. The pay was $9.25 an hour, with free park admission for family members and a 10 percent discount at the gift shop.

Olivia was issued a uniform, olive green like a park ranger's. By the time she attended orientation, Chrysler had declared bankruptcy, with General Motors soon to follow. The newly elected President Obama, who had continued George W. Bush's policy of using public funds to rescue the banks, earmarked even more money to save the auto industry.

The new hires at the Henry Ford sat in folding chairs and sipped coffee from paper cups. The trainer welcomed them and spent the morning explaining paychecks, timesheets, and the dress code. After lunch she took questions.

"What about the bailout?" was the first one.

The trainer explained that the Henry Ford was not owned by the Ford Motor Company or the Ford family or the Ford Foundation. Rather, it was an independent nonprofit. She also mentioned that while Chrysler and GM had accepted bailout funds, Ford had not. While on the topic of Ford, she thought a brief biography of Henry Ford was in order. Born right here in Dearborn on a humble family farm in 1863, Ford became one of the world's most innovative and successful men. It was no exaggeration to say he shaped the twentieth century. Although he invented neither the car nor the assembly line, he perfected them both. With the reliable Model T, which sold for just five hundred dollars, he brought automobiles to the masses. Cars granted the freedom of mobility Americans came to take for granted and ended the centuries-old confinement of village life. Ford single-handedly spurred one of the largest migrations to Detroit and helped to create the middle class. His own employees could afford a Model T! During World War II, Ford manufactured B-24 bombers at a rate of one per hour, and Detroit came to be known as the "Arsenal of Democracy." By the time of his death in 1947, Henry Ford—without so much as a high school diploma—had transformed America from the agrarian backwater of the late 1800s into an industrial superpower and guardian of democracy.

Someone asked about Ford's wife. The trainer said that Clara Ford, too, was raised on a Dearborn farm. She was hardworking, humble, and loyal, and a devoted mother to the couple's son, Edsel. Visitors were so interested in Clara that the museum had published her journal and sold it in the gift shop.

The questions continued for a full hour, until the trainer said, "Anything else, before we move on?"

A hand shot up in the back. A loud voice broke the silence.

"What about the Jews?"

The trainer blinked. Olivia craned her neck to see.

"I mean, all those things Henry Ford said about the Jews," said the man. "What if someone asks us about that?"

The trainer pressed her palms against the fronts of her khakis.

"That's an aspect of his life we choose not to focus on," she said. "How about a short break?"

THE SUMMER OF 2009 SWEPT over the Great Lakes warm and sticky, bearing swarms of fish flies and mosquitoes. Olivia rose before dawn and packed a lunch. Her stepfather chauffeured her to Greenfield Village by seven. The landscaping crew was split by gender. The men putted back and forth in restored Model Ts, rode mowers, and trimmed the hedges into geometric blocks with power shears.

The women bent over in the sweltering heat, planting flowers and tending the beds. Annuals. Petunias. Impatiens. Marigolds. Hydrangeas. Geraniums. Olivia didn't think much of the predictable choices, but she wasn't getting paid for her aesthetic. She had trained in white gloves at the Chelsea Flower Show, designed herbariums and terrariums, curated insect collections. At the topiary at Wisley Gardens she had learned to identify more than one thousand species of plants and flowers. She could sculpt a hedge into the shape of a spiral. Or of a squirrel. There would be no demand for those skills here. Her supervisors insisted that unplanted beds be turned frequently to keep the weeds down, which only sprouted more weeds. Olivia bit her lip. She was the only person under forty on the crew. Nothing would be gained by telling her boss that she knew better.

Olivia got her driver's license and applied for a $7,000 loan to buy her first car, a tomato-red Chevy. She assumed she would qualify. In her final year of college, instead of frittering away an elective on bowling or sailing, she had taken a class in personal finance, in which she had learned the importance of good credit. She'd dutifully applied for a card, used it to buy groceries and clothing even when she had the money in the bank, and paid off the balance each month. Nonetheless, she was denied the car loan. Her mother had to co-sign, and the loan she got carried an interest rate of 18 percent. Now in addition to her $150 monthly student loan, she was paying $235 for the car, plus $200 for insurance. Despite the fact that Detroit had one of the lowest median incomes in the nation, its insurance rates were among the highest. And Olivia was earning only $1,400 a month, above the poverty level but less than she'd made as an intern in London.

Olivia had taken out ads in the Grosse Pointe newspaper and picked up a few landscaping clients—an extra hustle. And she'd planted vegetables at her parents' home, hoping someday to turn a profit at a farmers' market. In the evenings she drove to Grosse Pointe to take care of wealthy people's yards, then with the northern summer days stretching out past nine, she came home to tend her own garden: a fifteen-hour workday.

Many of the Greenfield employees, especially the reenactors, were retirees who did the work as a hobby. They appreciated the free admission for their families. Olivia figured they would work till their hands fossilized around a doorknob. So she could not demand a raise. With Detroit's unemployment at 27 percent, she was easily replaceable.

All she was doing was weeding petunias, and she didn't even need a high school diploma for that. Although she liked the smell of the coal smoke from the locomotive, which made her imagine she was living in another time, by July Olivia could tell which engineer was running the train by the length and rhythm of the whistle blows.

A few hours into her shift one day, Olivia sneaked off to a wild, unmanicured part of the park, hidden behind the Greenfield church. She wandered to the creek and climbed down the rocks and inspected the old mill. Tadpoles darted beneath the rocks, and water bugs stretched their legs across the surface. Olivia checked over her shoulder. A steep hill was wooded with maples and oaks, and the turf between them was fluffy with duff. She climbed to the top of the hill as the creek babbled and the chipmunks chirped. And then she lay down across the slope and let herself roll down the hill, giggling despite herself, tumbling to a stop with leaves in her hair, just inches from the edge of a pond. She let out a squeal, then hushed herself. She still had a few minutes before the crew would miss her. She rushed back up and did it again. Then she picked the leaves and twigs from her hair and returned to work.

She knew she should be satisfied at the Henry Ford, or at least not complain. And yet so much of it just seemed fake. Greenfield Village was supposed to be a tribute to the old ways of farming, but not only was it too expensive to actually farm, it was too expensive to pay actors to *simulate* farming. This year the cornfield had gone fallow until some descendent of the Firestones pitched a fit and paid a crew of Mexicans with a tractor to plant it.

The more Olivia learned about Henry Ford, the more he seemed like a nut, sending off his minions to dismantle historical structures and reassemble them at Greenfield. Turns out he'd published his own newspaper, *The Dearborn Independent*, that was distributed at every Ford dealership in the nation, with articles like "The International Jew:

The World's Problem." In 1938 he accepted a high honor from the Third Reich, the Grand Cross of the Order of the German Eagle, and the company profited during the war from a subsidiary factory in Germany that enslaved its workers. Ford hired spies to investigate the homes of his factory workers, to ensure they were leading what he considered clean and healthy lives. Ford's thugs beat up union organizers at the Rouge in 1937. None of these facts was on display at Greenfield Village. And, also: independent nonprofit organization, my ass, it seemed to Olivia. The Henry Ford appeared to her just to be a hole into which the Ford and Firestone families dumped money to avoid taxes.

And Olivia couldn't even think about Clara Ford without getting peeved. Olivia loved history, loved learning about how people used to live, especially women. And she was annoyed when somebody's history was not properly told. In high school she had been assigned to write a paper on black history. Ms. Poku, her history teacher, who wore a dashiki to class and had lived in Kenya with her Kenyan husband, knew something about black history. She told Olivia that slaves in South Carolina and Georgia had been allowed to hold their own markets on Sunday because their Christian masters felt it would be wrong to forbid it. The slaves grew their own crops of rice and okra and sweet potatoes, and they competed for customers. They played drums and banjos and sang. Whites complained that these markets were unruly, an excuse for the Negroes to throw a party. They confiscated the instruments, but that didn't stop the music. The slaves drummed on their thighs and chests and bellies, invented a new music called "patting juba," or hambone. Still the markets were allowed. It was the Lord's Day, after all.

It sounded like a great topic: an overlooked corner of her heritage. Olivia's family came from Mississippi. They had been enslaved. This was their history. But when Olivia went to the library, she couldn't find a single book on the subject. None. You couldn't *tell* her that nobody cared about this subject. But the school librarians said, Good luck. That's a part of history they didn't write.

And now when she went to learn about the life of Clara Ford, she discovered another whitewash. She could only imagine what Clara's life must have been like, putting up with Henry Ford's shit all the time, especially in the decades before he got rich, when his first two car companies went belly-up. Her journal probably said things like *I'm sick of being poor, his inventions always fail, we have a kid, and all he does is tinker in the garage.* "And then he got rich and had his ass on his shoulders," Olivia told me, "and she had to put up with that." But Clara Ford's official gift shop diary said none of these things. It was not even written by Clara Ford, but by Henry! Or his minions, at any rate, pretending to be her.

Midsummer brought promising news. The Henry Ford was hosting its annual Ragtime Street Fair. Some of the world's finest pianists were slated for two days of music, dancing, and turn-of-the-century merriment. Despite her skeptical nature, Olivia was eager to go. The festival embodied two of the things she loved most: a bygone era and black history. Ragtime was the first African American music to gain international prominence. Scott Joplin and Jelly Roll Morton had played the syncopated African rhythms on the most European of instruments—the piano—and the result changed the world. From ragtime sprang boogie-woogie, then blues, jazz, R&B, rock 'n' roll, and hip-hop. You could draw a line from Scott Joplin straight back to the hambone, and straight forward to Duke Ellington to Billie Holiday to Miles Davis to Marvin Gaye to Bob Marley to Michael Jackson to Chuck D and Lauryn Hill. Any kid on the east side rhyming to a boom box owed a debt to ragtime, and any kid rhyming into his toothbrush—from Bloomfield Hills to Beirut—was the spawn of Jelly Roll Morton.

The headliner for the fair was Taslimah Bey, a pianist renowned as a ragtime master. There would be dance classes and funnel cakes and piano cutting and silent movies and sarsaparilla soda. The only problem was that the fair landed on a weekend, on one of Olivia's precious days off. But it was worth going anyway. She arrived just as Bey was beginning her set. In an instant Olivia realized what a mistake she had made. The piano playing was fine. That wasn't the problem. But what she found was an audience of gray-haired suburbanites, grandkids in tow, tapping their toes more or less in time with the beat. On the dance floor there were no flappers, no short-haired vamps in slinky fringe dresses kicking up their fish-netted calves. No Charleston, no rag, no shag, no hambone.

The only people on the dance floor were the usual cast of historical reenactors, two-stepping stiffly to and fro in their straw boaters and britches and petticoats and bonnets. They danced perfunctorily, with the same limited expertise and enthusiasm they brought to spinning yarn and cutting tobacco. Olivia knew these people. They didn't listen to ragtime. They didn't even dance. Indeed, mid-song, three pairs of dancers quit their shuffle, dropped each other's hands, beelined off the floor. Olivia glanced at her watch. The morning shift had ended.

Olivia counted precisely two other black faces at the fair: There was Taslimah Bey. And there was a light-skinned reenactor who compelled an apron-clad white woman in circles across the bricks. During one revolution his eyes caught Olivia's, and they exchanged looks that said, *What the hell are you doing here?*

IN THE SOUTH, the Powe family had been an anomaly: Southern blacks who owned hundreds of acres. Olivia's grandfather and uncles in Mississippi had run landscaping businesses for years. Even though Vicky had not wanted to be a farmer, she had good memories of growing up on a farm. "So I never thought it was like slavery," said Olivia, "because my mother tells wonderful stories, the black version of those

Lavinia Derwent stories, where kids are running around barefoot." She heard tales of Papa cooking bread and throwing scraps to the hounds, chewing sap from a tree and tossing a morsel to the children, taking them fishing at the spring-fed pond.

On a day off from the Henry Ford, Olivia drove downtown to Eastern Market, where farmers from across the state sold vegetables and fruits and meats. Although she'd been there many times in her life, she was surprised this time to find a table labeled "Grown in Detroit" and stacked with kale and arugula and carrots. The fare wasn't anemic and sickly, the way Olivia expected a Detroit vegetable to look. She tried a bite: robust and bursting with flavor. She was suspicious. The people working the table were pretty white for a pretty dark city. Olivia asked where the vegetables really came from. They told her that farmers were growing the stuff all over town, bringing it to the table, and getting paid.

"What's their cut?" Olivia asked.

"One hundred percent."

Yeah, right, she thought. Nobody just sold your product and let you keep all the money. It must be some kind of scam. Yet Olivia liked the idea of selling vegetables, so she offered to volunteer at the farm table. That way she could see where the money actually went.

She arrived at seven the next Saturday and laid out the produce. She was able to view the farmers with her own eyes. Many of them were hippies: guys on bicycles with scraggly beards, girls in carpenters pants and clunky boots. Almost all were white. One of the farmers, a clean-cut guy with flecks of gray at the temples, handed her a tray of his nasturtiums. Olivia arranged the tiny plastic pots across the front of the table.

"No, no," he said. "They have to be closer. Maximize every square inch."

Olivia shot him a look but he didn't notice.

"Hold my coffee," he said, and pushed a tepid paper cup into her hands. He redid all her work, squeezing the nasturtiums close and sliding in a second tray.

"Maybe you need your own table," Olivia said.

"Maybe I do," he said and flashed her a smile. Oh jeez, thought Olivia, now he's showing off his dimples. He repossessed the coffee cup, jogged back to his truck, and drove off.

After a few weekends at the market, Olivia had determined that Grown in Detroit was legitimate. She watched the money go into the till, and she watched the farmers collect their portions at the end of the day. Each onion and carrot was accounted for. Nobody skimmed off the top. Next spring, Olivia determined, she would sell her own produce here. Running the numbers, she decided that the most profitable crop would be garlic. It required little maintenance and resisted insects, and best of all, not many others were selling it. That fall she planted three hundred garlic bulbs in neat rows behind the gate on Mack Avenue. Come harvest time, she might make five hundred dollars. Not a bad hustle.

Food independence was nothing new to Detroit blacks. As early as 1896, Booker T. Washington had drawn a line from self-reliance to freedom: "It is through the dairy farm, the truck garden, the trades, and commercial life, largely, that the negro is to find his way to the enjoyment of all his rights." Decades before the phrase "urban farming" was coined, black migrants to the city began cultivating their backyards and side lots. In 1981, Coleman Young launched the Farm-a-Lot program, making city-owned tractors available to help Detroit residents till gardens on vacant lots. In 1992, African American elders from the South formed the Gardening Angels, mentoring young people in farming. The Nsoroma Institute, an Afrocentric charter school, planted a large garden in 2000.

"It's important to teach children that we're not reliant on the government or the corporate structure to eat," said the Nsoroma principal, Malik Yakini. "The deeper purpose of teaching gardening is connecting with nature: being whole human beings and really understanding our relationship with the rest of Creation."

Food security was a founding tenet of black nationalism, a movement deeply rooted in Detroit. During the Great Depression, an auto worker named Elijah Poole, a migrant from a Georgia sharecropping family, took the helm of the newly founded Nation of Islam. Poole, who called himself Elijah Muhammad, intuited a connection between food and freedom. In his book *How to Eat to Live*, he contrasted the "slave diet" with purifying "one's own body and controlling the food that enters it."

"We, the black people here in America, we never have been *free* to find *out* what we really can *do*!" said Muhammad. "All of our lives we have farmed—we can grow our own food. We can set up factories to manufacture our own necessities! We can build other kinds of businesses, to establish trade, and commerce—and become independent, as other civilized people are."

The Nation of Islam's most influential spokesman was Malcolm X, born Malcolm Little, the son of a Georgia Baptist minister thought to have been murdered by Klansmen after preaching black nationalism. Little was raised in Lansing, worked on a Ford assembly line, served prison time for larceny, and after shedding his "slave name," began his political life as Minister Malcolm X at the Nation of Islam's Detroit Temple Number One.

"The only way the black people caught up in this society can be saved is not to integrate into this corrupt society," wrote Malcolm X, "but to separate from it, to a land of our own, where we can reform ourselves, lift up our moral standards, and try to be godly."

In 1994 the Nation of Islam bought fifteen hundred acres of farmland in Georgia, with the ambition of someday providing one meal per day to each of America's forty million black people. The food is distributed and sold directly to African Americans through buying clubs in dozens of American cities. Detroit is also home to a Shrine of the Black Madonna of the Pan African Orthodox Christian Church, which teaches that Jesus and Mary were black, and whose founder, Albert Cleage, wrote, "White people have little value for black people other than the wealth that they can extract from us." Since 1999 the church has acquired a four-thousand-acre farm along the border between Georgia and South Carolina for growing fruit, vegetables, poultry, and cattle.

By the turn of the century, urban farming began attracting institutional support. The largest was Earthworks Urban Farm, a project of the Capuchin order of monks, which enlisted hundreds of volunteers to grow produce for its daily meals. In 2004, Earthworks, along with the Detroit Agricultural Network, the nonprofit Greening of Detroit, and Michigan State University Extension, won a $150,000 grant from the U.S. Department of Agriculture—a drop in the bucket for other cities, but which in Detroit represented significant economic investment. In 2007, Rebecca Solnit declared in *Harper's*, "Detroit may be the shining example we can look to—the post-industrial green city that was once the steel-gray capital of Fordist manufacturing."

But as the media and foundations swooned at the prospect of urban farmers resuscitating Detroit, the recipients of the press and grants were mostly white. Black people cried foul. In 2006, Malik Yakini of the Nsoroma Institute launched the Detroit Black Community Food Security Network, and the following year turned soil at its D-Town Farm on the site of a defunct city nursery.

"We are unapologetically focused on organizing for African Americans," Yakini told me when I met him at the farm. "While we realize that good food practice and policy benefits everyone, we also realize that Detroit's African American community is more severely impacted by food insecurity than the general population. There are some historical peculiarities that apply to African Americans that don't necessarily apply to other ethnic groups, because of the history of enslavement. Many people of African descent identify farming with enslavement, with sharecropping, and other forms of tenant farming."

When black teenagers arrived at D-Town Farm, within fifteen minutes one of them complained, "You're working me like a slave!" On the other hand, elders would sometimes stop by unannounced and offer to help. "I'm from Alabama and I did this as a kid," they'd say. "You're doing it all wrong."

"A large part of our work is reframing agricultural work as honorable work," said Yakini, "and putting it within a correct historical context, so black people can know we didn't just start farming as a result of being enslaved. We were farming for thousands and thousands of years prior to it." Africans were enslaved precisely because of their agricultural expertise, Yakini said, citing the rice plantations of the American South and the cattle ranches of Brazil as examples of African techniques transplanted to the New World. Few Americans, black or white, know that the community-supported agriculture phenomenon that has swept through enclaves of white liberals in recent years was most likely invented by a black man, Booker T. Whatley, an Alabama horticulturist and Tuskegee professor. "The farmer has to seek out people—city folks, mostly—to be members of the club," Whatley told *Mother Earth News* in 1982. "The clientele membership club is the lifeblood of the whole setup. It enables the farmer to plan production, anticipate demand, and, of course, have a guaranteed market."

In the early 2000s, a food justice movement led by urban blacks blossomed across the country. In Milwaukee, Will Allen, a former marketing executive, launched Growing Power, a farm that employed local youths and raised vegetables and fish. He won grants from the Ford Foundation, the MacArthur Foundation, and the Kellogg Foundation.

Similar food security programs sprang up in New York, Chicago, Oakland, and Los Angeles. In 2006, Chicagoans Fred Carter and Jifunza Wright Carter launched the off-grid Black Oaks Center for Sustainable Renewable Living in Pembroke Township, an hour south of the city, to teach permaculture courses and grow vegetables for Chicago farmers' markets. In 2009, First Lady Michelle Obama became the nation's highest-profile urban gardener when she planted fifty-five varieties of vegetables on the South Lawn of the White House as part of her effort to encourage healthy eating.

In Detroit, Malik Yakini's message resonated. In 2012 he won the James Beard Foundation Leadership Award, and in 2013 the Detroit Black Community Food Security Network received a $750,000 grant from the Kellogg Foundation. "We reframe this as an act of self-determination," Yakini told me. "We're not doing this to enrich somebody else but to empower our own community."

So when Olivia Hubert began to grow garlic in Detroit, she wasn't just continuing a family lineage that extended back centuries; she was carrying on the heritage of her people and her community. Still, growing a few hundred dollars' worth of vegetables was a far cry from earning a living. For Olivia, it was merely a hobby; with her college degree and loans, she still needed an actual job. When her position at the Henry Ford ended in November 2009, she searched the national databases for horticulture jobs. Nothing. She collected a hundred dollars a week in unemployment. Meanwhile her mother and stepfather gave up on Mack Avenue. They sold the loft at a tidy profit and bought for pennies on the dollar a stately mansion on one of Detroit's historic blocks. As they were both working full-time, Olivia spent the winter packing boxes and shuttling their furniture across town.

"But Mama, what about my garlic?" she asked her mother.

"Shit," said Vicky, "I ain't staying here for your garlic."

Nine

The story of Detroit is not complete without the story of the suburbs. Indeed, the origins of the back-to-the-land movement aren't so different from those of the suburbs. With the advent of commuter trains and freeways nearly a century ago, suburbs were envisioned as a place where people could be closer to nature, have a small garden or at least a lawn, free themselves from the pollution and crowding of the city. By the 1960s my own family had all left Los Angeles proper, my grandparents for an Orange County retirement village and my dad to Hermosa Beach with its bungalow walkstreets and sandal shops. But the suburbs also enabled sprawl and overconsumption, and resulted in isolation and segregation. And there simply aren't enough resources—not even enough land—for everyone to have a big backyard.

These days it's unclear exactly what a suburb is. A generation ago it was a bedroom town close to a large city, characterized by homogeneity of race and class (white, middle), low crime and good schools, and homes that were bigger and newer than their urban or rural equivalents. But all that has changed. Take Monterey Park, a suburb of Los Angeles, which is almost entirely Chinese immigrants, or Ferguson, Missouri, the suburb of St. Louis that is now predominantly lower-income blacks. Meanwhile, if Park Slope—a Brooklyn enclave

of whites pushing strollers between health food stores and wine bars—
is not a suburb, then what is?

Suburbs are defined less, then, by geography than they are by economics and demographics. They are a place where one can enjoy the
benefits of the industrial economy—high wages, good infrastructure
like roads and parks, and excellent public services such as schools,
libraries, and police departments—without confronting its by-products:
crime, crowding, poverty, pollution, blight.

I spent years fleeing the suburbs. Even though my family was have-
nots by the standards of Manhattan Beach, from a young age I could
see that we had it better than most people in the country, certainly in
the world. I had done nothing to deserve such advantages. If anything,
I had benefited from the sins of my ancestors who had owned slaves.
What had been bequeathed to me, however, was not land or even fortune, but this more slippery thing: privilege. It meant that I grew up in
a town with good schools and little crime, where when the police broke
up parties, they just sent us home, straight no Taser.

When I landed in Moab, Utah, in 1993, I felt I had escaped. The
"Uranium Capital of the World" was poor and undesirable after the
bust of its mine had left few jobs and a mountain of toxic dirt. But in a
decade that changed. As Superfund cleanup began, an economy of
tourism and second homes blossomed, and suddenly you could get a
latte and pad Thai and raspberry beer. A two-bedroom miner's shack
would eventually cost $250,000. I complained that the suburbs were
following me.

Later I moved to Missoula, also a postindustrial outpost with a
Superfund site and an air pollution problem. Then the rivers and skies
cleared, the loggers and millworkers vanished, and the price of homes
doubled. We had film festivals and farmers' markets. The newcomers
were telecommuters, freelancers, trust-funders, administrators of
nonprofits—people like me, white college graduates who earned their

living from the national economy but enjoyed the low crime, good schools, and natural beauty of a small town. Even in my bucolic homestead I was hardly roughing it, with high-speed Internet and grid power and, more important, freelance work that paid me out-of-state wages, which, if paltry by New York standards, in Montana were positively bourgeois. And then it struck me: The suburbs weren't following me, I was *bringing the suburbs with me.*

What I was fleeing was not a place or a lifestyle but the thing that can't be escaped: privilege. But now I was married to someone who didn't come from that level of privilege. Cedar had grown up in a busted logging town alongside kids who wanted nothing more than to get out. The neglected West had been her home long before I discovered it.

The difference in our backgrounds surfaced frequently. While planning our wedding, we'd had an argument about dinner plates. We had invited nearly three hundred people to a sit-down dinner in the willow grove in front of our house. Cedar had mercifully relented on her dream of having a potluck for that many people. The caterer would deliver, wash, and remove the plates required for fifty cents each, which I thought was a bargain. But my wife deemed the plain white plates the caterer would use boring. At an estate sale, she had bought a hundred or more mismatched vintage plates emblazoned with state maps and birds and flowers. But once you include dessert, we needed six hundred plates. Her mother knew a ceramist two hours north of us who stored crates of old plates in a shed and was happy to lend them. I mentioned that such an ordeal would require loading the plates into cars, driving them to Missoula, unloading them, washing them, serving on them, then rewashing and reloading them into cars, and driving back to return them. My arguments failed.

Our different backgrounds revealed different values. I just wanted to pay someone else to deal with the plates. Cedar thought that things done yourself were inherently superior to things bought in stores.

As for the labor of (twice) washing six hundred plates, that's what friends and family were for.

Cedar hadn't always seen it that way. As a child, she had assumed that her parents could not afford matching plates, and their mismatched ones had rankled her younger sister, who'd been mortified at having to use them for her birthday party in the barn. "Why can't we just have matching plates like everyone else?" she'd moaned. The meltdown had surprised their parents, middle-class college graduates who lived this way by choice. To Cedar's mother, the mismatched plates represented liberation from stodgy consumerism. Eventually Cedar came to recognize that what she'd seen only as poverty was also an aesthetic choice. The barn, the woodstove, the mattresses on the floor—these were what her parents *liked*. Eventually she came to like it, too. Hence, our six hundred mismatched wedding plates.

Yet voluntary poverty was poverty nonetheless. Cedar had sometimes felt poor as a child, and she never wanted to feel that way again, nor did she want her future children to feel it. The dirtbag life I had led for decades was a sort of pretend poverty, in which I could fall back on my Stanford degree and the generosity of my parents. It wasn't until I spent some time in Detroit, however, that I fully realized that what had felt for years like the renunciation of privilege had in fact been just another means of exercising it.

BECAUSE THEY LIVED outside the city, Dick and Jessica Willerer could not vote for mayor of Detroit. They paid little attention to the election. In 1989, Coleman Young was up for his fifth term, or maybe sixth—who could keep track? He always won by a landslide anyway. They didn't bother watching the coverage.

The Willerers lived in a woodsy subdivision on a winding lane by a lake in West Bloomfield, almost an hour north of the city, depending on traffic. Their three boys had graduated from the public high school. The youngest, Greg, would run the snow blower over the frozen lake to play hockey. The neighbors called to say, "Get that boy off the lake! The ice isn't thick enough!" But Greg was impatient and he loved being outside. At nineteen, he lived at home and attended junior college.

Lately he had brought to his parents' attention Coleman's latest scheme, a massive garbage incinerator that would spew pollutants not just over Wayne and Oakland counties, but across the entire thumb of southeastern Michigan. Criteria pollutants, acid rain, hole in the ozone—that boy could talk once he got started. None of it surprised Jessica Willerer. As far as she was concerned, Coleman had ruined Detroit. One scandal after the next. Recently a city employee had announced that the seventy-year-old mayor had fathered her child. Thinking about what Detroit had become simply broke Jessica's heart.

Like many white suburbanites, both Jessica and Dick Willerer had grown up in the city proper, in solid brick bungalows a few blocks from one another in northwest Detroit. Children played football in the streets and their parents left the doors to their homes unlocked. At twelve, Jessica walked by herself—after dark!—to the movies. Life was simple then. Jessica's father owned a barbershop on Twelfth Street and the Boulevard, a straight-shot commute down Grand River Avenue. Dick's father was a policeman and later worked for General Motors. They earned enough that their wives didn't have to work. Back then, in the fifties, Detroit boasted the highest per-capita income of any American city. While Dad commuted to work, the kids walked six blocks to Burns Elementary, and Mom walked to the shopping center at Greenfield and Grand. None of the families required two cars. On weekends they might drive downtown for a Tigers game or to shop at Hudson's. Jessica and Dick attended Cooley High School, a three-story manor of cream-colored brick, with twin turrets and an auditorium with two thousand red velvet seats. Cooley was true-blue Detroit—the Willerers went to school with Jimmy Hoffa's son. In 1961, the year after Jessica graduated, they married at St. Mary's of Redford, just a few blocks from home.

Dick apprenticed as a plumber and pipefitter at the Rouge and then got a good union job with benefits. His brother Joe was hired as an electrician, as were their two first cousins. A whole generation of Willerer men worked side by side at River Rouge. They joked, "Henry Ford has been very good to our family!"

And it was true. In 1914, Henry Ford shocked the world by doubling his daily factory wage from $2.45 to a whopping five bucks—$117 in 2015 dollars, about twice the current minimum wage. His competitors were outraged. The bankers called him a fool. Highland Park was flooded with thousands of men—not the shiftless loafers who had caused Ford problems by missing shifts and bungling tasks. The wage attracted men of talent and intelligence who were keen on raising their station, and productivity on the line soared. Ford's factories—along with those of General Motors, Chrysler, Packard, and Hudson—attracted Germans, Poles, Greeks, black Americans, Irish, and Italians, creating one of the nation's true melting pots. They siphoned farm boys from all across the United States, accelerating urbanization. In 1870 a quarter of Americans lived in cities; by 1920 half of them did. (The proportion has continued to increase steadily, reaching 80 percent in 2010.)

Among those who answered Ford's call were two German immigrants, Adam Heiler and Nicholas Willerer. Heiler had settled in Ohio with his parents when he was thirteen. He moved to Detroit to assemble Model Ts, bought a house in Highland Park, and eventually became a foreman at the Rouge. In the parlance of Detroiters, he "worked for Ford's" for forty-nine years. Nicholas Willerer came from Spokane and also found work on the Model T line, buying a house just blocks away. Willerer's son Joe and Heiler's daughter Anne met at the Carpathian Dance Hall, married, and bought the brick bungalow in northwest Detroit where they raised Dick.

Some historians consider Ford's wage the birth of the middle class. The auto industry—against Ford's adamant wishes—was where labor unions were strongest, pioneering the forty-hour workweek, pensions, and workers' compensation, which allowed common laborers a share of the owners' wealth. But even as Dick and Jessica Willerer grew up in idyllic prosperity, there were omens of Detroit's decline. In 1955, Hudson shuttered its Jefferson Avenue plant. In 1958 the Packard factory closed. As the United Automobile Workers began to command high wages in Detroit, the Big Three began to close plants. Between 1947 and 1963 the city lost 134,000 manufacturing jobs to automation and "runaway shops" springing up in the suburbs and smaller cities.

While some white flight was caused by the racism of whites who didn't want to share their neighborhoods with blacks, the economic and cultural forces that created suburbanization are far more complicated. As city property taxes increased to support the infrastructure of massive urban centers, the suburbs were actually more affordable, as they didn't have to provide services like public transportation. Federal government subsidized freeways to ease commuting, and the cost of cars and gasoline remained relatively low. The suburbs promised affordable home ownership for the working class, clean air and green trees, safety from crime, maybe even a vegetable garden in the yard.

Like virtually all white Detroiters, the Willerers left for the suburbs. In 1964, a baby in tow, they found a bigger, newer, cheaper home just north of Eight Mile Road, the city limit, and bought it with a down payment of only two hundred dollars. Better still, the property taxes were lower there in Southfield. As Dick commuted to Dearborn and Jessica raised three boys, chaos engulfed their native city. During the 1967 riots, the windows of Jessica's father's barbershop were smashed.

After that, his clients were afraid to go downtown for a haircut, and he closed the shop. The rest of the family trickled out of the old neighborhood. Joe and Anne Willerer's house was bought by the school across the street and torn down to make room for parking. They, too, moved to Southfield. The home of Jessica's parents was burglarized. They retired to Florida. Her uncle remained in the neighborhood a few more years, until Coleman tried to bus his kids all the way across town. The uncle took early retirement, sold the house, and left the city. Cooley High closed in 2010 and was picked apart by scrappers.

"I don't know where we went wrong," Jessica Willerer told me. "It was so peaceful and wonderful. Where did it go?"

Optimism was scarce in Michigan in 1969, the year Greg Willerer was born. The previous year, Martin Luther King Jr. and Robert Kennedy had been killed, police crushed protesters at the Democratic National Convention in Chicago, and the Tet Offensive in Vietnam indicated a long war ahead. Even as an American walked on the moon, many sensed that the country was lost in space. Detroiter Iggy Pop captured the mood: *It's another year for me and you / Another year with nothin' to do.*

While Detroit crumbled, Jessica Willerer still loved the city. Saturday mornings she hauled the three boys and a wagon downtown to Eastern Market for flowers and produce. But the decay crept closer. Factories fouled the air. Jessica observed students at Southfield High School smoking grass in broad daylight. Private schools cost a fortune. The family moved farther still from the city, to the rolling hills of West Bloomfield.

Despite the Ford legacy, Greg and his brothers were not expected to follow their father, uncles, and great-grandfathers into the factories. Throughout the eighties, newscasters spoke of layoffs and shutdowns. It would be a miracle if Dick's job lasted long enough to provide a full pension. The Willerers had not attended college, and they wanted their sons to have that chance and to be able to choose the careers they wished for. They were a family of hard workers, and so far each generation had had a better job, a better home, and a better life than the one before.

Which is why Jessica was so surprised, on the eve of the 1989 election, by a call from Dick's brother.

"You'll never guess who I just saw on TV!" Uncle Joe said.

He was right. She couldn't guess.

"It's Greg!"

"*Our* Greg?"

"Your Greg!" said Uncle Joe. "He and his buddies were getting stuffed into a paddy wagon on the nine-o'clock news."

"*Paddy wagon?*" Greg had told her he was spending the night at Monty's.

"They were down there protesting the incinerator and Coleman's goons scooped them up."

Jessica lobbied her husband to drive downtown immediately, but Dick took a more measured approach. While he wasn't exactly against what Greg was doing, neither did he think that a night in lockup would kill the boy. Might even do him some good. He agreed to sort it all out in the morning. Jessica worried the entire sleepless night.

"As a parent," she told me, "the last thing you want is to have your child in a Detroit prison."

"I KNEW THE SUBURBS were a lie," Greg Willerer told me, shoving a pile of greens into his mouth. "La-la land."

We were sitting at a picnic table nestled under a tree, beside a tractor and a heap of firewood, between his house and farm. Greg was in his early forties, compact and wiry, with flecks of gray in his close-cropped black hair, his arms and face leathery from the sun. A duffel bag with ice skates and pads and a helmet lay by his side while he forked up his salad.

"I eat it before I play hockey," he said. "It gives me so much more jump."

As he spoke, his leg jittered like a sewing machine needle, and I got the impression that sitting still was torture for him. He had little tolerance for writer types, no matter how well intentioned. "I get sick of fucking conferences," he told me, rotating his neck like a turtle, the vertebrae emitting a string of satisfying cracks. "The food justice movement gets on my nerves. They beg for corporate scraps under the table, but having meetings will not move us forward." As for visitors who seek the novel thrill of spending a few hours farming in Detroit: "There are a lot of people whose politics I like, but when they come to the farm, they're raking with one hand and talking on the cell phone with the other."

If Olivia hadn't put him up to it, Greg might have kept on ignoring my inquiries. Even after I made contact with him, most of our conversations occurred in moving vehicles, at his booth in the farmers' market, or as we hacked at weeds or laid irrigation hose through fields. As far as he was concerned, local food needed no more defense, just more defenders.

"How many people does it take to make an urban farm?" he asked in a Facebook post. The answer: "25 film makers and journalists to do pieces on urban farming, 63 grad students to study the farm, a few people from the not for profit complex to hold meetings about farming, a few elected officials to have their pictures taken at the farm, and about 5 people to do the actual farming."

Greg Willerer was as resolute about the organization of society as he was about the nutritional value of mizuna greens. Suburbia, he told me, was the greatest misallocation of resources in the history of the world: big, thin-walled houses that take loads of gas and electricity to heat and cool, acres of farmland and animal habitat bulldozed for useless lawns that guzzle water and gobble poisons, barrels of food scraps hauled across the county and buried in a landfill, sprawling subdivisions requiring cars and gasoline for the simplest of errands—mailing a package or buying a gallon of milk. What's more, he said, suburbs encouraged isolation, cultivated a fear of strangers, and created enclaves that segregated the white middle class from poor people and brown people.

As we sat there, a raggedy old white guy rode up on a bicycle, toting a handsaw and a sledgehammer, purple swollen fingers emerging from a cast on his wrist.

"Can I borrow your truck?" he asked. It was Greg's neighbor, a former Air Force mechanic, en route to salvage timbers from a condemned building up on MLK. Greg gave him the keys. But first he knelt with a screwdriver to switch the license plates from his other truck. Greg owned two trucks but only one set of plates.

With its skyline of empty skyscrapers and hollowed-out train station, Corktown was a cultural entity entirely its own: a mixed-race Appalachian holler plunked down in a detonation site. I was staying a block away at a cheerful hostel that had opened in 2011, hosting Ivy Leaguers interning at charter schools and European backpackers flocking to the ruin porn. On the lot across the street, a black Vietnam vet calling himself Liar had taken up residence in a fifth-wheel motor home, with a porta-potty and a Weber grill. On sunny afternoons he offered chopper rides to the Swedish girls on his three-wheeled Harley.

Recent news had put Olivia and Greg's creed of localism to the test: after a five-year absence, a national grocery chain announced plans to build in Detroit, setting up shop in the former skid row of the Cass Corridor, now rebranded as "Midtown." And it wasn't just any old chain. It was Whole Foods.

Until now, the irresistible narrative of urban farming went like this: Abandoned by the corporate food cabal, Detroit citizens had no choice but to grow their own. The arrival of a gourmet, all-natural grocery store upended this story. Now you wouldn't have to wait for the farmers' market to buy organic salad; you could get it cheaper seven days a week. Greg's allies at the Detroit Food Justice Task Force welcomed the arrival of the chain and got on board, consulting with the company on how best to serve Detroiters.

Greg disagreed. He had never totally accepted Detroit's label as a food desert. It was a hot phrase that attracted foundation money, but Greg saw Detroit as more of a "food labyrinth." Good food was there; you just had to know where to find it (and have the means of getting there). Just a mile from his farm, for example, was an excellent independent grocer in Mexicantown with fresh produce and homemade tamales and guacamole. More to the point, the movement was not just about vegetables but about economy, and restructuring society. He didn't want to be just the guy who brought arugula to the ghetto.

"I'll give Whole Foods about 1 year to last in Detroit," Greg posted on Facebook. "Not gonna complain, I just think they are part of the problem. Whether it's WF, Meijer, most grocery stores suck. Too expensive, have long lines and they enable Americans to keep harming the planet with our rich diet. We have Eastern Market (and a few more options). We can get better prices & quality and get things from the source!"

He posted ten reasons why Detroit didn't need Whole Foods. The last two were:

9. Detroit is on the verge of developing a unique local food economy that uses local farms and artisan food businesses. WF will use incentives from Detroit tax payers and that

money will go back to Austin TX where WF is based, while our local businesses cycle money throughout our community.

10. WF is part of this propped up image of a new downtown where Detroit is for the hipster, wealthier and whiter and at the same time diverting resources from neighborhoods where people have lived and struggled to improve their city for decades.

Before long, Greg received a proposition from a Whole Foods vice president. The face of this corporation was not some jowly white guy in a suit, but a young, ponytailed, eloquent Native American named Red Elk, for Chrissake, son of the founder of the American Indian Movement. Red Elk wanted to stock Greg's salad. It was part of the strategy built with the task force. Whole Foods had held meetings with church congregations. They were hiring local people—black people—at a good salary. They weren't merely stocking local vegetables and bread and beauty products on their shelves; they were offering micro-loans to help those independents ramp up production. Whole Foods could sell more salad in a day than Greg and Olivia could sell in a week. And think about the convenience. No more early mornings tabling at Eastern Market. No more CSA members dribbling in after dark to collect bok choy. No more clipping two ounces of chives and parsley to deliver to a chef. Greg could put the farm on autopilot: grow the salad, harvest it three times a week, and deliver it to Whole Foods, just a mile from home. Easy.

Greg refused. "Food justice isn't helping a corporation increase its bottom line," he told me. "Food justice is producing your own food, getting people to be food-independent." He dug in his heels. "Whole Foods just motivates me so much because I can't stand what they're about," he said. "They're still a corporation, they still have shareholders, it's still processed food, it's still taking the person out of the economic equation, it's still taking money out of our community."

I could have listened to him talk all day. He was headstrong, stubborn, and pugilistic in a way I admired. Greg and I were the same age, and our suburban upbringings and subsequent worldviews were so similar that I felt I'd met my doppelgänger, who, instead of ditching his home for the sticks, had steered for the heart of the city. And to understand how he'd resisted the Whole Foods offer required looking way back into his past.

Sheltered from the negative effects of the economy, kids like Greg—and me—came of age in the eighties and began to question the de facto segregation. And yet there were few channels of dissent in Reagan-era suburbs: no leftist newspapers or anarchist bookstores or union halls. Television and radio and newspapers and movies and popular music were increasingly owned by a small number of conglomerates. Indeed, the very design of the suburbs inhibited the gathering of citizens who might want to mount a protest. Instead of broad parks at the steps of city hall, there were four-lane streets without sidewalks, and malls that were not public at all but privately owned and patrolled by security guards.

Greg Willerer was as hell-bent on escaping the privilege of his youth as I was. For suburban teens convinced that there was something wrong with their world but unsure how to articulate it, one of the few lifelines was punk rock. Punk not only channeled anger and alienation but also was produced and distributed largely independent of the corporate media: indie records available only in indie record stores, advertised by word of mouth and a network of self-published fanzines. Just as I had discovered Black Flag and the Dead Kennedys through my brother, Greg raided his older brother's vinyl to hear the Clash, Minor Threat, and Angry Red Planet. *We had a hedge back home in the suburbs,* snarled Mick Jones, *over which I never could see.* Greg and his friends buzzed their hair and, as soon as they got their licenses, drove to punk shows in gritty clubs in Detroit—the town that spawned Iggy and the Stooges and the MC5. Greg loved the rawness and rough edges and racial mix.

Through the music scene he learned about the incinerator in East Poletown, a neighborhood that had already been seized by Coleman through eminent domain and bulldozed for a GM plant. The thing would burn fifty thousand pounds of refuse per year, and a group called Evergreen Alliance had formed to shut it down.

At rush hour the night before the election, Greg and company made their way to a freeway overpass and unfurled a banner that read BAN THE BURN! STOP DETROIT'S INCINERATOR. Greg and his friends didn't think they could actually tip the outcome—Coleman had it in the bag—but they knew that with the news crews on the street they could give the mayor a public black eye. Commuters inched along in traffic beneath the banner. And then the police arrived. "You all need to go home," said an officer. Greg knew they weren't breaking the law. They decided to stay put. The police ordered them off the overpass. They refused. They were arrested, handcuffed, and stuffed into a police van just as a news team arrived to capture it.

"What was it like in a Detroit jail?" I asked.

He dismissed the question with a wave. "We were bailed out by two a.m. by the Evergreen Alliance," he said. The charges of disorderly conduct were bogus, and a pro bono attorney from the American Civil Liberties Union had them quickly dismissed. Greg's parents were dismayed that he had been arrested, but what could they do? As for Coleman, he easily won a fifth term, serving as mayor for a total of twenty years. The incinerator opened on schedule.

Soon after his arrest, Greg moved to Detroit and enrolled at Wayne State University. He fell in with "the movement," the anarchists and

radicals who populated the decrepit Cass Corridor. The appeal of anarchism was perhaps stronger in Detroit than in any other American city.
New York and Washington, with their excellent subways, parks, and
museums, might inspire faith in government from even a libertarian.
Detroit had exactly the opposite effect. Here, it was the federal government that razed bustling neighborhoods for freeways that created suburban sprawl and expedited white flight. Government denied mortgages
in the slums and wrote whites-only neighborhood codes. Government
built segregated housing projects that became criminal dens. And city
government was as bad as the Feds. Detroit bulldozed Poletown for a
new auto plant even as dozens of abandoned factory sites pocked the
city. At the top of a long list of kleptocratic municipal boondoggles
were the incinerator, the sanctioning of downtown casinos, and a
multimillion-dollar "people mover," a tram that circled endlessly among
vacated skyscrapers, at a cost to the taxpayers of $4.26 per passenger
mile (as opposed to 30 cents on the New York subway). Immune from
these attempted improvements, the Cass Corridor was where the young
punks gathered.

Americans tend to think of anarchists as black-masked teenagers
chucking bricks at Starbucks from a speeding skateboard, or fashion-
ing pipe bombs from the instructions in *The Anarchist Cookbook*. The
ideology that captivated Greg Willerer, however, was the belief that
individuals and small communities, uncorrupted by power, provided
better leadership than government did. Before it was called anarchism,
principled resistance to the state appeared on American soil in the
refusal of Quakers to hold office in a government that condoned slavery and in Thoreau's going to jail for refusing to pay a war tax. Emma
Goldman, perhaps the movement's most impassioned advocate, said,
"Anarchism insists that the center of gravity in society is the
individual—that he must think for himself, act freely, live fully. The
aim of Anarchism is that every individual in the world shall be able

to do so." Anarchists condoned violence to destroy the state. Goldman was jailed for planning to kill a steel tycoon. The Polish American malcontent Leon Czolgosz, who assassinated President William McKinley in 1901, was an anarchist. In the resulting backlash, Congress banned anarchists—along with pimps, beggars, and epileptics—from immigrating to America. In 1927, Italian anarchists Nicola Sacco and Bartolomeo Vanzetti were executed for murder despite numerous doubts about their guilt; decades later, the governor of Massachusetts declared they had been unfairly tried and convicted.

In the 1960s, anarchism resurfaced as a critique of the bond between corporations and government, what President Eisenhower called the military-industrial complex. Antiwar protesters refused the draft and resisted taxes, and earth advocates like Edward Abbey declared government unfit for the task of protecting wilderness and urged citizens to do it themselves by destroying federal property such as dams and road machinery.

Greg met the editors of *Fifth Estate*, an anarchist magazine that had been in print for two decades. In the sixties, copies of *Fifth Estate* encouraging GIs to mutiny were sent to Vietnam. The paper's storefront on Cass Avenue was teargassed during the riots. In 1969 the editors wrote:

> We believe that people who are serious in their criticism of this society and their desire to change it must involve themselves in serious revolutionary struggle. . . . The Man will not allow his social and economic order to be taken from him by Marshall amps and clashing cymbals. Ask the Cubans, the Vietnamese or urban American blacks what lengths the system is willing to go to, to preserve itself.

By the 1980s, *Fifth Estate* had taken on a primitivist bent, condemning technology and modern agriculture. In a discussion of the best way to dismantle entrenched power, one of the writers told Greg simply, "I don't know what's going to happen." Greg preferred this worldview to that of other ideologies like socialism, whose proponents tended to begin with, *Clearly the bourgeoisie needs to . . .* "They have a football coach's playbook on what's going to happen with our country," said Greg. "And they want to see the left gain control by a mass movement and take control of the infrastructure, and so they have this playbook that will never be realized, and it's arrogant and stupid to think like that."

Greg and his friends changed tactics. "Instead of just showing up with a picket sign and doing the same old thing," he said, "a lot of people wanted a physical space where we could, at least in this zone, rid ourselves of racism and sexism and homophobia. And where, however temporarily, we could practice this world we wanted to see."

They formed a collective. In a storefront on Willis Street, just off Cass Avenue, they launched what they called an autonomous zone, or infoshop—a model popular among anarchists in London and Chicago. It was a place to distribute radical literature and ideas. They booked bands. "The punk thing was pulsing through our veins," Greg told me, "so we would have shows and charge five dollars, and that would pay the rent." They swilled beer from forties and got rowdy. One night some Christians parked out front and erected a cross in the open trunk of their car, hoping to condemn or convert. By night's end, their towering crucifix was littered with bras and panties.

On Sundays, when most places were closed, 404 Willis ran a coffeehouse. Guests who wanted to lounge at the tables and couches were not required to buy anything. Poets read aloud. All afternoon there was talk of the Gulf War, the incinerator, the corruption at City Hall, amid a mixed crowd: black and white, young and old, college kids and homeless men.

"We didn't like the typical Catholic idea of charity, so we weren't serving meals," said Greg. "We just had some food in the corner. People could serve themselves. We encouraged people to wash their own dish. For a lot of people it was liberating, because they didn't have that person serving them."

Greg Willerer rented a cheap room in the Trumbull Theatre, a dilapidated complex of two houses divided into flats and a one-story brick factory converted into a community stage. The owner was an oldster named Perry who resembled Santa Claus, and the denizens were chain-smoking pensioners and daytime drinkers, "guys like you'd see in Moe's in *The Simpsons*." The vacancies filled with punks and anarchists. The conditions were rustic. "You took a shit and left the door open" is how it was characterized by Tamara French, the then nineteen-year-old dreadlocked singer of a band called Dog Breath that pounded out thirty-second ditties in the basement. French was once mildly reprimanded for spray-painting "Make It Bleed" on the shower curtain.

There were few high-paying jobs south of Eight Mile, so Greg did the reverse commute to "some stupid deli in the suburbs" to pay tuition. Greg's mother had opened a bakery and Greg worked occasional shifts. He insisted on delivering the day-old loaves to the Capuchin soup kitchen in Detroit. The gap between city and suburb was widening. The population of Oakland County, with its sixty-two cities and townships, many of them quite wealthy, rose at roughly the same rate that Detroit's declined. In 1992, as Oakland voters began a long streak of voting for the Democrat in presidential elections, they also began a long streak of electing Republican L. Brooks Patterson as the county's chief executive. Patterson transformed Oakland into an economic hub larger than Detroit itself. "I love sprawl," Patterson said. "I need it. I promote it. Oakland County can't get enough of it." Patterson had grown up in the same part of Detroit as Greg's parents, but since relocating to the suburbs, he'd stoked the resentment of the diaspora by badmouthing their hometown—it was he who mentioned fencing Detroit and chucking blankets in for the residents.

In 1993, as he was finishing a history degree, Greg asked Tamara French and two others to pool their funds with him to buy the Trumbull Theatre. No bank would offer a mortgage in such a slum, so Perry financed it himself. They settled on a price of $33,000 for all three buildings, with Greg contributing $750 and the others about the same to hand over a down payment of a couple thousand bucks, with a contract to pay $400 a month for eight years. The Trumbullplex was born.

"Greg is the reason why that place happened," said French, now a prominent Detroit immigration lawyer. "Nobody would have thought to ask Perry to sell these houses."

Greg envisioned a space that would outlast him. He and his friends wanted to hand something real to the next generation of activists, just as they had been mentored by the old lefties from *Fifth Estate*. They transferred the deed to a nonprofit they created. The by-laws stated that rent would remain low so that residents could dedicate themselves to activism. Its mission statement read:

> We are a not-for-profit project dedicated to self-sufficiency in all facets of our lives; in our housing, our work, and our energy. We support other projects that share our goals of dismantling racism, sexism, homophobia, and the oppression of poor people through activities in our theater and housing collective.

They moved the music venue to Trumbull. The neighbors were mostly working-class black families, and Greg and his cohort made efforts to welcome them. They held family-friendly afternoon events like puppet shows and invited the neighbors to bring their kids. During punk shows—in which local parents showed little interest—Greg paid neighbors to watch attendees' cars.

Yet Greg wasn't satisfied with his utopia. As Trumbullplex became popular, the old-timers were displaced by punks, who tended to be white. It began to feel like an enclave. "Some of the white people living there didn't want to hear the rap music," said Greg. "There were neighbors complaining, because part of being punk rock is that you have to be loud as hell, and fuck the family that has a newborn baby across the alley from you." And the consensus model of governance engendered an endless process of meetings, infighting, and self-expression.

"What got focused on was interpersonal crap," Greg told me. "And punk shows."

Greg launched a career as an elementary school teacher. "I felt like if I really wanted to influence change," he said, "maybe young people would be a more productive use of my time." He spent the next fifteen years teaching at public schools in Detroit and Chicago. In 2001 he landed a plum job at University Prep Academy, one of the best charter schools in Detroit. The principal envisioned their work as that generation's civil rights movement. The teachers were given great freedom and encouraged to transform their charges into leaders who would build a better society. The students were mostly black, with a smattering of whites and Asians. Unlike at most Detroit schools, there was virtually no violence. "If I had a child, I would have sent him there," said Greg.

After a few years, his district hired a new superintendent who prioritized standardized tests. Greg and his fellow teachers resisted. "They got rid of some people without any kind of process," said Greg. He and his colleagues organized, with twenty-nine of the thirty teachers signing union cards. "They wanted to get rid of some of us, especially people like me who were already not teaching to the tests."

Greg had grown disillusioned with the environmentalists and then with the anarchists. Now he was disillusioned with public school reform. Little did he know that the movement he sought was right beneath his feet.

IN THE SPRING OF 2002, Greg planted vegetables in his yard on Farnsworth Street in Detroit. His mother had taught him the basics of growing food when he was a boy, so he knew enough to get started. Later that summer, his friend Kevin towed a bicycle trailer down Farnsworth and knocked on the door.

"Give me your vegetables," said Kevin. "I have an idea."

Greg loaded his friend's trailer with carrots and lettuce and tomatoes. Kevin set off down the cracked pavement in the sticky heat toward Avalon Bakery, two miles away. After two hours of street vending, Kevin returned sixty dollars richer. Greg was stunned. This could be more than a summer hustle.

Greg had discovered a side of Detroit even more inspiring than the classroom. He met Paul Weertz, a craggy, sandy-haired high school science teacher dressed like a farmer, in Carhartts and boots and a straw hat. A thin white guy who talked with a mobile Adam's apple and a Michigan honk, Weertz didn't look much like a revolutionary or a swami. Nonetheless, "the guru" was the nickname Greg would settle on for him, and Weertz, out of politeness rather than ego, tolerated it.

Weertz and his wife and two sons lived in Poletown, home of the cursed incinerator. In the early 1980s, the city had seized 465 acres for the plant and demolished 1,500 homes, 144 businesses, and 16 churches, displacing 3,500 residents. Hundreds more homes had been sold or abandoned as the working-class, mostly Polish American residents pulled up stakes. The incinerator proved to be the boondoggle that opponents had predicted. Children living nearby were hospitalized for asthma at two and a half times the state rate. The facility never filled city coffers and was sold to private investors for a fraction of the construction costs. Critics contended that city taxpayers were left on the hook for $1.2 billion from the original bonds and interest. Meanwhile, Poletown was devastated by eminent domain seizure, freeway construction, white flight, pollution, and arson. By the time Greg arrived, the stately timber-frame homes were mostly vacant, far outnumbered by weedy lots.

Weertz lived on Farnsworth Street, a startling exception to the blight. Every house on the block, both sides of the street, was still standing. Nearly all were occupied, and even the vacant ones were freshly painted, the grass mowed. Bunches of orange berries hung from mountain ash trees lining the sidewalks. Children played in the street, and their parents had transformed a corner lot into a verdant garden. They had also torn down fences between backyards to create a huge commons. Young adults lived across the street from their parents. In the heart of America's most dangerous city, crime was scarce. The street resembled the Detroit in which Greg's parents had grown up, with one anomaly: on the adjacent block, where not a single house stood, a tractor dragged a baler across a field of alfalfa.

It was the type of neighborhood that cities spend millions on planners and consultants to try to create, where buzzwords like "walkability," "diversity," "mixed use," and "pocket parks" are alchemized into "community." And yet this haven was built without a cent from—or for that matter, the notice of—any government body.

Farnsworth was created largely through the work of Weertz and his wife, a Wayne State professor. In 1985 they'd bought a rambling two-story fixer-upper with high ceilings and wood floors for just eight thousand dollars. When the Weertzes arrived, three European-style bakeries still lined McDougall Street, relics of the Polish residents, but they soon shuttered. As their neighbors fled, the Weertzes understood that vacant houses would attract drug addicts and scrappers, that crackhouses would be torched, and that unless they acted, their home might one day be the only one on the block. So they bought the house next door, and one across the street, turn-of-the-century Victorians that were selling for four figures. Unencumbered by a mortgage, the Weertzes, even with modest salaries, could pay cash. Before long, they owned ten houses on the block. They rented out those that they could and mowed the grass of the rest.

Weertz invited Greg to visit him at the Catherine Ferguson Academy, the public magnet school for teenage mothers where he taught science and math. Three hundred mothers attended and the school graduated 90 percent of them, providing daycare to two hundred babies. Weertz had started a small garden at the school, first as a means of teaching basic biology. Then, to teach entrepreneurship, he encouraged the girls to sell the peaches and apples and vegetables they grew. Greg wandered the grounds, his mouth agape. A fruit orchard—in Detroit! Weertz had acquired goats and horses, too, and Greg found himself roaming a pastoral farm in the heart of the rotting city.

As Poletown returned to prairie grass, Weertz bought a tractor and began mowing the hay, baling it, and feeding it to the livestock. Although ownership of the fields was uncertain—most of the land had become city property after the fleeing owners failed to pay taxes—Weertz did not apply for a permit at city hall, or anywhere else. "I don't ask permission," he told me one morning, sipping coffee in his kitchen. He was working with local government on one front, however; Weertz was seeding fields with alfalfa and putting up one thousand bales per year, some of which he sold to the Detroit Police Department for its horses. Meanwhile he pulled down all the fences between the backyards of his properties, creating a private park. He shared his garage full of tools with his neighbors. When each of his sons turned eighteen, he gave the boy his own house on the block.

"I grew up in the suburbs," said Weertz, "which back then was the country." He was a baby boomer, one of ten children, and when he moved to Detroit in the 1970s, he saw programs to serve the poor fail because of the gap between helper and helpee. "To understand poor people you have to live with them," he said. He felt powerless to affect the course of American foreign policy he disagreed with, but he saw that he could do good work right at home. "I can't do anything about Vietnam, or wherever," he remembers thinking. "I can do something here." And Weertz was more drawn to action than to planning or philosophizing. "We were meeting to death," he said of his short-lived membership in some well-intended association. "It took six months to come up with a name."

Greg Willerer rented one of Weertz's houses. It was the world he had long envisioned: a mixed-race, working-class village built out of reach of the tentacles of banks or government. And Paul Weertz was enacting the sort of decentralized change that Greg had heard activists and educators theorize about for decades now.

Greg expanded his garden. He met Ashley Atkinson, a Flint native who had just rented a table at Detroit's Eastern Market and called it Grown in Detroit. With the help of the nonprofit that employed her, the Greening of Detroit, she gathered produce from city farmers, sold it, and handed over all the proceeds to the growers. It was a hit. She invited Greg to sell his vegetables.

Eastern Market was a Detroit institution, run continually since 1891. Greg remembered getting hauled there in a wagon by his mother on flower day. But now he saw the place with new eyes. Even as the city tanked, Eastern Market was bustling, one of the few places where suburban whites and urban blacks mingled. Between thirty thousand and forty thousand shoppers came each Saturday morning. It was not strictly a farmers' market. Much of the produce—avocados and mangos and pineapples—was grown by God-knows-who in God-knows-which banana republic and shipped to Detroit by conventional means. But there were also local products from Michigan farmers: beef and pork and chicken, cheese and milk, and of course corn and grapes and berries. Amid the industrial detritus, Greg was surprised to learn, Michigan held some of the most fertile ground on the continent and was second in crop diversity only to California. The state grew cherries and apricots, kohlrabi and broccoli and corn. An entire shed was devoted to cut flowers and garden starts.

When I visited Greg and Olivia at the Eastern Market, the place was buzzing. Vendors sold homemade soaps and salves and sauces, buskers strummed Bob Seger, circles of drummers pounded djembes. Across the street, lines ran out the door at the omelet joint, and when I wandered into Bert's Motown Room for a midmorning beer, I was not alone. A cloud of sweet smoke enveloped muscled chefs wrangling brisket and baby back ribs on a curbside barbecue, their shirts stamped with the slogan WHY YOU ALL UP IN MY GRILL? The place was packed, and as we all tore into platters of pork and greens and black-eyed peas, the regulars queued up at the karaoke machine for pitch-perfect renditions of tunes by Smokey Robinson and the Righteous Brothers or pushed back their chairs and danced at their tables. *To the right, to the right, to the right. To the left, to the left, to the left.* A woman about my age sporting a white satin graduation cap and gown arrived with her parents and her small children. When I offered them my booth, she beamed and said, "May I give you a hug?" and I happily received it.

Greg piled his produce on the Grown in Detroit table each week. Shoppers loved the idea of buying a carrot grown within city limits, even if it was smaller and cost more than one from California. After all, what had grown in Detroit lately besides crime and despair? A carrot was progress. He loved proselytizing about local food. Though the money was little, he was putting fallow soil to good use. He wasn't using chemicals or pesticides. He was replacing vegetables trucked in from California that wasted millions of gallons of fuel each year. And when people bought lettuce from Grown in Detroit, their money wasn't shipped off to a corporation in the Salinas Valley or Mexico. It stayed right in Detroit. In his pockets, in fact.

Meanwhile, he and his girlfriend were engaged, looking to move in together and renovate a house. As much as he loved his block on Farnsworth, it had come to resemble the back lot of a Hollywood studio: rows of houses facing one another, backed by emptiness. Greg was more drawn to Corktown, one of Detroit's oldest neighborhoods, directly west of downtown. To the untrained eye, North Corktown was a wasteland, with its toppled roofs and weedy rubble. In the 1950s hundreds of homes had been demolished by the city with federal "urban renewal" money, but never rebuilt. A huge swath was razed in the 1960s for the Fisher Freeway, now Interstate 75, whose ten lanes of roaring traffic had divided Corktown ever since. Additional homes on the north side burned in 1967, never to be rebuilt. On the south side, buildings were leveled over the decades to provide parking for Tiger Stadium, but then the baseball team moved to a new park in 2000, and the stadium was demolished in 2009.

Greg saw beauty and potential: a neighborhood whose sharpest decline was far behind it. Whereas other neighborhoods were in the midst of collapse, with houses burning and water mains gurgling, Corktown had collapsed decades ago, and had now stabilized with its handful of survivors. "It was almost mystical what attracted me to this neighborhood," he said. "I loved the realness of it." There were even signs of renewal: on Michigan Avenue were an upscale barbecue joint and an espresso house. Which is not to say the place was gentrified.

One day while Greg was peeking at shuttered homes and inspecting vacant lots, an old black man came out from a creaking door and shuffled up the walk.

"Can I help you?" the old man said.

Greg told him he was looking for a house to buy. The man was perfectly pleasant. He made some suggestions. They chatted amiably.

A few minutes into their exchange Greg realized that the long narrow object in the old man's hand that he had assumed was a cane was in fact a rifle.

In 2005, Greg borrowed money from friends, and he and his fiancée paid $11,000 in cash for a two-story wooden cottage on Rosa Parks Boulevard, formerly Twelfth Street, the same street where Greg's grandfather used to cut hair, the same street where cops and revelers sparked the '67 riot. Built from a Sears kit a hundred years before, the bungalow listed a bit, but it had three bedrooms. The block had just six other houses, and fourteen or so vacant lots.

Greg and his fiancée began renovating. The fenced yard was quite small, so Greg claimed the vacant lot next door and began planting. "It was almost like God told me to build a greenhouse," he said. He expanded into additional lots, and spent as much time in the garden as he did in the classroom.

Before long the couple's visions for the future diverged. She didn't want to be a farmer. They weren't ready to commit. She moved out. Trying not to give in to self-pity, Greg channeled his efforts into his garden. He didn't have to look very far to see that a movement was afoot. Local-food manifestos like *The Omnivore's Dilemma* and *Animal, Vegetable, Miracle* were bestsellers. Ashley Atkinson's organization determined that Detroiters were tending seven hundred gardens within city limits.

By the end of 2008, Greg had bought out his ex's half of the house. He owned it free and clear. He had paid off his car and his credit card debt. His expenses were just $500 a month. He had operated the farm for three years, expanding into more vacant land each year, and that summer he had sold $10,000 worth of produce. He wondered how much more he could make if he invested all his time. He was making $45,000 a year as a teacher. If I can't make more than a teaching salary, he thought, I must be a fool.

And besides, the thrill of teaching was gone. More exciting were the things rising out of the soil, on Farnsworth Street and at Earthworks Urban Farm, without the help of government.

"I used to think education was the way to change society," Greg told me. "Now I think it's the local food movement." As a teacher, he felt hamstrung by administrators who not only were a nuisance but in some cases—such as their focus on standardized testing—were actually doing the wrong thing. As a farmer he had complete autonomy. In the classroom he sometimes felt that the curriculum was too theoretical; but when schoolchildren harvested food on his farm, they instantly understood concepts like urban renewal and sustainability. The raspberry was mightier than the pen. And he didn't have to explain why a thriving garden was an improvement over lots filled with junk cars or crumbling houses. As for the activism of his youth, slogans about clean air, saving the whales, and protecting "the environment" seemed frankly irrelevant. Growing food inspired people with more tangible rewards—like being outside, earning money, eating delicious carrots—and just happened to improve the planet. While protests felt to him like a string of losing battles, of begging the government to change its ways, local food had the potential to actually win.

That winter, after fifteen years in the classroom, Greg Willerer walked away from his teaching job, its health insurance and salary. His goal: to wrest a living from a single acre.

THREE PRINCIPLES GUIDED GREG'S VENTURE. The first was to bring a new product to market. In 2008 it was impossible to find gourmet organic greens in Detroit. Those things might be available in the suburbs, but in the city you'd be lucky to get a head of iceberg. The one place for excellent salad was fancy restaurants, and they were sourcing from out of state. So the second principle was import replacement: selling a local product to those restaurants, which would keep the money in Detroit as well as eliminate the carbon costs of trucking produce in from the West Coast. Third, Greg saw that salad greens were a uniquely profitable product. Most row crops—corn, broccoli, tomatoes—deliver their harvest over a period of one or two months, leaving ten months without income from that source. But salad greens could be harvested every week between March and November and sold for thousands of dollars per month. Working the rows alongside his dreadlocked housemate, Larry, Greg came up with the name for his new venture: Brother Nature Produce.

First Greg had to secure water. To irrigate his growing acreage, he initially ran a hose across the street to the fire hydrant, watering at dawn and dusk when it was less likely to be discovered by a meter reader. The collapsing Detroit bureaucracy was a mystery. On the one hand, it lacked the resources to put out fires, turn off broken water mains, or respond to 911 calls. On the other hand, it routinely issued tickets to farmers for having chickens. He eventually began collecting rainwater instead.

Next Greg needed dirt. While reporters and ecotopians loved to say that Detroit had twenty or so square miles of vacant land, they rarely mentioned what was required to make that ground fertile. Much of it was industrial wasteland, polluted with heavy metals and chemicals. On residential lots, demolition crews sometimes merely bulldozed the charred timbers into a pit, along with all the metal, brick, concrete, plaster, and plastic. Just as prairie pioneers had to clear timber and stumps and roots before pulling a plow, urban farmers had to excavate their "free" lots of detritus. What's more, much of the soil in Detroit was fill dirt that had been trucked in when the houses were built. It lacked nutrients.

Greg set out to fertilize his lots. He planted sunflowers to draw lead from the soil. Commercial mulch was available, but it was expensive. And besides, why truck in soil from across the country when you could make your own, for free, from things that would otherwise go to landfill? He found allies in the beer breweries and coffee shops, whose spent grains and grounds made excellent compost. He bought a full-size pickup so he could haul it himself. On Craigslist he saw an ad from a guy who raked and hauled leaves. Greg called and asked what he did with the leaves. The guy paid a fee to dump them at a landfill or at one of Detroit's composting services. "I'll take those leaves for half of what you're paying," said Greg. It was a deal. The truck arrived and tipped a load of maple gold. Greg wasn't just getting free soil, he was getting *paid* for it. A win for everyone. The landscapers saved fees and gas money—they no longer had to drive across town to tip their loads. And the nutrients in the leaves helped produce food instead of being preserved in the landfill with bubble wrap and Barbie dolls.

This arrangement lasted about a week. A woman from the city knocked on his door. As it happened, landfill operators and compost companies paid a yearly fee for a tipping license. When one learned that Greg, an unlicensed competitor, was underselling him, he blew the whistle, and the city that couldn't fix streetlights was able to send an inspector to shut Greg down.

"But what if they don't pay to dump?" Greg asked the inspector. "What if I let them dump for free?"

The inspector didn't see how that would require a license. It wasn't a business transaction. So Greg continued to collect leaves, now without a fee, amassing mountains of them in the far reaches of his farm. Even that system was plagued with urban-specific problems. Lawn clippings, which theoretically made excellent compost, were usually tainted with chemical fertilizers. He specified to his suppliers that he would not accept grass. (He opted not to have his farm certified as organic by the USDA, a process that could cost $6,000. Instead he marketed his produce as "chemical-free.") On one occasion an inexperienced crew scooped up concrete chunks with the leaves, then dumped that on Greg's farm. It was not only useless; it would require money and labor to move. The pile of rubble sat there for years.

And there were unique challenges to being a farmer in a poor city. One time an old man showed up with a sack and began to harvest collard greens. Greg confronted him. "I thought this was a community garden," the man said. On a sweltering summer day, just after Greg and Larry and their friend Doug, an older man from the neighborhood, had planted a row of zucchini and covered it with a huge mound of compost, a car pulled up. Two black men emerged with cans and shovels. Greg recognized them as local weed dealers. They began scooping up the soil and loading it into the car, presumably for their own growing operation. Greg tore across the yard, with Larry and Doug—both black—at his heels.

"What the hell do you think you're doing?" Greg said.

"Step back," said one of the drug dealers.

"I just planted that."

Greg's pulse throbbed in his temple and sweat trickled down his face. "I would give you some if you just asked," he said. Larry was urging Greg not to let the bastards have anything. It was about to get ugly.

Then Doug stepped in. "We're sorry," he said. "Take what you got. But if you want some in the future, just ask."

That defused the standoff. The compost thieves drove off. And a few months later, when Greg bumped into one of them, there was no tension. "Doug realized these are the motherfuckers you don't piss off," said Greg. "And that's a very valuable lesson either for living on the frontier or living in the hood."

Greg's work was paying off. On a good Saturday he earned three hundred dollars at Eastern Market, selling out by eleven in the morning. He sourced directly to high-end restaurants. And it was fun. He invited his friends and neighbors to bonfires and held you-pick afternoons. Old-timers on the block called him Garden Greg. By the end of his first year as a full-time farmer, Brother Nature had grossed $30,000. Along with his savings, it was enough to live on, and a big step toward independence.

A documentary film crew arrived to chronicle the movement. In 2009, Greg was named by *Time* magazine as one of eight members of its "Committee to Save Detroit." The members were photographed downtown, overlooking the river. Greg posed beside his old boss from the Academy, the man whose arrival had precipitated Greg's departure. His decision to quit teaching had been vindicated. Also on the committee: L. Brooks Patterson, the sprawl-loving boss of Greg's native Oakland County.

Ten

In 2010, Olivia's dream job appeared: she was hired by her former mentors at the Belle Isle Conservatory. By now many of her colleagues were approaching their fourth decade working for Detroit. With the city's finances failing, the workload had increased and raises had halted. Her mentors apologized for the piddling eight dollars per hour, half of what workers there had made a decade earlier, but promised a career with health insurance and a pension. It was also half of what she'd earned interning in London and a buck less than at the Henry Ford, but she believed she would make it work somehow.

On her first day on the job, Olivia realized that Belle Isle was in bad decline. Four of the old-timers—the experts who knew every leaf and branch and leaky pipe on the premises—had been nudged into retirement. Fallen leaves went unswept. Goose turds stained the flagstone. Litter fluttered across the yard. Spiderwebs clung to overgrown shrubs. The walls traditionally used for seasonal displays were overgrown with philodendron. The palms had outgrown the atrium, and fronds pressed against the glass ceiling. Now and then one busted a pane trying to escape. Scratchiti was etched on the fernery windows as if by desperate convicts. In the Cactus House, in the soft flank of the silver-dollar cactus, someone had carved I LOVE MIMI. The queen of the night clung to the overhead bars, gasping for air. In an effort to reduce the work hours required to grow saplings from seed, mature trees had been transplanted, bringing with them an epidemic of cockroaches and mealy bugs.

"They wanted instant stuff," said Olivia, "and the instant stuff comes with instant problems."

She lowered her chin and did her job. One advantage of the staff reductions was that the new supervisor had been transferred from city hall and knew nothing about horticulture, leaving Olivia relatively free to pursue her own projects. In the old days, when it came time for seasonal shows, the horticulturists would propagate the flowers from seed in the greenhouses: lilies for Easter, mums for fall, poinsettias for Christmas. Now, since nobody knew how to propagate, they simply bought the flowers from a distributor, even though the city was broke. Olivia thought that with some hard work and initiative she could restore the conservatory to its glory days—and save money to boot. She cultivated a few hundred geraniums in the greenhouse, months in advance of the summer show, rather than buying them at the last minute. She spent weeks at it, germinating them in two-inch pots, then transplanting them to five-inch pots. She instituted a strict schedule to prevent overwatering. She even defended her sprouts from a fox that had found its way into the greenhouse. And then one weekend, her colleague who had been transferred to the conservatory from the city zoo took it upon himself to give the geraniums a little extra water.

"He drowned the bitches," she remembers. "They rotted."

Olivia's four-generation family saga from farmer to college-educated professional was almost complete. Her family had played by the rules, worked hard, and Olivia had found a good job—a city job—with the kind of benefits that were supposed to secure a place in the middle class. Jaded as she was, at her core Olivia actually believed in the system—wanted to believe in it. What she had not anticipated was that the system itself—in this case the city of Detroit—would go bankrupt.

As it teetered on the brink of insolvency, the Belle Isle Conservatory grew more dysfunctional than ever. Sometimes Olivia was the only worker on duty, color-coding orchids in some drafty greenhouse with a broken boiler. Someone outside pounded on the door. She didn't open it. Occasionally her superiors pulled her from the conservatory and shuttled her to the mayor's mansion to give landscaping advice. Another time a lady from the power company demanded to see the electrical meter. She wanted to write the conservatory a bill.

"There's no meter," Olivia said.

"Of course there is."

Olivia led her down to the clammy dungeon and showed her the place on the wall where someone had ripped out the meter and reconnected the wires.

Olivia's wage was raised to ten dollars an hour. At the same time, the city furloughed its workers, forcing them to take an unpaid day off every other week. Then everyone took a 10 percent pay cut. Now Olivia was barely earning minimum wage. And she was still paying off student loans. "If you get an education and still can't get a job with a living wage," Olivia said, "then the education is not worth the cost." One of the Belle Isle old-timers told her she was getting ripped off. Her stepfather said she was being exploited for her knowledge and suggested that instead of taking initiative, she simply follow instructions from the higher-ups who didn't know anything about horticulture. Her mother suspected a plot from the governor's office to run Belle Isle to ruin so that the state could wrest it from the city. After work, Olivia parked her car on the far side of Belle Isle and sat there for hours, watching an old man fish in the Detroit River.

"The age of the aesthetic was over, and people didn't care about me being able to make topiaries or any of these things that I had bothered to learn," Olivia told me. "Now people show their wealth by gadgets instead of having a really nice garden, so they're unwilling to pay a highly skilled person to make a topiary garden, or maintain a kitchen garden. I was about fifty years too late."

ALL WINTER HE ASKED about her: that girl at the Grown in Detroit table who had sharply suggested that he get his own table. He figured he'd see her the next Saturday, or the next. But their paths did not cross. He asked if people knew her. They didn't. Or if they did, they weren't giving out her phone number.

A friend invited Olivia to a brunch on a farm. The current resident had expanded from his own yard to colonize a row of vacant lots. Amid the towering weeds, Olivia could make out tomatoes and lettuce and kale and broccoli. It was a pretty nice spread, she observed. A bit sloppy and in extreme need of attention, but for an amateur it was not a bad garden. As they were being seated she recognized the farmer: it was that white guy from Eastern Market, the one with the nasturtiums, Mr. Hold My Coffee and Look at My Dimples. They ended up seated together, and she told him her dilemma: three hundred garlic plants on Mack Avenue in need of a new home.

"Transplant them over here," Greg suggested. The next weekend he arrived with pickup and shovel, and helped her dig up the garlic. They tilled a fresh row and pushed the green shoots into the soil. Afterward he invited her to join him at a symposium on Detroit farming. She agreed.

As it turned out, Greg was one of the speakers. Not much of a date. Olivia watched him take the stage with the others. Not a black face among them. Apparently nobody had told them this was a symposium *about Detroit*. The white people talked and talked: local food, food desert, food justice, greening the city. When the farmer's turn arrived, he said, "I'm flattered to be asked to speak here, but we really have to get a more representative group of people to discuss agriculture in Detroit."

Olivia wasn't exactly impressed, but at least someone had said it. Afterward, she struck up a conversation with another man, but Greg shooed him away and whisked her off to a nice restaurant, where they ordered wine. Maybe it was a date. Sipping, Olivia told him how tired she was of living with her parents, and how she wasn't too thrilled to move into their next renovation project. And yet she wasn't earning enough to get her own place.

"I've got an extra bedroom," he said.

They dated for a month, and Olivia found the farm a lovely respite from the constant hammering at her parents' house. Soon Greg's housemates moved out. "I was over here all the time," Olivia said. "I didn't really notice that I had moved in." Yet moved in she had. She was up at six each morning for her job at Belle Isle, and then helped on the farm afternoons and weekends. "After a couple of months it dawned on me she is all about living a certain way," Greg said. For Olivia, natural farming and food justice were not political slogans, but values she embodied through her work. "And she worked her ass off," he said. "People on the left always talk a good game about how they feel politically. She was one to just show it without saying anything. I felt really at ease with her, in a plain way."

As it happened, Greg had been inside Vicky Ransom's resale shop on Mack Avenue back in his college days. The two got along swimmingly. A month after Olivia moved in, he took Vicky to lunch to formally ask for her daughter's hand. The two conspired to choose a ring. He pocketed it and took Olivia to Cliff Bell's, a historic jazz club and restaurant and one of his salad greens customers. The maître d' whisked them to a private booth where a chilled bottle of champagne waited.

"Damn," said Olivia. "They must have really liked the salad."

As an engagement gift, the couple bought themselves a twelve-gauge shotgun: a symbol, as they saw it, that their farm and their future were worth protecting. They carried it down to the old train station and shot off a box of shells for target practice.

At the end of 2010, Brother Nature had grossed $40,000. Greg had made a living off his acre. That winter he married Olivia at the church at the corner of Martin Luther King and Trumbull, and for the reception a horse pulled the couple on a sleigh to the old ice rink on Belle Isle.

THE FOLLOWING WINTER was a cold one. Out on Belle Isle, Olivia bundled up in the greenhouse. She could see her own breath. She caught strep throat. Making her way through the atrium, she was poked by punk tree and scratched by screw pine. The crown-of-thorns cactus could draw blood. One glimmer of hope was a grant the conservatory won to install new boilers. But without access to the know-how of the old crew, the contractors placed the new units a few inches too low. Pipes froze and the basement flooded. The boilers failed.

"A plant massacre," said Olivia. "I was crying at work."

Yet she remained optimistic. If she could work hard and get her inner house in order, then perhaps Detroit would follow. She dedicated herself to the orchids, taking on small projects she could complete without interference from above. The orchids were rare triple crosses: cattleyas mixed with dendrobiums mixed with vandas. Someone, back in the glory days, had invested years to breed then. With a large glass carboy that she found in the basement and could hardly lift, Olivia set out to make a terrarium, a display for kids whom she imagined would ask all sorts of questions. How does a flower grow in glass? What does it eat and drink and breathe?

It was like building a ship in a bottle. First she poured a layer of gravel to serve as a drain. She covered that with sand, then cork pebbles to which the orchids would attach their roots—orchids are epiphytes and naturally cling to something solid, like branches. Then a layer of Spanish moss. Now came the orchids. She wasn't sure which would survive in her experiment, so she planted a dozen different varieties. Brassavolas. Cattleyas. Dendrobiums. She eased the orchids into the narrow mouth, then maneuvered them with sticks to sit upright on the bottom. It was pretty damn cute. And it needed only the moisture that was already inside its tiny, closed ecosystem.

Just days before the terrarium was to go public, a coworker stuck a garden hose down the mouth to water it. He drowned it.

"I was losing my humanity," Olivia said. "I got to see the collapse of things firsthand."

She gave notice.

"Once I realized that there would be no conservatory or garden jobs," Olivia told me one day as she pulled weeds at her farm, "the next logical thing was to grow food, to do something that people need."

In East Lansing and then London, she had come to believe that Detroit's problems were the world's problems, and running away from collapse was one of the things that caused it. She had to stand her ground somewhere. She'd come full circle: she was a full-time homesteader, like her Mississippi forebears. Barefoot, in a battered straw hat and a cotton dress, she looked the part. She honed old-time skills: canning, pickling, pressing cider, saving seeds, drying herbs, rendering stock from beef bones.

When Olivia's grandmother stopped by Brother Nature for the first time, she saw crops in long rows like she hadn't seen since Mississippi. "That's some *hard* work," Granny murmured, and retreated to her truck. Olivia built a coop for chickens and ducks, named them Bubbles and Screech, Max and Buffy. "It takes a lot of shooting to kill a possum," said Olivia, recounting how Greg had blasted a predator with the shotgun. "It's kind of surprising." She preferred to kill varmints with bow and arrow.

Growing food in marginal soil with limited resources in a city often referred to as "post-apocalyptic" and a "war zone," Olivia took her lessons from an actual war zone: Britain between the world wars. "That was the last time people put modern scientific method into low-tech ways of doing things," she said. "They were on rations for fourteen years. They had to make do, and they had to ask grandpa what he used to do. That was the last time that people really took that stuff seriously. After the wars it was *chemical this*, and *spray that*, and *Why don't you just monoculture?*"

Olivia not only believed that such chemicals and techniques destroyed the soil and were unhealthy for people; she was sure that the petroleum-based fertilizers upon which modern agriculture relies would eventually run out. It's a view she shared with the thousands of preppers stocking their rural bunkers with a three-year ration of food-stuffs. Yet Olivia viewed the apocalypse from the other side: she and Greg were figuring out how to farm without reliance on the industrial technology that, in their opinion, had brought about the collapse of their city in the first place.

Olivia set about whipping the farm into shape. For all her husband's enthusiasm and success, his methods were not up to the standards of the Royal Horticultural Society. In Olivia's professional opinion, he merely threw a bunch of seeds in the dirt, watered, and hoped for the best. With Olivia's guidance, crops were planted in straight rows, with neat handmade trellises, and weeds were pulled on schedule. The salad mix was standardized. Instead of a bucketful of whatever grew, there were equal parts arugula, mizuna, pea tips, sorrel, lettuce, bekana, and spinach. Olivia sorted the harvest into three mixes: mild, medium, and spicy.

Meanwhile Greg had already launched Detroit's first CSA. Members bought a share for $600, and then received a basket of vegetables each week for twenty-three weeks. But when Greg decided that his partner in the venture, who one day distributed store-bought tomatoes, was steering the operation aground, he severed that relationship and

Olivia stepped in. Over the course of the growing season, members received herbs, eggplants, hot peppers, sweet peppers, heirloom tomatoes, broccoli, four varieties of kale, Swiss chard, raspberries, and melons. As the CSA grew to forty members, the enterprise grossed $24,000.

Greg and Olivia spent ten hours a day in the fields. Volunteers pulled weeds in exchange for produce. Saturday was market day, and on Sunday they tried to rest, but often found themselves sorting seeds or canning or doing laundry. Olivia provided the practical counterweight to Greg's exuberant idealism. "Greg thinks hard work is supposed to pay off in a relatively short period of time," she said. "I think it will pay off *eventually*. You might have to be poor for ten years."

They had complementary strengths and weaknesses. Olivia had limited patience for dealing with customers, their penny-pinching and ignorance. It incensed her when someone asked, "What do you put on the salad to make it spicy?" That's just what arugula tastes like. "I'm what make it spicy," she growled.

"I'm not a people person," she explained. "If I was a people person, we wouldn't get anything done."

But Greg had a knack for marketing and for salesmanship. At Eastern Market, the Brother Nature table nurtured a distinct aesthetic. Instead of plastic banners and dry-erase boards, they listed their wares on chalkboards in vintage picture frames. One said NATURAL CHEMICAL FREE, and another, referring to the state's food assistance program, said BRIDGE CARD TOKENS ACCEPTED HERE. Greg imagined the entire operation, from the growing on through the presentation at market, as a creative endeavor.

One day a middle-aged woman with long dreadlocks stopped in her tracks, surveyed the product, and murmured, "I see you've got that sexy lettuce." When a straight-laced white dude approached, Greg dangled a ribbon of mizuna from his tongs and said in his nerdiest voice: "Would you like to taste my sexy lettuce?"

"This stuff won't go bad on you overnight," he said as he doled out samples with a pair of tongs to a queue of curious shoppers. "I cut it this morning. It didn't sit on a truck from California."

"Five dollars a bag?" someone said. "For real?"

"In the store it's four dollars for a five-ounce bag," he countered. "Ours is five dollars for eight ounces."

Greg launched a new venture. The Detroit Zoo was in the midst of a conflict with the landfill, and as a result, mountains of manure were piling up. It was more than Greg could take all at once. But he knew that other farmers needed manure. He and a partner started Detroit Dirt. They leased a parcel of unused land by the railroad tracks and wrangled a tipping permit from the city. The zoo delivered thirty-four hundred cubic yards of animal dung and wrote a check for $34,000. There was money in this hustle. "I got the work ethic from my dad," he said. "And I learned not to put all my eggs in one basket."

Part of Olivia's role at Brother Nature was simply reining Greg in when his enthusiasm threatened to spread him too thin: doing favors for any beginning farmer who asked, lending equipment, talking to reporters, attending meetings. He had recruited interns for the farm, but when he was away, they didn't know what to do. Olivia persuaded him to focus on the farm. Greg sold his share of Detroit Dirt and bought a tractor.

A tractor! It was majestic, watching her husband putt along Rosa Parks Boulevard in the old blue Ford. Now and then people who bought heroin across the street parked alongside the farm to sample the product. Greg bore down on them in the tractor and chased them off. During winter the Ford enabled an additional hustle: Greg earned a few hundred dollars plowing parking lots after snowstorms. Yet tilling the rows of raised beds with a tractor presented a whole new set of problems. A single brick or timber or piece of concrete could bend the plow—and often did.

Ultimately, the secret of Olivia and Greg's survival was simple: they worked.

Whenever Olivia felt overwhelmed cultivating an acre with just her husband, she thought of her ancestors: a father and son—and a mule—on forty acres. "If you're going to be a farmer, be a farmer," she said. "You have to bite the bullet, and be really cheap, and not go watch the Wings lose to the Blackhawks at the bar. How can you farm part-time? You're not going to be taking your kids to ballet. If you want to take the kids to ballet, you need to get a job and work for someone else so you'll have plenty of excess time to drive them around, and the ability to work overtime and make a bunch of money."

"A lot of younger people are looking for a way to get into it, but don't want to work that hard," she continued. "If you'd just work, you'd get somewhere, but always trying to get a grant, or always trying to work for Wayne State on the side, you're wasting your time. I think it's hard for Americans to accept that we really have to work this hard. It's like my grandmother says: it's some *hard* work."

Greg was similarly dismissive of fledgling farmers who expressed shock at how little money was to be made. "I wonder what farmers in Brazil, Mexico, Ethiopia, or Korea would think of these Americans complaining about their income," he posted on Facebook. "All I gotta say is that some people don't hustle. Out in the country we know farmers who usually have a side hustle. Maybe they trim trees, carpentry, or our friend Bruce has a tractor repair business as well as growing hay. Most North Americans have a side hustle. The day and age of having one job that takes care of you is over. Our parents lived like this, but those economic times are gone. We plow snow in winter and provide tilling to other gardeners. I wish we could just farm and make enough money doing that, but that is not gonna happen. These are hard times for most people. Resilient people will make do."

Eleven

On my third visit to Detroit, the place was showing signs of actual recovery. Quicken Loans had moved its eight thousand employees from the suburbs to a vacant downtown skyscraper. Suddenly, young, college-educated white people were flooding across Eight Mile on fixed-gear bicycles, harvesting kale, and brewing kombucha. Art galleries opened, techno collectives were formed. A boutique hawked thirty-dollar tank tops that read DETROIT HUSTLES HARDER. Two young farmers from upstate raised $5,000 on Indiegogo to start an aquaponic fish operation where a school once stood. And nobody loved it more than the media.

At the Wayne State farmers' market, I watched a film crew interview a man in a tie, and the director called out, "Start a sentence with 'What people don't know about Detroit is . . .'" The man did not miss a beat. "What people don't know about Detroit is that it is a city on the verge of transformation, and it's happening here, right now. Lots of positive things are under way. Occupancy is near an all-time high. It's thriving! It's vibrant!"

As Brother Nature succeeded, the movement grew. New farms sprang up. More markets were established. A white family with two small children and no car homesteaded near Farnsworth Street, shuttling their "carbon zero" sprouts to market in bicycle trailers. They called it Rising Pheasant Farms, a nod to the upland bird that had begun to populate the Detroit prairie.

Although to its boosters the rebirth appeared a grassroots reclamation of abandoned America, to many black Detroiters it smacked of old-fashioned gentrification, and crowdfunded tilapia was a meager trade-off for a functional public school. "We live in a society where white supremacy is still the dominant narrative," Malik Yakini told me, "where people with white skin still have unearned privilege. Lots of young whites moving to Detroit have not really studied racism and how they have internalized it, so they bring a lot of that with them."

Olivia Hubert had mixed feelings about the new arrivals. On the one hand, she liked the local food, the network of progressives, and the farm-to-table cafés. (As for the trendy barbecue: "It's *okay*, but it's not like my grandmother's.") And yet: "The perk of being black in a black city is no longer a perk. These newcomers, they don't like black people, but they don't know it yet." She did not experience overt racism, but something subtly insidious. A new coffeehouse, in a city that is 80 percent black, hired only white baristas. And there was a double standard. "When someone who is well educated and comes from a middle-class family comes down here and whips their Bridge Card out, it's okay," Olivia said. "It's just, *You need a little help right now, and that's what the government is for.* But when black people who have been in Detroit and have been poor all their lives have a Bridge Card, it's, *You're just a drunk or a drug addict, or you're a baby mama and you shouldn't have had those kids if you can't take care of them.*"

What's more, the urban farming movement continued to be largely white. Olivia Hubert might have been the only black woman in the city making a living on a farm, a farm she came to own by marrying a white guy. I asked Yakini if he knew of any black couples or families in Detroit who were "going it alone" like Brother Nature. He considered for a minute, then shook his head. "Not yet." The reasons for this are as complicated as the history of Detroit: the historic discrimination against blacks owning homes, mistrust of the city, lack of black capital. Olivia offered that most black people with the where-withal to start their own enterprise required a steadier income than farming offered, and that white farmers were more likely to have a financial cushion to fall back on in lean times.

Yakini was careful not to condemn the new arrivals. "The vast majority of them are good people and have great intentions, but the problem is, sometimes when you come into an area and you don't really have an understanding of the history and culture, you can start doing that work in opposition to the aspirations of the community. If white people don't become aware of that and how it impacts them, then they move like a bull in a china shop. If you become aware of your privilege and acknowledge it, you can move in a way that's more supportive, and be an ally."

Olivia's young white neighbors rode skateboards and let their dog off leash. When the dog went after her ducks, she whacked it with an iron bar. Like farmers from time immemorial, she minced no words: "You let that dog jump my Buffy again, I will kill it!" She resented the newcomers' flaky self-congratulation at "discovering" Detroit after Brooklyn or Oakland or Portland was played out. She suspected they would soon skedaddle for the next cool place. "What the hipsters don't get, what they never hang around long enough to figure out, is that we look out for other people in the neighborhood."

Still, plenty of the sort of anarchism that Greg championed flour-ished in Detroit. Renegade farmers appeared where you'd least expect them. Out on the east side I met Donald Jones, who sourced salad greens to Greg and Olivia when demand ran higher than their supply during peak weeks. Donny lived in a relatively intact bungalow of cream brick with a small porch. The grass was uncut but the yellow tulips made the place look occupied. He wore a loose white T-shirt that hung over baggy jeans, and the calligraphy of a tattoo rose from the neck of his shirt. He had a scruffy beard and short cropped hair.

"I used to be part of the problem," Donny told me. "Now I'm part of the solution."

I had driven north on Van Dyke, one of Detroit's main drags, with the boarded-up tire shops and crumbling brick storefronts and burned-out bungalows. Donny's block, shaded by leafy elms, appeared to be about one-quarter occupied. As for the remaining half of the homes on this block: they were gone. Prairie grass shivered beneath elms and sycamores. Pheasants clucked and nestled in the reeds. It would have been an idyllic scene but for the end of the block, up against the train tracks, where the street was blocked by mounds of flotsam: televisions, twisted bookcases, piles of demo debris, bricks and timbers.

Donny was thirty years old and had grown up on this block. He told me that he'd "rescued" his current residence. "The people got foreclosed on, so I waited and watched," he said. "I moved in the day after they left." Even with that scrupulous planning, he was a day late. Scrappers had already wrenched the furnace from the basement, in the process snapping the water pipe and flooding the basement. Donny had a friend turn off the main, and eventually the water drained. "At least it was clean water," he told me. "Not sewage." The downside: no more running water.

I followed him through the side door, which lacked a knob or a lock. The house was bare and tidy, with white walls and hardwood floors and no furniture. From upstairs I heard voices, and I asked who was up there. "That's Uncle Bobby."

Donny lived in the small back bedroom. A mattress lay on the floor. A half-filled plastic bottle glistened with yellow liquid. The only other furnishing was a folding chair on which a television flickered. A tangle of wires snaked out a window.

"Power company don't care if you own the house," he said. "They only care if you pay the bill."

Donald told me that he had lived the last two winters without heat. But he didn't mind. He saw it as a challenge.

He led me to three acres of vacant land up against the train tracks. Tall grass fed by the spring rains lined the far end of the property. But closer, along the curb, green shoots of onion rose out of mounds of soft earth. A hand-drawn sign announced Donny's domain: OCCUPY YOURSELF FARM.

"Those are garbanzos," he said, pointing to a low shrub. "A dry-land crop."

Donny Jones was an enthusiastic innovator. He used no power tools or gasoline and experimented with no-till, no-irrigation perma-culture. He wrapped the porch of a condemned house in clear plastic to build a budget greenhouse. (It didn't work.) He took me to meet a prospective member of his co-op, Edith Floyd. A sixtyish woman with a Carolina lilt whom Donny addressed as Miss Edith, she stepped out on the porch to meet us, a hospital bracelet on her wrist. She told us in a hoarse whisper that she'd just been discharged from surgery that morning. A purple scar enclosed her neck. I could see tubes taped to her other wrist with medical tape. She listened politely, occasionally nodding, as Donald expounded on his plans to dominate the Detroit broccoli market. Miss Edith and her husband, recently passed, had been growing vegetables on vacant lots on their block for decades, over the years colonizing an entire city block.

"As a house go, I take it," Edith whispered. This year, because of her hospitalization, she hadn't plowed some of the lots yet, and it was hard to tell what was garden and what was merely grass. She told me her empire ran all the way to Van Dyke, clear over to the tire shop. I commented on the good fortune of so much available land. Miss Edith turned her head toward me. "Suit me fine if *nobody* stay over there."

Back at Donald's, it was raining, and he and I waited in the car for the rain to stop. A thin, white-haired guy arrived on a mountain bike. This was another member of Donald Jones's co-op, by the name of—wait for it—Donald Jones. The black Donald Jones stepped from the car and greeted his doppelgänger with a hug. The white Donald Jones removed from his shoulder a bright blue mountaineer's pack. He unfastened the cord and scooped out the contents: clear grocery bags of leafy greens. Ten bags. Half a pound each. The outsource was outsourcing.

Black Donald Jones removed his T-shirt, revealing the words LONG SUFFERING tattooed across his chest, and ambled across the street with a knife in hand as the clouds opened up. He bent low in the green patch, filling a big plastic tub with salad mix. When he joined us on the porch ten minutes later, his tub overflowing with lettuce, his jeans were soaked. He mixed the bags of lettuce supplied by white Donald Jones with his own greens. "These are looking a bit wilted," he said. He fluffed them with his hand, as if to breathe new life into them.

"They look pretty good to me," said white Donald Jones.

"Maybe I should just go cut another five pounds from my garden." The White Donald Jones exhibited a look of despair.

"Nah, it's all good," said black Donald Jones, breaking into a smile. He continued dumping the plastic bags of arugula into his tub. "I told you I'd buy it, and I'll buy it. I'm a man of my word. I can't do anything without my word."

He leaned into his task, and told us about a plan to supply the Detroit public schools with 250 pounds of greens a week. "I was sitting in a meeting with the *people*," he recalled. "You know what they said? *Donny, you're a fucking young pup. You don't know what you're talking about.*"

His voice rose and his hands flew through the greens. "I said, That's cool. But you know what, you gonna *beg* me to buy from me."

He stomped his feet and his shout startled us. "You gonna *beg*!"

"Whatever you say, Donald," said white Donald Jones.

He stepped off the porch and paid white Donald his twenty-five dollars. Buy for a nickel, sell for a nickel. White Donald pedaled off on the rainy street. Donny and I walked back to the porch, where he sorted through the tub, carefully removing most of the lettuce he'd just bought from white Donald.

"I didn't think it was good enough," Donny said. "I have a reputation for high quality."

Minus what he paid the other Donald, he would earn fifty dollars. In the meantime, Donny had already spent his last cash on lettuce that he would leave to rot.

"Dude, lend me a dollar," he said. "I want to buy a couple of cigarettes."

OLIVIA AND GREG continued to dream. Yes, they had succeeded in earning a living on a one-acre homestead. But their goal was not just to change *what* people eat; they wanted to change *how* they eat. "I want the garden to replace the café," he said. "The garden to replace the grocery store." They also wanted to give people a way to participate in the urban farming movement without devoting all their time to farming. "If you want to get people to stop funding Monsanto and the GMOs, then you have to provide an alternative," she said. "Not everyone's going to have twelve ducks and nineteen chickens and four guineas." Really what they wanted was to build a new economic model of food distribution.

But if Greg and Olivia were going to undersell Whole Foods and any other health food chain that came to Detroit, they would need a lot more than one acre. They began searching for land to expand the farm. And they began to bump against the limitations of urban farming. In 2012, the city had finally passed an ordinance allowing itself to sell vacant lots as agricultural land. There was plenty for the taking, and it was cheap. But it would take five years, give or take, to make an urban homestead fully functional, in the best of conditions. Greg and Olivia wanted land that they could buy on a Monday and plow on a Tuesday. They didn't have the energy or time to excavate another acre of rubble.

And there was an even stronger disincentive for committing to another plot of Detroit soil. They didn't trust that the city would let them keep it. Like many black Detroiters, Olivia feared deep in her bones that if she were to build something great, the city would take it away.

"You can't ever own land in the city," she said. "In the Black Bottom neighborhood, all those people owned houses, and when the city wanted to build a freeway, they just took it. They did this with Corktown. They did it to Mexicantown. And if you're farming, it's not like a house. Even though you love your house, you can live in another house. But I can't go break ground someplace else and then just pick up and leave."

After working for the city bureaucracy and observing how bad decisions were made, Olivia was convinced that even their current farm was in danger of seizure. "Being across from the elementary school, they probably won't let this land stay like this. Eventually they'll say they're going to build low-income housing, and they'll say, *How can you hold out against that?* I think we'll probably be put off, or we'll be squeezed down to the point where we just won't be able to farm here." They needed land zoned for permanent farming. Such land did not exist within the city limits.

AND THERE WAS THIS: Olivia and Greg were talking about having a baby. But Olivia, the girl who had pined for a secure home all her childhood, wasn't sure she could have a baby here. One winter night shortly after they were married, she and Greg had been ensconced in the upstairs bedroom beneath a warm blanket, watching an apocalyptic thriller on the laptop. They'd squeezed each other as the zombies attacked, amid gunfire and explosions.

"Hold on," said Greg, bolting upright. "Turn it down."

Olivia hit the mute button.

The gunshots continued.

They ran to the window and threw back the curtains. Across the street at the crackhouse, shots rang out. Two men were fleeing as a third fired at them. The whole entourage rushed toward the farm. Dressed only in boxers, Greg grabbed the shotgun and pounded down the stairs. Olivia watched from the window. She saw a man driving an SUV that hauled a trailer, shooting out the window at his pursuer. The block was split by a wooded dirt road that was once an alley. Just as the men raced into the alley, Greg burst through the back door, threw open the fence and met them, shotgun pointed at the ground.

"I hope you're not running through here," he said.

The appearance of a white guy in underwear toting a shotgun stopped the runners cold. "We didn't do anything," one cried.

"Take that shit somewhere else," said Greg.

They wheeled around and sprinted off. Greg stomped through the snow into the kitchen, and when the street was quiet, he and Olivia resumed their movie.

Unlike their rural counterparts, Olivia and Greg regularly confronted the crime, pollution, and addiction of urban living. Was Detroit safe? Critical Mass bike rallies and farmers' markets indicated yes. The high rate of murder and assault, and a rash of burglaries at the aquaponic farm, would indicate no.

Olivia still felt afraid. When Greg was away, she would work the rows alone, visible to anyone who crept along the block. Sometimes she hid in the raspberry thicket. But as the months rolled past, she found that people were not interested in harassing her. She had several theories. "The work repels them," she said. "And when you're working hard, and sweating and panting, and having to go sit down in the shade, they don't want to bother with you. They don't want to be around work, like it's some kind of sickness." Another theory was that thieves saw fewer prospects in a black person. "The brown camouflage works every time," she said. (The statistics disagree: Blacks in Detroit and the rest of the nation are much more likely than whites to be victims of crime.) To further dissuade passersby, as she sat on the picnic table distributing bundles of CSA vegetables, Olivia sharpened her kitchen knives.

For a long time, Greg had believed in diffusing tension peacefully, as he'd learned from his friend, Doug. "You have to kill people with kindness instead of being aggressive," he used to say, "because people do really crazy things." His view hardened over the years, especially after marrying Olivia. "If you're a man, kindness works," said Olivia, whose grandmother kept a hatchet stashed beneath the seat of her pickup. "If you're a woman, it's seen as weak."

Greg and Olivia came to agree that certain situations required a show of force. "Fight crazy with crazy," Greg said. "These are the people who know the people who will be breaking into our house, or will be breaking in themselves." A neighbor boy, child of a drug dealer, had been peeking through the fence, perhaps stealing from the yard. Greg's dog bit him. "That sent a message to him and all his thieving friends that these dogs are fucking crazy here," said Greg. "That this was one of the last places on the list." Other houses on the block were burglarized numerous times, while Greg and Olivia's was untouched. Their immediate neighbors, known to carry concealed weapons, were also left in peace.

As for the hipsters moving in, they tended to revel in the lawlessness. "They can play sax on the porch until midnight, even if they don't know how to play," said Olivia. "They can do whatever they want. They haven't had it undermined yet. Or tore up. Or spray-painted."

Olivia had never been attracted to her city's lawlessness. She would like to see more law and order, more authority: "These politicians today are weak as water. What we need is to clone Coleman Young."

"That's the problem in new Detroit," she said. "Nobody gets judged. People do whatever they can get away with. For human beings to live together, there has to be some judgment, or else there will be chaos."

She disagreed with the idealistic young white newcomers who tended to believe that human nature was generally good. "We're just a bunch of chimpanzees," she said. "People have the potential to be good, but when you live in a society that doesn't groom any goodness, this is what you get."

AND SO THE POSTER COUPLE for Detroit farming had gone looking for farmland outside Detroit.

The ideal property would be no more than an hour's drive from Corktown. It would require a well, electricity for a pump, and no trees. They wanted land not surrounded by genetically modified corn and soy, from which pesticides would seep. It needed to be cheap, which was a realistic stipulation, given Michigan's massive real estate slump. And they wanted to find an owner who would finance the land himself. "We don't want to share our wealth with the bank," said Greg. There was another criterion: they eliminated one excellent farm after seeing the Confederate Stars and Bars flying from the neighbor's roof.

They finally found a place in the tiny township of Riley, not far from where Greg had grown up. They bought 6.9 acres for just $32,000 from a flower grower who was willing to carry the note. Riley was in the country, boasting not even a stoplight. It lacked its own police and fire departments. And yet Olivia was boggled by its efficiency. "The paper gets picked up on the side of the road. Mail gets delivered. Garbage *and* recycling." Some of the three hundred residents sold tomatoes by the side of the road on the honor system, with an unattended cash box.

With a few passes on the tractor, Olivia and Greg quickly doubled their growing operation. They left the remaining six acres fallow for future expansion. They continued to live in Corktown, reverse-commuting to the country to tend their other farm. There was no house or barn on the property, but Olivia, a self-professed country girl at heart who had never lived in the country, allowed herself to dream. "You can't have a childhood when you can't tell if those are fireworks or gunshots," Olivia said. They could build a little solar-powered cottage and raise children and not cheat them, the way Detroit had cheated her, of that barefoot idyll of Lavinia Derwent. "We could have a place of childhood."

PART THREE

Montana

Twelve

I was unsettled. On the one hand, I wanted to be like these people. I owned an acre of tumbleweeds and cottonwoods along a desert creek, a perfect place to plant cherry trees and build a straw-bale house. Yet even as I fantasized about some future Eden, the weeds in our existing garden cried out for pulling, and I gazed at them through the window with little interest. Hot and buggy out there! As much as I admired Ethan and Sarah, and Greg and Olivia, I wasn't flinging myself on the barricades or, for that matter, the compost heap. When I mentioned this to my wife, she said, "You don't really want to live like that."

"I don't?"

"I know people who want to live like that, and you're not one of them."

"Like who?"

"Like all the guys I went to college with," she said. "You're attracted to the ideas, but living back-to-the-land is not an intellectual decision. People do it because they love it. Once I was out in a cabin in the winter with my friend Graham and he saw two pygmy owls in a tree across the meadow. And he was so excited that he ran out across the snow, his boots unlaced, filling with snow, to go see them, and I thought: I just don't care enough about seeing those owls to get snow in my boots."

I could think of nothing to say.

"You don't like to rough it. You don't like to be cold, or to split wood in the snow. You don't like to garden. You don't like to fix things. You like to hire someone to do it. You like to take a hot shower every night."

It was true. I was not the type to fill my boots with snow just to get a closer look at an owl. I was the type to read a book about such a person. Or write one. I was in the category of most simple-life dabblers: seduced by the idea of it, repelled by the hardship.

About the time Cedar's book was published, her sister won a Fulbright to study painting in Nepal. "Growing up in a barn in Whitefish," Cedar said, "we just weren't the sort of people who published books and won awards."

Her reflection startled me. I, of course, was the exact sort of person who published books and won awards, always had been, and as an adult was insulted when I didn't. While my parents had refinanced the house to pay my college tuition, Cedar had balked at loans for private college, and instead took a scholarship to the University of Montana. It wasn't merely that we made different choices for college; it's that we were products of different upbringings: mine valued education most highly, even if it meant taking on debt, and hers valued autonomy and freedom, even if it meant forswearing membership to the academic elite.

It was a moment where my love for Cedar deepened, not in a swoon of romance or a desire to get something I wanted, but in a longing to help her get the things she wanted. And of course it surprised me that after finding her back-to-the-land upbringing so alluring—it was one of the first things I loved about her—I saw that she didn't find it alluring enough to want to return to it.

Something was happening in our marriage that came as a shock to me, a confirmed selfish person. Cedar was turning me not merely into a kinder person, but also into a deeper thinker and better writer. She intuitively understood what I was trying to say, and articulated it better than I could. She likened marriage to two stones in a polishing machine: they tumbled against each other—and it hurt—but they emerged smoother and more beautiful than they would ever have become sitting alone on the ground.

And perhaps I was having some effect on her. She had carried inside her a dream that she rarely shared: to be a poet. And when she revealed this dream to me, far from explaining all the reasons why being a writer was silly and impractical (a topic in which I was well versed), I said yes, do it! I wanted her to have as much opportunity as I'd ever had.

We found ourselves dissatisfied with our little piece of paradise. Cedar wanted to study poetry, not just to write it in isolation in our provincial town. As for me, I wanted the fruit orchard and double-paned windows with natural sunlight. I wanted to own my own home and land. So we found ourselves choosing between a version of the simple life and a not-very-simple life.

The simple option: We would go live in my trailer in the desert, which was paid off. We wouldn't be homesteaders exactly, but we'd reduce what we had. We'd build flood berms and a big garden. Scraping together a little bit of money at a time, we'd build more structures, little straw-bale studios with woodstoves, perhaps a casita with solar panels on the roof.

To finance this dream, I had my eye on my wife's pot of savings. Through hard work and frugality Cedar had squirreled away $25,000 in case she ever wanted to do something risky. The way I saw it, twenty-five grand could buy a lot of adobe.

The not-simple option: Cedar would study poetry in graduate school. She knew this wasn't a wise financial move. She already earned a better salary than nearly every living poet. She had always wanted to study literature, but had taken a detour to biology in college from which she had never fully returned. Growing up with little money, she had always been careful and practical about the stuff. She had assumed that a degree should get you a better-paying job. But now, perhaps influenced by me and my non-remunerative education, she was changing her mind. Wasn't the love of literature reason enough to study it?

Her motivations might seem counterintuitive. If she wanted financial security, then why become a poet? But Cedar never felt that living in a shack and driving a twenty-year-old truck were symptoms of disadvantage. Like her parents, she loved those things. What felt like disadvantage to her was that she had never had the privilege, as I had, to shamelessly study literature, to fling herself recklessly into her creativity. And weren't education and art—as much as Jeffersonian agriculture—the pinnacle of what civilization has to offer? "I must study politics and war that my sons may have liberty to study mathematics and philosophy," wrote John Adams. "My sons ought to study mathematics and philosophy, geography, natural history, naval architecture, navigation, commerce, and agriculture, in order to give their children a right to study painting, poetry, music, architecture, statuary, tapestry, and porcelain."

Well, then: bring on the tapestry and porcelain.

She sent off her applications.

IN THE MEANTIME I'D BEGUN to wonder about the longevity of the simple life. I didn't know how long Olivia and Greg and Ethan and Sarah would last at it. They still had much of the work of childrearing in front of them. None were financially secure, and all exhibited moments of doubt and discouragement. We talk a lot about renewability, but if a way of life is too difficult to endure for more than a decade, then it's not sustainable. I wondered what it would look like to maintain a vision of simplicity for an entire lifetime.

A friend suggested I meet some people just forty miles down the road from Missoula, organic farmers in a tiny town called Victor. "They've been at it forever," my friend said. "Their first son was born in a teepee."

A few days later I followed Luci Brieger as she stomped in old Levi's and ditch boots and a canvas coat through the mud and snow to a shimmering stand of solar panels cocked toward the southern end of the Bitterroot Mountains. Jagged white peaks tore the blue sky, and afternoon sunlight dappled the rolling fields of green clover and mowed yellow grain. Down the middle of the valley the lazy Bitterroot River wound between bare cottonwoods.

Fifty-six years old, Luci Brieger (rhymes with *eager*) was all sharp edges, including elbows and cheekbones, a knit cap pulled low above piercing blue eyes, graying hair braided down her back. She and her husband, Steve Elliott, had earned a living growing vegetables without pesticides or synthetic fertilizers for three decades. They did not appear to be impoverished. They'd amassed forty acres in this spot, complete with a tidy home, a rustic barn, two large greenhouses, sheep in the pen and cows in the pasture, a pastoral spread fit for the cover of *Sunset* magazine. I saw a newish four-door pickup truck, a compact German station wagon that ran on vegetable oil, and a pond that in winter froze into a hockey rink where their three children had learned to skate. Luci and Steve ran their business without cell phones or computers; neither had ever sent an email.

Fastened to a steel pole as thick as a pine tree, the surrounding soil still disturbed from its installation, the solar panels looked like a small drive-in movie screen plopped down on the farm. Luci explained that their electrical meter now ran backward, that the power company paid them, instead of vice versa. I expected her to tell me how satisfying it was to be self-reliant. Instead she did something with her lips that made me think she was going to spit.

"I despise adding more electrons to the system so that other people can waste them," she said, "so people can plug in and play electronic solitaire and look at porn."

She told me she had paid $6,000 to build the panels, a sum that was matched by a grant from the state. The arrangement involved contracts with the government and negotiations with the power company. She reckoned it would take a few years to recoup the investment.

"In order to get out of the money game," she said, "we have to play the money game."

I followed her back to the house, where we saw Steve departing by bicycle, bumping down the long dirt driveway toward town.

"Where are you going?" Luci cried after him.

"To the dentist," he called back.

"Do you have the checkbook?"

Steve Elliott waved his hand casually and pedaled off. Inside the house, kale chips baked in the oven and yogurt heated on the stove. Luci glanced at a thermometer poking out of the pot. "Who left the bathroom light on?" she called, but got no answer. She turned off the switch herself. Seeing that she had tracked snow across the floor, she said, "Fuck." Then: "I use that word too much." The phone rang and she picked it up and listened and then said, "We'll pick it up the next time we're in town." She hung up.

"That was the butcher," she told me. "We killed the llama."

Turned out that the animal, intended to protect sheep, had allowed a dog to kill one. Worse yet, Steve had witnessed the llama using the ewes as a shield to protect itself. It had to go. Luci showed me the greenhouse and I asked if it was warm enough to grow lettuce in the winter. She shot me a look.

"We don't eat lettuce in winter."

Thirty years ago she and Steve had pitched a teepee along Sweathouse Creek, not far from where we were standing. They lit the place with kerosene lanterns. They hauled drinking water in five-gallon jugs on a bicycle trailer. They cooked on the woodstove in winter, a propane burner in summer. They dipped in the creek. In the winter they heated cauldrons on the fire and sponged themselves clean, or filled a cast-iron bathtub with creek water and lit a flame beneath it. Steve fashioned a plush sofa by draping sheepskins across three folding chairs. The teepee had no telephone or electricity. They used an outhouse.

In those early years they ate their own radishes and lettuce, spinach and peas, broccoli and cucumbers, tomatoes and beets, and squash and potatoes that they cellared for winter. They helped run a dairy that produced milk and cheese, a farm that grew beef and pork. They foraged for huckleberries and asparagus. They traded for Flathead cherries. They gleaned apples in the fall and pressed barrels of cider, but when that was gone, they went without fruit. They did not eat packaged snacks or sweets. Anything else—like grains and oils—they bought in bulk.

For their fifty-hour workweek, they allotted themselves an annual salary of $2,000 each. Their expenses were gasoline for the pickup, propane for the campstove, kerosene for the lanterns. On frosty mornings they pedaled bicycles down the icy road to the dairy to work their shift on the milking stand. They cut and split their own firewood. They owned only a few changes of secondhand clothing. They filed tax returns but did not earn enough to owe taxes. They didn't have health insurance or life insurance. "We don't like the idea of insurance companies getting rich from us," Luci said. Saving for old age was not discussed. They rarely went to restaurants or the movies.

And yet when I told her I was writing about the simple life, Luci Brieger almost shouted: "Nothing simple about it."

She insisted that she had not gone back to the land. She would say that we all live on the land, whether we know it or not. She did not drop out. There was, to her way of thinking, nowhere to drop out to. She never yearned for a simple life, a sun-filled yoga studio, a coop full of chickens, tomatoes reddening on the windowsill. She is not vegetarian, vegan, macrobiotic, or gluten-free. She does not practice TM, est, or Gestalt. She is not the serene earth mother who accepts the world and its inhabitants just as they are. Even after birthing a child in a teepee without hot running water, she insists that she is neither radical nor extreme. She is merely sensible.

It's one thing to choose a life of restraint for yourself and your spouse. It's another to impose it on children. But for Luci Brieger, parenting was not cause to compromise. Having a family was an integral part of her vision of household—and an occasion to double down on her beliefs. She took exception to a society in which individuality trumps all else.

"We choke on our freedom," she told me. "Our children choke on their freedom. We tell them to follow their dreams, but fulfillment doesn't come from fully doing whatever you want all of the time."

But how to raise a family with restraint in a culture that encouraged gratification?

There were going to be rules.

Each Easter she bought a basket of oranges and grapefruit, but for the most part, once the autumn apples were eaten, there would be no fruit until summer. The family did not want for food—Luci fed them steaks, burgers, bacon, and chops from animals that grazed in nearby pastures. But she would not buy them soda pop or California strawberries. Although she eventually bought a washing machine, there was no dryer, even though one could have run for free on the power generated by the solar panels. In the dead of Montana winter, Luci hung laundry on a rack in the bathroom. Each night after sunset, she fastened insulated curtains over the windows to contain the heat. The family ate together around the table, without televisions or computers. There was no microwave oven or dishwasher or frozen entrées; meals were cooked from scratch, and pots and plates scrubbed by hand. The children soon learned that if they delayed washing dishes by only a few minutes, their mother, whose hands never rested, would leap to the sink and wash them herself.

Another rule: no matter how busy the farm was, they tried to take Sunday off for hiking, skiing, or playing hockey.

At Lifeline Produce, the rules were firm. Indeed, the rule against idleness even applied to me. When I proposed to Luci that I corral her for a dozen or so conversations over the course of a year, she said, "I don't have time to sit down for interviews. But I'm happy to answer your questions while I work." And thus I spent the better part of a growing season double-stepping after her, pen and notebook in hand, as she raced between greenhouse and kitchen and fields. The recordings consist of us hollering to each other over the hiss of water hoses and the whir of greenhouse fans and the rumble of a tractor. One day when the operation was understaffed, she even roped me into sitting on a transplanter, a trailer pulled behind a tractor, to plug lettuce starts into the earth.

But beneath her sharp edges, Luci was warm and nurturing, a trait masked in gentle and not-so-gentle mockery. One day I showed up in shiny black wingtips. "Look at his shoes!" she cried with a giggle. "Do you think you're in the big city?" After that I wore boots. At the end of our days together she pressed into my arms a gigantic cabbage, or a bunch of fresh-cut beet greens, or a sack of potatoes, and sent them home with her regards for my wife. Telling me about a farmer friend who had had a stroke who had received a check for a thousand dollars in the mail from another farmer who didn't even know her, Luci's eyes filled and her voice cracked: "He's just such a fine human being."

Steve returned from the dentist, rubbing his jaw. He had ruddy good looks and a full head of gray hair. He looked different from when I'd seen him earlier in the morning. He had shaved. "I think it's rude to go to the dentist and ask them to touch your beard," he said. "I always shave before I go." Then he looked at my beard and clarified. "I mean, it's not rude to have a beard. Just to have stubble. When you go to the dentist." For an anarchist farmer-rebel who didn't care what anyone else thought, he was unfailingly polite. But he carried himself with the irony of an autodidact, someone who never went to college but over the years figured out that he was smarter than many of the people who did, and he presented his brand of philosophy with a glint of mockery.

At lunchtime, for example, Steve said, "Let me show you how to make a sandwich." Over the years, he deadpanned, he had engineered the perfect sandwich. He had discovered that while untoasted bread became soggy, toasted bread was dry as plywood. The optimal sandwich bread was toasted on the inside for structural integrity—to prevent the mustard and mayo from making it soggy—yet left soft on the outside for mouthfeel. Steve had devised an elegant solution: he inserted both pieces in the same slot of the toaster, browning the flanks while protecting the middle. He slathered one side with Grey Poupon, the other with peanut butter, slices of raw onion between them.

I took a bite and had to admit it was tasty.

In the ensuing discussion of scientific innovation, Steve told me he was constantly amazed at how technology adapted to meet his needs. "Just when I was reaching the age where I couldn't drink a lot, we got microbreweries that only allow you three beers and close at eight. And just when I started to gain weight, they came out with relaxed-fit jeans." Although he didn't use email, he now had an iPod that he filled with music from his children's laptops and listened to while driving the tractor. When I asked him what he thought was the most significant technological innovation of his lifetime, he tapped his chin for a few moments and finally said, "The salad spinner."

Luci and Steve had become the leaders of the state's local food movement and were often asked to join committees and speak on pan-els; they were the matriarch and patriarch of an extended family of former apprentices, many of whom had started their own farms in western Montana. Some of them still dropped by for dinner and were always referred to as "the kids." Steve had even performed the wedding ceremony for the one-time apprentice who'd introduced me to them.

The next time I visited the farm, the pond had frozen, and hockey season had begun. At least two days a week, the Brieger-Elliott family geared up in helmets, kneepads, and elbow guards and took to the ice. Other farmers and friends and apprentices drove all the way from Missoula. A boom box on an extension cord from a dilapidated camper blasted old soul for the adults, MIA for the kids.

"They gave away the Super Bowl!" Steve howled to his buddies as he laced up his skates. "This young kid, this cornerback, just stopped running! Didn't cover his man! He thought the game was over. And of course the pass was a Hail Mary, and the guy caught it, and just walked into the end zone. It will go down as the worst choke in the history of the Denver Broncos, or maybe of the NFL."

The hockey game was not for novices. Luci and Steve's sons, Emmet and Wendell, and their daughter, Ali, were naturals, and all played in the Missoula high school league, with Ali already on the boys' team in eighth grade. The action at the rink was fast and the hits hard. Steve and Luci's aging bodies ended up splayed out on the ice more frequently than the others' did. But it was clear they'd won by a more important measure: their three teenagers, whatever luxuries had been denied them, had willingly, and by all appearances happily—spent a Sunday afternoon with them.

This miracle was not lost on Luci, whose parents had divorced when she was thirteen, and whose sister had then left to live with an aunt. Nor was it lost on Steve, whose father had died young.

"Almost everyone will tell you that family's the most important thing," he told me, "but so many of us live life the opposite."

He bristled at the suggestion that our happiness depends on the quantity of things we have. "As long as we perpetuate that myth, then we're never going to be happy. And that has to do with fear, because the more you have, the more you're afraid of losing it. Anyone who's a parent figures that out. That's kind of a mindfuck because you have to be afraid for everybody else. But fear of losing things will never make you keep it a minute longer."

And yet no amount of intentional living could entirely insulate the family from the economics of the modern world. The eldest son, Emmet, had recently decided to attend a college that cost fifty thousand dollars per year, in order to pursue his dream of becoming an artist. The couple had set aside a modest college fund for each child, but it would not begin to cover this much tuition. Fifty thousand was about as much as Luci and Steve made in a year.

"Somehow we raised a metro kid in Victor, Montana," said Luci. "With upscale-hipster taste."

"I will love my kids whatever they do," said Steve. "And I approve of what they do as long as it's practical and frugal. But we don't know if a hoity-toity art school is the right thing for him."

I wanted to know more about what it was that had sustained this couple in their way of life for going on forty years—how they had found their version of right livelihood yet also engaged and integrated with the world enough to prosper and to raise and educate children. I wanted to understand how they'd kept their ideals intact, and how they dealt with what challenged those ideals, like Emmet's decision. Was a vengeful god punishing them for the hubris of believing they knew what was best for their children? Thinking about my own future, I wanted to find out.

Thirteen

For Luci, the values set early. Virtue was efficiency and thrift and, most of all, work. Vice was laziness and indulgence and, worst of all, waste.

This spartan response to a Hobbesian universe may best be explained thus: Lucianne Brieger was Texan. Her parents descended from German immigrants who settled in Central Texas in the mid-nineteenth century. Her father, Emmet, had grown up on a few acres with a few cows in South Texas during the Great Depression, the youngest of ten, or maybe twelve, but Luci could name only ten. Babies died all the time back then. Emmet was the last; his father committed suicide before he was born, and the farm failed. As he grew up, he found ways to help support the family and to make his way in the world. He rode his bicycle to town and got a job mixing malts. He enlisted in the navy and shipped out to the South Pacific, then got a college degree on the GI Bill.

Luci's mother, Merle Jean Fischer, had grown up on a horse farm, eight hundred acres of mesquite and rocks in Central Texas. It was pretty country if you squinted just right, but hard to make a dollar off. When the market for fancy horses collapsed during the Depression, her parents switched to goats. When the price of mohair sank, they switched to cattle. They kept a few acres in hay and oats. As a girl, Luci's mother had collected sticks to cook meals on the woodstove.

Emmet found good work as a mechanical engineer in the oil-well service industry and bought twenty-five acres outside Houston. Luci's mother became a nurse. The area was fast becoming a suburb of Houston, but the family had a cotton allotment, grew alfalfa and hay, kept stock. "I got me some cattle out there," is how her father put it. "A break-even deal." In an era when fast food and TV dinners were ascendant, her mother kept a vegetable garden and cooked from scratch.

Emmet Brieger was not raising debutantes. He gave Luci and her sister, Leesa, little hammers and screwdrivers. When he shot doves, Luci ran and fetched them. The family ate every single one. The girls tromped a trailerful of cotton in the hot Texas summer. If something broke, a fence or a truck or a water pipe, Emmet fixed it himself. As a man walked on the moon, he saved steel cans to store nails and bolts and washers. Food scraps went to the chickens. Emmet had grown up hauling water from a well, and even when it came from a tap he could not bear to pour it down the drain. If the Briegers weren't entirely living off the land as their forebears had, they were still practicing traditional skills and enforcing traditional values—frugality, hard work, land stewardship.

"My parents being real products of the Depression, in my household we never wasted anything," Luci told me. She was made to see that everything came from somewhere before you got it, and went somewhere when you were done with it. "If you have to haul the wood to heat the water, and you have to haul the water, you're a lot more careful about what you use. I didn't grow up hauling water, but they did. They understood the value of things—not in dollar terms. They understood what was precious."

Luci continued to visit her grandparents' ranch, and felt more connected to that scrubland than to the green fields of home, especially after her parents divorced. "The land ethic of my family was so tied to that place in Central Texas," she told me. It was fragile and marginal land, where growing things had to be prickly and gnarled to survive. Yet Luci was careful never to claim that she grew up on a farm. "A hobby farm, maybe," she told me, implying that only the worst brand of pretender would falsely claim to be a farmer. Her parents had not been at the mercy of weather and crops to make it to the next year.

And they certainly had not intended for a daughter of theirs to become a farmer. As much as Luci was the product of bootstraps pioneer stock, she was also a product of decades of postwar prosperity and Great Society government expansion. Before the GI Bill, a farm boy like her father would likely have not been able to afford an engineering degree. In the 1970s, Texas, with its good public schools, offered more opportunities to Luci than her mother or grandmother could have imagined. She excelled at chemistry and calculus, competed on the debate and speech teams. She grew into a gangly tomboy, joined the cycling club, and took long rides on the weekends. At Southwest Texas State University in San Marcos, she majored in geography and minored in chemistry. Although tuition was low and her parents helped pay it, they'd ingrained in her the belief that she must earn her own way. Through high school she had worked evenings at the local Pizza Hut, biking the seven miles home when her shift ended at midnight. In college she supported herself working twenty hours a week at a burger joint.

In the America of her youth, in which resourceful citizens seemed to work hand in hand with innovative government, Luci felt a sense of purpose and responsibility. Even as she took college courses about looming problems like carbon emissions and greenhouse gases, she expected that government would take the lead in solving them. President Jimmy Carter was blocking the construction of dams and encouraging Americans to wear sweaters indoors and dial down the thermostat. Before him, Richard Nixon had signed the Endangered Species Act and chartered the Environmental Protection Agency. It felt to Luci that the country was on the brink of great change, and she wanted to join the effort. She applied to graduate programs in environmental studies to prepare for a career with a government agency or a nonprofit.

But before she continued her pursuit of meaningful work, she allowed herself a taste of the freedom that lay off that path. The summer before grad school, Luci invested $239 in the best bike around—a Motobécane Grand Touring. She strapped a tent and a sleeping bag to it and embarked with a friend on a tour of the country. They pedaled along the Blue Ridge Parkway and landed on the Atlantic shore in Virginia. They rode to Washington, D.C., and took in the museums, then went up to the Finger Lakes, through Boston, as far north as Acadia National Park. With their long hair stuffed under ball caps, they were often mistaken for a pair of teenage boys. They camped out and were invited to sleep in strangers' fields and on their floors. How lovely to see that the world opened wide when you trusted that it would! They budgeted ten dollars per day each, scanning the horizon at dusk for an all-you-can-eat buffet, stuffing their pockets with leftovers for tomorrow's lunch.

And as they rode, Luci saw evidence that America was, as she had suspected, on the brink of big change. But it was not the kind of change she had anticipated. It was the summer of 1980, and as she filled her bicycle tires at service station air pumps, cars waited around the block for gasoline. The hostages in Iran began their second year. The economy sputtered as inflation and interest rates soared. In her admiration of President Carter, Luci was in the minority. Ronald Reagan was up in the polls, promising to make America great again. Unlike Carter and Nixon, he did not believe government's role was to safeguard the air and water, but rather that a free market would protect those things on its own. Reagan declared that government was not the solution but the problem, and promised to "use all the resources now available to us—including more of the oil and natural gas."

In September, Luci and her friend ran out of time. School was starting. They leaned their loaded bicycles against a highway sign on the interstate in Pennsylvania and stuck out their thumbs. Cotton candy clouds collided overhead, grasses yellowed on the rolling hills. The girls wore grease-stained shorts and threadbare T-shirts, their calves and shoulders browned by the sun. They had ridden three thousand miles in one hundred days.

Within five minutes an eighteen-wheeler shuddered to the side of the road. The driver was headed far south, but he called on the CB for another trucker to meet the girls at the junction and convey them west to St. Louis. "We'll buy your supper!" cried Luci. The girls wheeled their bikes around to the cargo door at the back of the truck. Inside were dozens of identical cardboard boxes in neat stacks, each containing a brand-new cash register. There must have been more than a hundred of them. As the trucker heaved their bikes on top, it struck Luci: What is someone going to do with a hundred cash registers?

"Where these things going?" she shouted over the roar of passing trucks.

The trucker slammed the door and fastened the latch and yelled back: "Walmart!"

WHEN LUCI BRIEGER STEPPED off the Greyhound in Missoula to attend the University of Montana in the autumn of 1980, the scenario that greeted her bore little resemblance to Yellowstone and the Big Sky of her imagination—and little resemblance to the hip college town I moved to a quarter century later. Missoula was dreary and cold, an aging mill town of sooty brick warehouses and clanging train yards, already coated in September by a film of grimy snow. Incinerators burned slash from the mills, and smokestacks belched yellow clouds that instead of floating off on a crisp breeze settled into the beige valley, a damp haze that burned the eyes and stank like rotten eggs.

The pollution provided Luci further evidence that her decisions were valid. With proper training she would help find a remedy. After her first semester she took an internship with a nonprofit watchdog group in Helena, the state capital, working on energy and waste policy. Even though Reagan had been elected, there was still a sense of invincibility among conservationists. For two decades they had won one victory after the next: the Clean Air Act, the Clean Water Act, the Wilderness Act. Luci's confidence was not the woozy passion of a tree-hugger with a romantic yen for mountains and animals but the logic of a scientist who had considered the data and engineered a sound solution. When the session ended, Luci took an internship with the United States Department of Agriculture. "We thought we knew everything," she told me.

But in fact, just as she was beginning her career, the seeds of its undoing had already been sown. The era of good public schools and high wages and a national consensus on conservation was ending. In the years that followed, manufacturing was shipped overseas, the gap between rich and poor widened beyond that during the Great Depression, and Americans consumed more food, oil, and electricity than did any society in the history of the world. The welfare state launched by Franklin D. Roosevelt was crunching to a close, heralding a new era of deregulation and privatization, in which the desires of the American consumer would fuel the entire world economy.

Luci's first hint that the orderly world she put such stock in was collapsing was the weariness she detected when she made her rounds to allies at the Environmental Protection Agency and other regulatory offices. They were under attack. The Sagebrush Rebellion—a movement of local governments in the West defying the federal protection of public lands—had stormed the national stage. "Count me in as a rebel!" Ronald Reagan declared. He appointed as secretary of the interior James Watt, who announced, "We will mine more, drill more, cut more timber." Watt quintupled the amount of land leased for coal mining and opened the seas to offshore oil drilling, actions unusual enough to land his balding pate on the cover of *Time* magazine with the headline "Land Sale of the Century." Meanwhile, at Reagan's EPA, enforcement cases were down by 79 percent.

In Montana, legislators blamed the agencies for the closing of lumber mills. "They weren't correctly identifying the problem, so the solution was always to lash out at environmentalists," Luci remembered. "It was always that there was too much regulation—that's why the mills were closing. They weren't interested in reality. It didn't matter about facts."

Luci attributed the crash of the lumber industry not to regulation but to global market forces: American mills were being undersold by those in other countries. This could be attributed to lax labor laws in those countries, or free-trade agreements that benefited multinational corporations, or a strong dollar that encouraged imports. Now, instead of pushing for more protection, activists were playing catch-up, trying to force the government to obey its own laws.

Luci fidgeted at her desk, whether in the statehouse or at the university. To pay tuition and rent she waited tables, and she liked the work: it kept her hands busy. She lived in a small room, didn't own a car, and cooked her own meals. And yet, doubts began to creep in. What if the conservation movement—the scientists and professors and regulators—were not saving the planet? She had long perceived that the world was steered by experts armed with good facts and good intentions. What if this was false? In the best-case scenario, the well-meaning experts were being whipped by superior opponents. In the worst case, the experts were twiddling their thumbs, drawing salaries from universities and government while the planet burned.

On the periphery of this ominous vision, Luci glimpsed a different path. In the fall of 1982 she learned of a farm south of Missoula where one could volunteer in exchange for vegetables. It was forty miles away. She hopped on her bike Friday after classes and rode up the Bitterroot Valley, the clear sunny peaks a welcome break from Missoula's haze. She camped at the farm, then spent the next day wrestling squash from the vine. These farmers looked like nobody she had ever met. They were neither the gentleman hobbyists from the outskirts of Houston nor the bucktoothed hicks of television's *Green Acres*. Nor were they flower children. The place was run by lean, hungry-looking guys, college dropouts and Vietnam vets, with beards and Levi's and leather boots and flannel shirts. They were attractive, charismatic, and had a seriousness of purpose about them. They were rougher around the edges than the university and capitol crowds. Some lived in teepees. They worked on their knees, elbow-deep in soil, ten or twelve hours a day, in a way that made them appear powerful, connected to the land. This bunch of dropouts had a better idea of what needed to be done than the whole lot of professors at the university, Luci thought.

Although the farm was cooperatively run by seven men and women, it appeared to Luci that the visionary among them was Ernie Harvey. Ernie was clean-cut and ruggedly handsome and commanded respect when he spoke. He was a Montana boy who had grown up raising shorthorn beef with the Beaverhead County chapter of Future Farmers of America. After high school he had drifted from his roots and begun bicycling, making pottery, working as a stonemason. "I was disillusioned making luxury fireplaces for rich people who might just use them two weeks a year," he told me. "I wanted my life and work to be socially redeeming, to have a purpose." He dabbled in meditation and yoga, but found that the practices were limited to human experience and did not incorporate the natural world that so evidently meant something. He enrolled at the University of Montana, but dropped out before graduating, took a job on a farm up the Bitterroot, and in 1978, along with a few partners, founded Lifeline Farms.

Ernie Harvey and the Lifeline crew had caught the tail end of the back-to-the-land movement, but by the time Luci Brieger arrived to pick squash, most of the communes and homesteads had fizzled out. Nonetheless, the crew at Lifeline cast some doubt on her professional ambitions. As she wavered on her career track, Luci read the book that derailed her. The author was Wendell Berry.

The Unsettling of America appeared to be an innocuous collection of essays on a topic—farming—too stodgy to garner discussion among grad students drawn to sexier causes like wilderness and endangered species. Yet Berry declared that the conservation movement of which Luci was a fledgling member suffered a deep split between what its adherents thought and what they actually did. "As consumers," he wrote, "they may be using—and abusing—more land by proxy than they are conserving by the intervention of their organizations."

Luci became convinced that farming and conservation were the same. The conservation movement, as such, had long focused on protecting "the environment," a place outside people's homes, populated by whales, owls, rivers, forests, and air. To protect these things, laws were passed to limit human activity such as mining, drilling, damming, and logging. Yet none of the laws offered advice on how humans themselves were to live better. After all, mankind's most impactful—and important—activity was not mining or logging but farming. Over the eons, humans had lived without gasoline and electricity, but they could not survive without food. It seemed to Luci that the real work in conserving the planet was in figuring out a permanent way to feed ourselves. But in Luci's graduate program, agriculture wasn't even allowed as a concentration.

Luci returned to Helena. This time, her frustration doubled as the Montana legislators ramped up their attacks. "You would have been better with a bucket of nails," she said of the leadership. "They were just bags of shit. So stupid. So selfish. The worst politicians imaginable— and I'm from Texas. The legislature meets ninety days every two years; for all the trouble they caused, it would be better if they met two days every ninety years."

"I grew to hate it," she said. "You have to be so patient. The ones who succeed at it are much better people than me."

Luci struggled with the Protestant work ethic of her upbringing. Before the Reformation, Catholics were taught to do "good work"— that which served the community—as a means to salvation. But Luther and Calvin taught that salvation was predestined—that you couldn't work your way into heaven. The result was the opposite of what one might expect. Instead of becoming rank libertines, Protestants led lives of temperance, frugality, and productivity, not as a way to punch their tickets to heaven but rather to measure up to the godly standard established by their predetermined salvation. As a result, the European Protestants, and especially their American brethren like Luci's forebears, were perhaps the most industrious souls in the history of the planet.

And yet America has always been pulled from opposing poles on the question of whether the purpose of work is to maintain virtuous simplicity or to gain material abundance. "But the question," John Adams mused in 1775, "is whether our People have Virtue enough to be mere Husbandmen, Mechanicks, and Soldiers?" To Adams's likely chagrin, the new nation's free trade, bounteous resources, and labor-saving inventions delivered what virtue could not: an escape from village toil and an entrance into the propertied class, complete with the milled coats, beaver hats, and silver spoons previously reserved for aristocrats. Shortly after independence, Samuel Adams lamented, "We are exchanging prudence, virtue and past economy for those glaring spectres luxury, prodigality and profligacy."

In the modern era, however, hard work does not always equal good work. The dilemma that Luci faced—that most of us have faced—is the creeping dread that the work offered us is, in fact, bad. Bad for our fellow humans, bad for the planet, bad for justice. The centralization of power in government and corporations creates a scenario in which many of the available jobs might conceivably hasten the demise of the human race, whether through war, destruction of farmland, or spoiling the air and water.

So while Wendell Berry extolled the virtues of labor, his brand of work was not precisely the same as that which defined previous generations. In an echo of John Adams's fear of "ignominious domination," Berry argued that most modern careers required submitting to "specialization, degradation, trivialization and tyrannization." In other words, the protestant work ethic had turned sinister. How could we derive satisfaction from our work if it diminished ourselves and helped destroy civilization?

Berry declared that good work is not working "for a living" or "to support a family." Good work *is* living. And the place to perform such work was not in an office or factory but in our own home. "If we do not live where we work, and when we work," concluded Berry, "we are wasting our lives, and our work, too."

Luci quit grad school to apprentice at Lifeline Farms.

Like me, Luci found that her worldview was rocked by reading Berry. But instead of just wrestling with his ideas in her head, she acted on them. In fact, three decades later, having embodied the essence of

Berry's philosophy, she could not correctly recall the name of the book of his that had changed her life. As Cedar had told me: people who live like this might be drawn to the ideas, but more important, they loved the work.

Around the time she quit school, Luci had a chance to meet Berry himself at a conference.

"Wow!" I said. "What did you say to him?"

"I don't remember." Luci blinked and smiled. "That was a long time ago."

FARMING WAS CERTAINLY NOT the life expected of Steve Elliott. At the Oakmont Country Club in Glendale, California, he and his parents and sister golfed on Saturday mornings, then ate prime rib buffet in the clubhouse. There was no question that Steve would attend college and become a professional. Conservative Christians who voted for Ronald Reagan for governor, his dad had graduated from UCLA and owned a manufacturing firm in Los Angeles, and his mom stayed home in La Crescenta with the kids. One day a week she volunteered arranging window displays at a thrift store while a Mexican maid named Carmen cleaned the house and tended to Steve and his older sister.

Steve didn't mind caddying for his father and his father's friends, but you couldn't pay him to swim at the pool with their sons. Neither did he want to hang out with the rich boys from church. "Rich people are a bit like dogs," he told me. "One is always great, it's when you get them in a pack that they cause trouble."

Wealth was not a hardship Steve Elliott would have to endure for long. When Steve was thirteen, his father was diagnosed with cancer and died within a year. His mother took a job selling women's wear in a department store. She let Carmen go. While his sister went off to UCLA, Steve took a job stripping furniture. His grades dropped but nobody asked to see his report card. The year was 1969. On weekends he told his mom he was staying at a friend's house but instead hitch-hiked with a buddy to Yosemite.

Steve's father had spent his life juggling balance sheets in anticipation of some future reward. His dream had been to cash out for a ranch in Colorado. Then he died at fifty-three. Steve wanted his life to mean something *now*. He wanted to work with his hands, master tasks that *needed* to be done.

But artisan apprenticeships available to L.A. teenagers were few. Steve was hired at the Gifts and Gadgets warehouse. He assembled boxes of Christmas tree-top angels, plastic reindeer, spools of ribbon, and strings of tinsel and loaded them onto a truck. He liked the sputter of the forklift's diesel engine and the power of the hydraulic levers as he moved pallets around the yard. But manual labor did not necessarily translate to meaningful labor. After a few months, Steve quit.

When he told his mother, she said, "I never took you for a quitter." That cut to the bone. Steve resolved never to be called that again. He took a job tossing pies at Straw Hat Pizza. The boss told him to cut his hair. Steve was rebel enough to grow it long, but not so stubborn as to lose a job over it. On Hollywood Boulevard he bought a short-hair wig, which he pulled over his locks.

Steve did not bother applying to college. Three days after high school graduation in 1972, he and three friends thumbed up the coast to the Olympic Peninsula and took the ferry to Canada. Steve had been assigned a draft number, but it was high, and even if the number was called, he didn't intend to show up. Over the next few years he hitchhiked across the country eleven times, maybe twelve. One night in Maine, after a breakup with a girl, Steve stayed up till dawn reading *On the Road*. In the morning he stuck out his thumb. Fifty-one hours later he was in Reno, perhaps some sort of record. Hippies may have been passé by then, but Steve Elliott still believed in living simply, being close to nature, not grinding away his life in pursuit of money.

The one part of being a hippie that he got tired of was sitting around doing nothing. He preferred to work. In New Hampshire he took a job scraping the bottoms of boats and rented an uninsulated beach cottage for the winter. He loaded ovens in a mica factory. He knocked on doors and interviewed people for the Census Bureau. He swept warehouse floors at a submarine base, a government-funded job. The first day he finished sweeping one warehouse in two hours. His boss told him that was impossible; the task was supposed to take four hours. Here was another meaningless job. Yet Steve was determined not to quit. The next day he packed a parka and a paperback, and when he finished sweeping, he bedded down on a pile of fire hoses in a closet and read some Vonnegut.

He wanted to discover the realm beyond the material, if there really was one. And yet some strain of Southern California smart-ass skepticism stopped him from leaping headlong into spirituality. After his friends took up Transcendental Meditation, he noticed that they started whupping him at ping-pong, so there must be something to it. Yet whenever he went to a meeting or a class, there was always some catch—giving money, donning garb, chanting foreign words—that prevented him from joining. Instead he tried sitting in the woods by himself, listening, praying. His mind raced with pointless thoughts. He was sure he was doing it wrong.

In 1975, Steve thumbed into Atlanta and was hired to hang wallpaper at a Holiday Inn. From a fifty-four-inch roll, he was taught to cut a strip of paper eight feet, two inches long. He fed it into the mouth of the pasting machine, pulled it out through the roller. He folded the sheet in thirds, stepped up a small ladder, then spread the top third onto the wall. He smoothed out the bubbles with a trowel and sliced the excess off the top edge with a razor. He stepped off the ladder and applied the middle third and the lower third and smoothed them with the trowel. He trimmed the bottom edge. Snipped around any sockets or switches. Pressed the edges with a seam roller.

Steve Elliott liked the work. Each series of motions was identical, and he trained himself to be efficient. No movement or effort was wasted. Some guys carried a utility knife in their belt, but constantly reaching for it was an inexcusable waste. Instead, Steve bit down on a naked razor blade and used that, saving hundreds of motions a day to draw a knife, and hundreds more to sheath it. Money was good. In 1976 this dharma bum was making one hundred ten per day.

When Steve focused on hanging paper, time ceased to function. It was the sensation he had read about, the transcendence of the material world, that he could never find sitting cross-legged, staring at infinity. But when he held tools in his hands and put them to use, he achieved a meditative state. Hanging paper was his martial art, and he became a master. The young man walked the country alone, a wallpaper samurai, bandanna knotted around his locks, a simple pack containing the weapons of his trade: a Marshalltown trowel, a seam roller, a carton of razor blades. He embraced the Tao Te Ching:

> Manifest plainness
> Embrace simplicity
> Reduce selfishness
> Have few desires

Not all the bosses liked longhairs, and some hesitated to hire him, but even they were silenced once they saw his hands flying, the silver blade in his teeth. They had to admit: that hippie could hang some goddamn paper.

Eventually Steve Elliott bought a Bel Air station wagon that he lived out of. Yet it was evident to him that the modern American way of life was doomed, a feeding frenzy on limited resources. Water, food, forest, soil—we were consuming it all faster than it could be replenished. He had studied enough history to conclude that societies did not collapse overnight, not even in the lifespan of a single person. He wasn't worried that the apocalypse would arrive and that he would have to fend with a bow and arrow. He simply did not want to participate in a civilization bent on its own destruction. Lame Deer wrote that to participate was to give tacit approval. Well, Steve Elliott didn't approve, and he wasn't going to help sink the ship. Neither did he want to be a freeloader. He vowed not to vote, serve in the military, or accept government handouts.

And yet, the simple life got more complicated. After Steve got a girlfriend, the Bel Air was too small. In Kalispell, Montana, he landed a union job, and the couple rented a cabin. As a union man Steve was paid by the hour, not the square foot. A fourteen-dollar wage was good money, but once you minused the dues, it wasn't any more than he'd earned five years before. And it drove him crazy that no matter how many square feet he hung, he'd still make $112 a day. There was no challenge, no incentive. The ability to work fast should be rewarded, first by making more money, and second by getting to go home sooner. But on the union crew, time did not disappear. Instead, the clock ticked by in maddening increments.

Time.

Slowed.

Down.

Still, Steve would not quit the job.

Eight years after high school, Steve Elliott's quest had ground to a halt. He was no mystical kid on an epic journey toward right livelihood. He was a contractor who paid rent and insurance and hung wallpaper in laundry rooms. What's more, his plan to embody the simple life was clearly not working. He and his girlfriend left Montana.

That spring, Steve heard Gary Snyder speak in California. The former guru had cut his hair. He was not advising anyone to drop out. "There is no place to flee to in the U.S.," said Snyder. "There is no quiet place in the woods where you can take it easy and be a stoned-out hippie. The surveyors are there with their orange plastic tape, the bulldozers are down the road warming up their engines." Snyder preached responsibility. He told his audience to join the school board and run for city council. We were all in this world whether we liked it or not. Integrate with your values intact.

In the summer of 1982, the couple drove to the Bitterroot Valley. Snow-covered mountains soared up along the western edge of a flat valley. He came across a farm stand. A chatty old Swiss woman was selling the season's first lettuce and spinach. Her son, Ernie, ran an organic farm just up the road. Steve asked if they needed any help.

Fourteen

A young man pedaled a bicycle along Wyckoff Avenue in Brooklyn. He passed New York New York Barber Shop, where a placard advertised NECESITAMOS BARBEROS. In the window of a salon, a hand-scrawled paper sign announced:

BIG SALE
UNDER ARMS WAXING
FOR BOTH ONLY $8.50

On the sidewalk, bicycle frames leaned against stop signs and bus shelters, fastened with U-locks, picked clean of their saddles and wheels. The young man's bike, in the style of the day, was a vintage fuchsia Schwinn with a single gear. Bright pink grips capped the handlebars. The young man wore a thin beard and a thrift-store orange corduroy cap, slightly cocked, embroidered with "Denver Broncos." He wore an untucked slim-fitting dress shirt beneath a black hoodie, and skinny jeans pegged above bare ankles. Passing from Bushwick into Ridgewood, he lunched on a ninety-nine-cent bean taco prepared by chefs who might have been Chinese or Korean. He ate one of those tacos nearly every day. It was the best deal in Queens.

At precisely 1:15 in the afternoon, Emmet Elliott's smartphone vibrated, and he found an empty stretch of sidewalk. He scrolled through his library of images to a photo of an old postcard, a shot of the modernist Chapel of the Holy Cross protruding from the red-rock cliffs of Sedona, Arizona. He had acquired the postcard, and hundreds like it, by browsing flea markets and stoop sales. The Sedona card was postmarked 1:20, June 12, 1972—precisely forty-two years ago today, two decades before Emmet was born in the teepee in Victor, Montana. At the stroke of 1:20, he posted the photo on Instagram. For the caption, he typed what was written on the card itself: *We were up here today with friends. Brought Ingrid and Oscar here when they were out in January. Enjoyed your letter and will write soon.*

Next, he searched for the most recent Instagram post in a mile radius. Just seconds before, someone named Mohammed Sahib had posted an image of the Brazilian flag in celebration of the opening day of the World Cup. Emmet captured a screenshot of the flag. Then he searched for the most recent Instagram activity in Sedona, Arizona. He found a post. His app gave him the approximate street address of the poster, which he recorded.

Later, when he had some time, he would print Mohammed Sahib's Brazilian flag on sturdy card stock and, on the back, handwrite the caption in pen: *#brazil #worldcup2014*. Then, to complete the circle, he would affix a postage stamp to the handmade postcard and mail it to the Arizona address. He wouldn't be able to do it today, though, because beginning at four in the afternoon he worked a nine-hour shift waiting tables in a pub.

Emmet Elliott had performed this ritual for 163 consecutive days, dropping whatever he was doing in order to post at the correct time. He had archived 365 old postcards with original postmarks that corresponded to every day of the year. He would continue until the final day of 2014. As for the unwitting Instagram users around the globe who received the paper postcards, he was not sure what they thought. Nobody had yet responded.

The project, which Emmet archived online, had begun as an art school assignment. Emmet was twenty-one years old and had just finished his first year at Parsons, the art school that was part of the New School in Manhattan, to which he bicycled daily, dodging cars as he made his way across Brooklyn and onto the Williamsburg Bridge, a commute of thirty-five minutes in good conditions. He looked and talked the part of a New York City art student.

"The conceptual jumping-off point is the remarkable similarity between a postcard and an Instagram post," he told me as we walked though Queens. "I juxtapose two different but similar forms of communication. It raises questions about *performativity*."

Emmet spanked that jargon with a bit of backspin, suggesting that although he had learned to use it correctly, he questioned whether it was a real word. Nonetheless, the professors were impressed. "I did this for a final project," Emmet told me, his eyes brightening and his lips spreading into the same deadpan smile his mother used when examining my shiny wingtips. "I got an A."

Emmet Elliott was perhaps the only student at the New School born in a teepee. And unlike his fellow students who also use the Internet as a medium for conceptual art, Emmet grew up climbing into the seat of a tractor to intercept the neighbor's WiFi. "I hate the Internet," he said. "I do this to negotiate my own relationship with it."

The irony was delicious: the child reared in frugal worktopia fled to the most spendthrift city on the globe, where he trafficked in ideas so abstract that they required tenure to appreciate.

"My parents are bemused," Emmet said.

The conflict had been not whether Emmet's parents would approve of art school, but whether they would help pay for it. Emmet had applied to colleges through a program for low-income students that subsidized the fees. He didn't know much about Parsons—he'd never been to New York. But once he'd been accepted, he fell in love with the idea of moving there. He was offered a partial scholarship, but the tuition was still more than his parents could pay. He knew that they doubted the value of higher education anyway. When their apprentices considered taking loans for ag degrees, Luci told them not to. "You shouldn't be afraid to go into farm debt, because if things go bad, you've still got the land and the equipment, and you can liquidate," she said. "But if you go into debt for a degree, that's all you've got."

Steve and Luci stressed that they were not opposed to art school. They just weren't sure that the price of tuition was worth it, compared with other alternatives. Emmet had been offered a scholarship to another college in Brooklyn, and could have attended the University of Montana with low tuition. Steve had helped Emmet to run the numbers. After four years, he would amass between $100,000 and $200,000 in debt. After that he would find himself in New York with an art degree, and perhaps the only high-paying jobs he could find would be in advertising: the belly of the beast. And Emmet didn't want that.

To be practical and frugal, Emmet had deferred admission for two years and had taken a job with City Year, an AmeriCorps program that rewarded community service with a tuition stipend. He arranged online to rent an apartment in Brooklyn's Bed-Stuy neighborhood with some coworkers. He flew to the city and picked up his key at ten p.m., then found his way to the building, half a block from a housing project notorious for homicides. It was dark. He carried his belongings in a backpack. The other housemates had not yet arrived. Heavy basslines thumped from a hip-hop club next door.

It wasn't until he approached the front door that he realized that, while he had used keys for cars and bike locks, he had never, as far back as he could remember, used one in a door. The farmhouse in Victor had never been locked.

He inserted the key. It wouldn't turn. He jiggled it. No luck. He looked over his shoulder. It was a sweltering August night, with a dank humidity he'd never known in Montana. He could smell himself. Still the damn key would not turn. Finally he forced it. The key snapped, and Emmet was left with a useless shard of metal between his fingers.

NO ONE KNEW BETTER than Luci Brieger that taking a path different from that of your parents tended to vex them. During the summer of 1984, Luci's mother visited Lifeline, with its ramshackle buildings, battered machinery lying around, half-drunk cups of coffee scattered in the crop rows collecting rain. She took a withering look at Luci's clothing: a faded men's work shirt and torn jeans with stains on the knees.

"Of course my clothes are dirty," Luci said. "I work in the dirt."

"I'm a nurse but I don't go into town with shit on my uniform," said her mother.

As for the new boyfriend, Luci's mother observed that Steve was the one with the biggest mouth. Each morning he organized crews, determined which crop to harvest, which deliveries to make.

"Big fish in a small pond," she said. "Maybe his parents will send him back to college."

"He's too smart for that," said Luci.

But it hurt. She had thought that choosing to be a farmer would please her parents, given their own upbringings. But that's not how they saw it. They had worked their way up from the fields, into the comfortable life, and when Luci rejected that world, they took it personally. Besides, they knew that real farming was a rough life, could break your back and your spirit. Her stepmom's fingers had been stained black from picking pecans on the Concho River. What's more, farming was a poor life. Her parents had worked their whole lives so they didn't have to bend down in the dirt to make a dollar.

The Briegers were a family of letter writers, and Luci sent missives on fossil fuels and consumption. She debated her father on his work in the oil industry. He shot back that even an organic farm like Lifeline was dependent on burning gasoline in its tractors and truck. Luci sent a copy of *Small Is Beautiful* to her nearest aunt. "But what's wrong with indoor plumbing?" replied her aunt Dora, who had grown up with an outhouse. "I like flush toilets."

The fact that her parents had walked away from the farming life did not dissuade Luci from thinking that farming was the right thing to do. She told them they had simply not done the critical thinking about what was being thrown out in their shift away from production to consumption. Luci's mother retorted in a letter, "You are too pretty, too smart and too knowledgeable to be a farmer."

Lifeline was deep in debt, having borrowed $70,000 to buy a dilapidated suite of potato-harvesting machines. Yet Ernie Harvey was not cowed. He grew the business by launching a dairy. The buy-in price for new partners was zero. What was required was sweat equity and assuming a portion of the debt.

Her family never explicitly told Luci what to do. "I wouldn't have had enough sense to listen to them," Luci said. "I didn't know I was fallible. I didn't even know what money was back then." Her ignorance of finances and farming was outweighed by her certainty that she was doing right and that things would work out. "I never would have signed on if I thought it wouldn't succeed."

As morning crews were divided, Luci would all but jump up and down in front of Steve: *Pick me! Pick me!* Day after day, he chose her and they pulled weeds, cut cauliflower, delivered truckloads of lettuce to Missoula. By then his girlfriend had gone back to California. Steve didn't exude the intensity of the others: he told jokes, goofed around, told stories about his years hitchhiking and working odd jobs like hanging wallpaper while living in his car. He was a few years older than her, had barely missed the Vietnam draft, had never gone to college. Luci could have done without his long beard, which made him resemble the Ayatollah Khomeini, but beneath all the hair he was quite handsome.

In Steve's memory, the two had connected the first day they met, when Luci rode her bike down from Missoula for a harvest party. They sat across from each other at a table, and amid the beer drinking and platter passing, he caught her eye, and for a moment everything else fell away. It wasn't lust, but something much deeper. Corny as it sounded, Steve felt like he had experienced true communication. Years later Luci would have no memory of this moment. No matter: Steve fell for her.

On their days off, Steve and Luci rode bicycles down the Bitterroot Valley to a diner and sat on the banks of the river eating homemade pie. For her, committing to the land and committing to the man were part of the same package. She was twenty-seven years old. She stuck a fork in her dessert and turned to her boyfriend.

"We should start talking about getting married."

Luci and Steve became part owners of an old potato harvester, three beat-up trucks, a splintered fiberglass grainhouse, a rusty hopper, and a rickety loading contraption called Spudnik—and signatories on a $70,000 note.

They had become farmers.

LUCI'S PARENTS WERE CORRECT in their warning: the 1980s were an unwise time to start farming. During the Great Depression, as the number of farms peaked at 6.8 million, 25 percent of Americans—

including Luci's parents and grandparents—lived on farms. Over the next decades those numbers plummeted. Older farmers—such as Luci's grandparents—died or retired, and their children did not replace them. Often families sold farms for reasons other than financial failure: farm boys drafted to World War II, Korea, and Vietnam; the GI Bill allowing those veterans a college education; and high-paying jobs that drew them to cities and suburbs. By 1970 the number of farms had dropped by 60 percent, and only 4 percent of Americans lived on them.

At the same time, the average size of a farm doubled. With big machinery, chemical pesticides, and petro-fertilizers, fewer farmers were growing far more food. Nixon's secretary of agriculture, Earl Butz, furthered this trend by pressuring farmers to "get big or get out." Getting big entailed borrowing money for industrial-scale equipment and transitioning from a variety of crops to monoculture grains—corn, wheat, soy—much of which was exported. Farm debt burgeoned from $71 billion in 1970 to $215 billion in 1984, fifteen times the 1950 level.

Just as farmers were mortgaged to the hilt to compete on the international market, forces beyond their control caused its collapse. When the Soviet Union invaded Afghanistan in 1979, President Carter meted out punishment with a grain embargo. The result was a surplus of grain for American farmers and a sharp drop in prices. Meanwhile, a series of economic events further crippled farms. With their new machines, the farms were dependent on gasoline and diesel, and the OPEC embargo sent the price of fuel soaring. The low interest rates of the early seventies that had enabled easy lending now led to spiraling inflation. Nobody, least of all farmers, liked to see the price of groceries double. And yet, inflation actually benefited debtors, as the dollars used to pay back the debt were worth less than the dollars borrowed. Inflation's losers were the banks, which had lent money at 8 percent, only to see their profit eroded by inflation of 9 percent. The Federal

Reserve, bolstered by President Reagan's promise to strengthen the dollar, enacted policies that would aid the lenders (and punish the borrowers). The Fed raised interest rates, which tightened lending and stalled inflation. Farmers, however, were in a business that *required* borrowing money for seed, fuel, and machinery every year, no matter the interest rate. At the same time, the dollar rose against foreign currencies, a boon for Wall Street and American tourists but another blow to farmers, who had been persuaded by government to sell their product overseas; a strong dollar effectively raised the price of American grain, causing foreign buyers to shop elsewhere.

The combination of massive debt and plummeting income proved too much for many farms. More than three hundred thousand families lost their farms in the decade, and the farm population was cut in half, from six million to three million. Not even Willie Nelson's star-studded Farm Aid concerts, launched in 1985, could save them. Unlike those in the previous generation, who had left the farm for better opportunities, these farmers were forced out of their livelihood by foreclosure and bankruptcy, and left with few options.

Most of the farms were not purchased by other family farmers. They were either subdivided to accommodate sprawling suburbs or bought up by bigger farms with the deep pockets to survive. The 1980s were not so bad for big farms, or corporate-owned farms, but they were terrible for small farms, those with fifty acres or fewer that threw off less than $50,000 per year in income—that is, the exact type of farm that Luci Brieger and Steve Elliott were trying to help run.

Having staked out her path, however, Luci was determined to prove it was the right one by succeeding. As long as Lifeline lost money, the doubters would be right. Agribusiness would win. And so it came to pass that the way Luci would prove that she had built an ethical household (and done her part to save the planet) was to make money.

But Luci and Steve and their partners were new to full-time farming, and they were learning the skills on the fly. They employed techniques termed biodynamic, a system developed by Waldorf School founder Rudolf Steiner that is widely considered the precursor to organic. After a bumper year of potatoes, Lifeline broke one of the first rules of organic farming and reseeded forty acres with the same crop. A heat wave spawned a plague of beetles. As Steve and Luci picked the bugs with their fingers, most of the plants died.

What Steve and Luci lacked in skills, they tried to make up for with frugality, by creating the sort of household envisioned by Wendell Berry and Gary Snyder.

And yet they were not homesteaders merely trying to feed themselves. They weren't trying to opt out of society so much as to find a principled, constructive way of living in it. Luci never felt that quitting grad school or politics was dropping out; rather, she felt that becoming a farmer was a better way to achieve the goals of making a better world. So it wasn't enough for them to get good at farming. They had to find a way to scale up and feed the multitudes.

The dilemma presented itself starkly in Steve's first season. Lifeline grew enough potatoes to blanket a basketball court four feet deep. Innovators like Ernie Harvey had figured out how to grow tons of organic food, believing that "if we grow it, they will eat it." But Lifeline hadn't devised a plan to get the food to people's plates. No one had stayed in the position of marketer for more than a year. Even Ernie had quit the job—he said phone calls gave him ulcers. Now Steve became marketer, and what to do with a million pounds of potatoes was suddenly his problem.

In 1983, organic food was more a dream than an industry. The first Whole Foods had opened just three years before in Austin, with a staff of nineteen. The closest thing to an organic foods infrastructure was a small network of health food stores and distributors on the West Coast. They happily placed orders with Steve. Selling hippie food to hippies was easy; problem was, there weren't enough hippies to eat it all. No distributor was large enough to order a full truckload, and no trucking company would bother with a partial load. The solution: Lifeline hired an entire tractor-trailer. Steve and the others stayed up all night on either end of Spudnik, loading twenty tons of pallets into the eighteen-wheeler. In a five-thousand-mile odyssey, the truck dropped potatoes in Seattle, Portland, Eugene, San Francisco, Santa Cruz, Los Angeles, Austin, and finally the East Coast.

Still there were tons of unsold potatoes. Steve set his sights on Missoula, population thirty-three thousand, the only city within 150 miles. A small distributor bought a few loads. Steve made one visit to the farmers' market. It should have been called the gardeners' market: little old ladies selling bunches of carrots for a quarter. The farm stand in Hamilton kept Ernie's mother busy but didn't move much product. Steve had a mountain to offload.

To do it, he would have to tap into the biggest market around: Montana grocery stores. But while a one-pound Lifeline potato fetched twenty cents in California, its conventional cousin grown next door brought only a nickel in Butte. Thus, Steve set out to sell a mountain of hand-weeded, cosmically fertilized potatoes for the same price as the ones that Gramps next door was coating in petroleum, showering with pesticide, dousing with weed killer.

Steve was the right man for the job. As a contractor he had developed some business sense: made bids, sent invoices, collected payments. After a decade on construction sites, Steve could talk John Deere as easily as John Lennon. He shaved his beard and kept the mustache. He told jokes. He shot the bull. As for his opinions about consumerism and the galling waste of the capitalist machine, he kept them to himself. He had never been dogmatic. For example, he had been a vegetarian for three years, but when he started hanging wallpaper in the South and was invited into people's homes for dinner, he simply couldn't refuse their collard greens with fatback. It was ungracious. He had eaten meat ever since.

His flexibility was an asset when he cold-called the Safeway in Butte. The produce buyer didn't want to hear some rap about astral energy and healing the earth. He just wanted cheap potatoes. When Steve announced that he had a truckload of organic, he could almost see the buyer grimace.

"Well, I guess we could take them anyway."

A deal was struck. "You give good phone," a Lifeliner remarked after eavesdropping on a sales call.

Far from feeling ripped off, Steve Elliott was elated. He sneaked organic food into Safeway in Butte, Ryan's in Great Falls, SuperValu in Billings. It was more gratifying than feeding the fussy health-store shoppers. Copper miners and cowboys and captains of industry were eating biodynamic—and didn't even know it! Steering them toward health and enlightenment without their consent was subversive, like dosing the drinking water, but instead of pouring chemicals in, Steve was taking them out, and SuperValu shoppers were none the wiser. He sold potatoes through the fall and winter, and by the time spring rolled around, only twenty thousand pounds remained, which he unloaded as goat feed to a farmer down the highway.

Steve and Luci and Ernie considered the great potato sell-off a victory. Yet it was not exactly profitable. By selling potatoes as conventional commodities, they were literally working for pennies. The profit from trucking potatoes to California was eroded by the freight costs. They knew the farm lost money, but didn't know how to fix it.

Financial troubles mounted. Another partner, with his wife and new child, packed it in for an actual salary, leaving more work and more debt for the rest of them. Steve still took wallpaper jobs for extra cash. Even after incorporating, the remaining partners could not get a bank loan. They borrowed money from friends and family—five hundred here, a thousand there, shares of ownership that someday might be worth something. After a below-zero cold snap in October destroyed most of the potato crop, Lifeline received a federal farm disaster loan to make it through to the next year. The loans pulled them from the brink, but the debt grew to $150,000.

Meanwhile, the drawbacks of Lifeline's cooperative structure were becoming evident. Group decision making stretched for hours and gobbled up useful daylight. Steve declared that he believed in consensus—just not the amount of time it took to achieve it. Luci chafed against some of the farm's unscientific methods. The woman in charge of the greenhouse would meditate in order to germinate the seeds. "You can meditate your ass off," Luci said later, "but if it is too hot, you're not gonna get the fucking lettuce to germinate." Finally two more partners left, leaving just Steve, Luci, Ernie, and a few part-time workers.

Although the path to profit was unclear, Luci and Steve still enjoyed the work—it was the meaningful vocation they had aspired to. And even on a subsistence budget, Luci did not feel that she was suffering. She found the life abundant and beautiful, filled with fresh, delicious food and long days in the sunshine of the mountain valley. Asked to house-sit for a neighbor, she and Steve staked the teepee outside the cottage and used only the kitchen and bathroom. When Luci's family visited, the arrangement struck Luci's stepmom as odd. Were Steve and Luci just trying to prove a point? To show everyone they could do it the hard way? Luci's sister, however, immediately understood why Luci lived this way. Leesa poked her head into the teepee and saw a magnificent master bedroom—a palace three times the size of the bedroom in the cottage, a plush queen-size bed beside a roaring woodstove, 360 degrees of luminescent walls.

As for Steve, he did not find in farming the sense of timelessness he'd experienced hanging paper at the Holiday Inn. Although there were some mindless, repetitive jobs, like weighing spuds into ten-pound sacks, his mind raced toward the other tasks that awaited: fix an irrigation line before the heat, deliver lettuce before it wilted, collect an invoice before drawing pay. He felt overwhelmed and incompetent, wondering which machine would break next. But he liked being part of something bigger than himself. He described it to me as a physical rush, partly the power of seeing how much food he and his partners could produce on their plot of land, and partly the humility of realizing that his role was actually limited, and that nature did most of the work on its own. What kept him on the farm was not some pastoral love of the labor but the belief that the work extolled the virtue of life.

And he believed that the stars and moon and the soil were spiritually connected to the people who tilled it. Steve had not been part of any congregation or religious group since high school, but neither had he become an atheist. He sensed the divine out there, and the closest he came to it was in the soil.

But unless Lifeline stopped losing money and paid its debt, there would be no farm, no household, no livelihood, right or otherwise. With Ernie running the dairy, Steve and Luci needed a better plan for the produce. Luci stayed up late poring over back issues of *Organic Gardening* beside a kerosene lantern, employing one experiment after the next to increase yields and quality.

A seemingly unrelated geopolitical event changed Lifeline's course—and finally revealed one path to profit. When communists took over Laos in 1975, a Montana smoke jumper turned CIA operative helped relocate a Hmong general who had fought for the Americans. Several hundred Hmong refugees settled in Missoula and the Bitterroot. As it happened, they were excellent farmers.

Luci still remembered the first time she saw their produce at Mr. Natural's Good Food Store, a fledgling shop run by Missoula's Covenant Church that had begun buying from Lifeline. "The Hmong would have ten bunches of spinach, and they'd be glorious and radiant and just make you weep," she said. "The amount of work and toil you could see represented by these spectacular bunches of spinach, and tied with a single thread, so elegant and beautiful. And ours were all crumpled and ham-fisted and not that clean, but they had ten bunches and here we were busting out *ten cases* at a time." The Hmong set up shop at the weekly farmers' market—not as a hobby, but as a livelihood. And it was evident they were making money.

Following the Hmong's lead, Steve and Luci packed the truck with spinach and cauliflower and gave the farmers' market another shot. They sold out in a few hours and earned four hundred dollars— for them a small fortune. Each week they loaded more produce into the truck, and each week they were greeted by an increasingly long line of loyal shoppers.

Without realizing it, Luci and Steve had arrived at the vanguard of the food movement, as its emphasis began to switch from organic to local. In its first decade, Lifeline had been most concerned with replacing pesticides and petroleum-based fertilizers with "appropriate technologies" such as crop rotation, compost, manure fertilizer, and biodynamic preps. In the late eighties, as climate change emerged as a more significant problem than pesticide pollution, organic was not good enough. The carbon reduction of eliminating petro-fertilizers was likely offset by trucking vegetables a thousand miles. As Luci's father pointed out, Lifeline was still dependent on petrol for its tractors and trucks. While they had created a local economy in the sense that they were making a living in the Bitterroot—and allowing thousands of Montanans to eat local food—they were still trucking potatoes all across the country, and milk to Washington state. Of course the most appropriate technology to distribute food was to reduce the distance it had to travel.

In other words, Lifeline's small, local enterprise would have to become smaller and more local. And the only way to grow less produce and earn more money was to sell it at a higher price. Luci and Steve needed hundreds—or maybe thousands—of local customers who would buy their produce for twice as much as the California conventionals cost in the grocery store. But Americans were accustomed to cheap food. In 1949 they spent 40 percent of their income on food; by 2011 that had dropped to 15 percent, replaced with higher expenditures on housing, transportation, and medical care. Americans spent less of their income on food than nearly all other countries. The market Luci and Steve required did not yet exist. In the 1980s there was no such thing as a local food movement. This was decades before Michael Pollan's *The Omnivore's Dilemma*, before farm-to-table cafés and CSAs and the surge of urban farmers' markets. To succeed, Luci and Steve would have to change the eating and buying habits of all western Montana. And then they would tailor the farm to match the markets.

As it happened, Missoula was an ideal testing lab for a local-food economy. Since the nearest major city—Seattle—was some five hundred miles away, it made sense to produce as much as possible nearby. In 1987 a microbrewery opened—one of the first in the nation. Moreover, the culture of the city was changing. As recently as 1969, Missoula's pulp mill, nicknamed "Little Hiroshima," had appeared along with New York and Los Angeles in a *Life* magazine photo essay on air pollution. Montana novelist Jim Harrison put a finer point on it: "The whole place smelled like a stinking pile of shit which required an absolute mutation of the senses to live with."

Civic leaders took action. Having been in violation of the Clean Air Act since 1978, the city banned woodstoves. The Brad Pitt movie *A River Runs Through It*, which had had to be filmed two hundred miles from Missoula's ochre skies, had already mythologized the city's clear, green fly-fishing rivers. Now, as the skies cleared, they revealed a cutish college town with bike trails and ski hills. As logging yards closed and mills scaled down, millworkers and lumberjacks were replaced by professors and outdoor guides. This being Montana, they naturally owned rifles and shot an elk each autumn, but instead of heaving the carcass in the bed of a Chevy, they lashed it to the roof of their Subarus, alongside their mountain bikes.

The city's transformation from mill town to recreation center continued to attract more of the people who placed a premium on healthy living—and healthy food. Little Hiroshima was rejiggered from pulp to cardboard, and the rotting-egg stench evaporated. Citizens voted to preserve open space, and the city council built more bike paths and traffic circles. The Internet enabled the arrival of telecommuters like freelance writers, software developers, and administrators of national nonprofits. Bistros and bakeries and breweries and wine bars sprang up in the weathered brick buildings clustered around a defunct train station—which had been remodeled into the office of a financial services firm. While industrial hubs like Butte and Great Falls fell into decline, Missoula's population doubled in three decades. By 2001, merely thirty-two years after Missoula was listed in *Life* as one of the nation's most polluted cities, *Outside* magazine ranked it alongside Santa Barbara and Santa Fe as a "Dream Town": "America's last best place to ski, kayak, and rock climb."

The new breed of Missoulian had perhaps read a Wendell Berry book, and decades before anyone had heard the word *locavore*, they were willing to pay an extra dollar for radishes grown nearby. The Good Food Store, having outgrown the church that founded it and having dumped Mr. Natural, moved to a larger storefront, then remodeled to accommodate its base. The store remained a nonprofit and gave preference to local food over the organics now available from California. One day Luci was delivering to the Good Food Store in the old panel truck when she looked at the mirror and saw cauliflowers bouncing along the road behind her. She pulled over and gathered them up, then arrived at the store ashamed of the bruised vegetables.

"They're beautiful," said the buyer. "I want them all."

A loyalty was forged. Lifeline would fill any order from the Good Food Store, even a single box of carrots. Meanwhile, Lifeline scaled way back on potatoes, becoming leaner and more nimble. They dropped from fifty acres to ten. They grew the vegetables that fetched a high price: lettuce, spinach, cilantro, herbs. By selling directly to stores they got the price that the distributor got, instead of what the distributor paid. In a period of fifteen days Lifeline sold nine hundred cases of lettuce, and Steve calculated that for that period every salad tossed in Montana was Lifeline's. They were finally able to phase out shipments to the West Coast and most conventional grocery stores. In addition to being a more ethical model, selling local also made business sense, reducing the losses incurred from trucking and selling on the commodities market.

Lifeline became a truly local business. Each Saturday at the stroke of nine the bell rang in the farmers' market and the mob clambered to the spinach. Between Steve's joking and Luci's teasing, they became something of a comedy duo, using their broccoli pulpit—and their unofficial slogan, "The customer is always wrong"—to educate and harass both loyal patrons and innocent passersby. After all, Luci had to not merely sell produce; she had to teach them about why it was important to buy local. Useful advice about when and how to prepare vegetables was mixed with mockery. Woe to him who purchased iceberg lettuce! He would hear from Luci about its nutritional poverty compared with that of the robust romaine.

One regular was the director of the University of Montana's Environmental Studies program, and Luci never missed a chance to berate him for not including agriculture in the curriculum. An acquaintance named Dan Baum purchased a kohlrabi—"a problematic vegetable at any time," he said—and found it tough as a croquet ball. He made the mistake of complaining the following Saturday. "Luci just tore my face off," he remembered, for lacking some quality essential to its preparation.

Luci's ferocity aside, it's easy in this era of small-batch kombucha, single-source honey, and artisanal lard to forget that the local food movement was driven first by producers, not consumers. Nowadays we associate local food with foodies—the wealthy gourmets who buy the stuff. It's easy to dismiss these changes in appetite as mere snobbery— to surmise that as the nation got wealthier over the past half century, a segment of the population merely determined that frozen peas and carrots were beneath them and that they would henceforth dine exclusively on rainbow chard and endive and arugula.

But it was in fact producers like Lifeline that spawned the local food movement. In trying to replace industrial monoculture with a small-is-beautiful local economy, they were free to plant a row of kohlrabi seeds to see if they could grow one. Their approach was strangely like that of Steve Jobs, who famously remarked that it was not the consumer's job to know what he wanted; the customer would understand what he wanted only after Apple invented it.

Consumers were ripe for the picking. Farmers like Luci Brieger did not invent kohlrabi or arugula, nor for that matter persuade people to like those vegetables. But the desire Luci and her fellow farmers were learning to tap into, if not for interesting vegetables specifically, was for being something other than a consuming cog in the industrial machine. In other words, the local food movement was not about healthy or gourmet food per se, but about ethical economic behavior. It got lumped in with luxury indulgences like fancy cars and smartphones in that it required spending more money on food than Americans were used to. But that was really only returning sustenance to the place it had occupied in Americans' budgets until very recently, with the advent of mass-produced food. Paying two dollars for a head of lettuce at the Missoula farmers' market (or four dollars at one in New York) was not really a cultural aberration, even though you could get it for ninety-nine cents at Walmart.

Along with a more personal engagement with what you were eating came, as Dan Baum discovered, a personal engagement with the person who grew it.

"She did not want her kohlrabi impugned," Dan Baum said, recounting his confrontation with Luci. "She was very good-natured, and it was funny as hell, but it's not like she was kidding. It's not like she later said she was sorry." Awkward though it was, the event marked not the end but the beginning of a long friendship. Baum never complained about the brassicas again.

As for Luci and Steve, a decade into their quest to put their house in order, they had done so, and the effects were rippling across western Montana. Their customers wanted to get *their* households in order, and buying local healthy food from actual farmers seemed an easy first step.

In 1990, after six years of chipping away, Luci and Steve finally made the last payment on the banknote. By then they no longer even possessed the potato machines that had incurred the debt. The business didn't amount to much: a few trucks and tractors, some milking stands, word-of-mouth agreements with stores, and an enthusiastic crowd at the farmers' market. Nonetheless, they owned it all, free and clear.

With two more years of saving, Steve and Luci squirreled away $40,000. They found a twenty-acre farm with dilapidated outbuildings and an old mobile home. The Bitterroot Valley was becoming a destination for second-home owners. Steve and Luci offered $105,000, which seemed exorbitant to them, and the owner agreed to carry the note. They were landowners.

Averse to debt and amenable to rustic conditions, they immediately sold the trailer, applied the $10,000 to the mortgage, and pitched their teepee. It sat on a high spot overlooking a small pond, backed by the sharp-toothed Bitterroots. They dug a four-foot pit beneath the structure, to gain extra space and a higher ceiling for a loft. Their new property already had water and gas and electricity. Steve wired the teepee with lights and a telephone. He built a bathhouse with a flush toilet and a hot shower. Living in the teepee saved them money, but Luci did not feel like she was roughing it. The teepee was pretty. She was building the household she wanted. They rented their land back to Lifeline—a tax advantage—and that spring they began tilling their own soil.

For the first time it appeared that they might actually succeed.

"IF THEY HADN'T HAD CHILDREN," Steve's sister told me, "they probably would have stayed in the teepee."

Luci and Steve had not arrived at parenthood easily. In the late eighties, they sat in the waiting room of an obstetrician's office. Luci was pregnant. Without health insurance, they would pay cash.

It was not Luci's first pregnancy. That time, she and Steve had spread the happy news to their parents and friends. They found a midwife in Missoula to deliver the baby at home. But Luci suffered a miscarriage. They didn't tell anyone about the second pregnancy. That one miscarried, too.

Now they were going to see a real doctor. As Luci read the waiting-room magazines, an ad from the American Sugar Council explained how excellent its product was for newborns. Luci flung the thing on the table.

She was called to an examination room where a nurse pressed a cold stethoscope to her forearm and pumped the cuff. The doctor arrived. She asked Luci a few questions. Literature provided, the appointment was over.

Luci and Steve walked to the truck.

"The doctor didn't lay one hand on me," she said. "Didn't feel my belly, didn't even ask what I'd been eating."

Steve had what he called a healthy mistrust of Western medicine, but Luci had no particular ideology about the benefits of homebirth. She simply thought the midwife provided better care than the doctor. She did not go back to the obstetrician.

The miscarriages continued. In 1990, after eight of them, Luci brought a pregnancy to the seventh month. Then the heartbeat went silent. The midwife arrived. Luci went to the hospital and delivered a stillborn baby.

When I asked Luci about these losses, she brushed it off. "It was hard," she said. "Not much else to say."

Neither was the type to dwell on misfortune. "When things go wrong, I don't let myself go to certain places," said Steve. For instance, although Steve was adopted, he never searched for his birth parents. "Never gave it a minute's thought," he said. They did not entertain the possibility that a different approach to medical care might have avoided some of their pregnancy difficulties. In their grief they poured themselves deeper into the farm.

Soon Luci was pregnant for the tenth time. She did not return to a doctor. "I had white-coat syndrome," she told me. She was not afraid of giving birth in a teepee; she was afraid of doctors. "We would have a baby, or we wouldn't," Steve said. "That Luci wanted to keep trying was enough for me." She would not compromise on her dream of having both a farm and a family; nor would she rely on medical procedures that she doubted. Luci wanted what she wanted so badly that she would risk her life to have it.

The midwife visited the teepee at the end of the long dirt road and determined that it was an adequate birthing place. She plotted a route to the hospital in case of emergency. Her one requirement was that they purchase a portable gas heater. When labor began in May 1993, the midwife arrived. Luci lay in the bed and pushed against Steve as he stood behind her. Just as the baby arrived, a woodpecker hammered on a lodgepole overhead. Luci bore a healthy son, whom they named after her father, Emmet.

Luci and Steve did not practice the helicopter parenting that was becoming common. Luci carried the baby in a sling as she worked in the fields, and let him nap in a bike trailer that she hauled to the shade of a tree. Just about everyone who visited the young couple had an opinion on their parenting approach, however. "I thought it was really stupid to have a child in the teepee with the wood-burning stove," said Steve's sister. "Yet it seemed *so Steve*." Dan Baum brought his family to visit. "My parents were gobsmacked that they had a newborn in a teepee," he said. "Beyond belief." As for Luci's family, they bit their lips. "My mom may not have liked it," Luci said. "But she didn't say so." What she did say was, "I'm not coming back until you have a house."

Three years later Luci was pregnant again. When she was a week past due, the midwife determined that the baby was breech. The midwife manipulated the baby with her hands, turning it in utero. "Now you're going to squat until the baby is born," she said. Luci squatted as much as she could, and at the end of three days, she delivered a healthy ten-pound boy. This one she named Wendell. ("That's so sweet of you," her father said. "You named him after my Navy buddy." Luci did not correct him.)

In 1999, Luci was pregnant again. "I always knew I was going to have a girl when I was forty-two," she said. "That's what my grandmother did." She contracted pneumonia and had to spend a night in the hospital. When the delivery date arrived, the midwife discovered that the cord was wrapped around the baby's neck. The Missoula hospital was forty-five minutes away. They didn't have that much time. The midwife untangled the cord and helped Luci deliver a healthy girl, Alianne.

Raising kids was the point at which most radicals gave up the dream. And perhaps the reason Steve and Luci persevered beyond that point was their flexibility; they were willing to make some concessions without fully sacrificing their ideals. After nearly a decade in the teepee, they built a house. Unwilling to borrow more money, they saved for two years, and in 1995 erected a modest home of thirteen hundred square feet. The ground floor included a living room, kitchen, and bathroom. Upstairs were three bedrooms and a bathroom. The house was heated by south-facing windows and a woodstove. They installed a gas furnace in the basement but ended up not needing it.

Land-rich and cash-poor, they did not prioritize buying things for their children. Instead they bought cows and llamas and sheep, tractors and plows. Meanwhile the children were outfitted at Goodwill. When their aunt came for a visit, she offered to take them to Walmart for school clothes and a new pair of Nikes. Luci refused. How about a gift card to Target? Negative. When Emmet reached middle school and discovered skateboard fashion, his aunt inquired about his birthday wish list. "Anything with a name brand on it," he pleaded.

Refusing your children trendy clothes may not seem like radical parenting. But Luci and Steve also declined what had become the cornerstone of the middle class: health insurance. Raising three children on forty thousand dollars a year, they applied for a federal health plan for working families. But the value of their property had soared, and they were denied. With too much land for a subsidy, yet too little cash to pay premiums, they went without a policy.

The first time Wendell broke his arm, they took him to the doctor in Victor, who didn't have an X-ray machine. The doc sent them to the veterinarian for the X-ray, then set the bone. The pain was excruciating when the doctor sank the needle into the bone to numb it, but the bill was only two hundred fifty dollars. The second time Wendell broke his arm was on a Sunday, and they took him to the emergency room. The doctor suggested Wendell be put under to avoid the pain of the needle. This time, the bill was for two thousand dollars, which Steve and Luci begrudgingly paid. Steve did not countenance suggestions that going without health insurance irresponsibly placed a burden on the system. "Fuck 'em," he said. "Make a reasonable system and we'll join." (In 2014, with passage of the Affordable Health Care Act, he and Luci did just that.)

Strict as they were, Luci and Steve were not purists. Their house was connected to the gas and electricity grid. They bought a television. They owned a tractor and a big truck and a station wagon. Sometimes they drove the seventy miles round-trip to Missoula for the kids' hockey games. As much as they detested the oil industry, they were aware that without gas and diesel they would grow a lot less food, and people would instead buy it from California, which would require even more fossil fuels. And yet their indulgences were restrained, or at least intentional. Eventually Steve learned to refine biodiesel from used vegetable oil, and fueled the tractor and car with that. Their television received only the three local channels. Through severe frugality, smart borrowing, and a $40,000 inheritance, they managed to live debt-free and pay virtually no interest to banks. They constantly felt the financial paradox: money bought freedom, but acquiring money compromised that freedom.

They sent their children to public schools. Products of public education themselves, both Steve and Luci believed that its mix of social class and background was the underpinning of democracy. "I don't believe in removing them from the public school system just because we have problems with the public school," Luci said. Besides, they didn't like the other options. Private schools cost too much, and would require driving the kids each morning. "And homeschooling is not my calling," Luci said. "To do it well I'd have to spend an enormous amount of time. And there's always been too much financial pressure to make money on the farm." And as Steve put it: "I wanted them to be from Victor." So the children walked to the local schools.

"We didn't necessarily pass on our love of efficiency to our children," said Steve. Instead they motivated them with capital, letting the kids cultivate their own cash crops. In ninth grade Emmet earned over two thousand dollars growing parsley. He bought a laptop.

Steve and Luci pinched pennies and paid off the land early. Aspiring young farmers applied to be apprentices. Steve and Luci brought in two per year, paid them a stipend, and provided a cabin. The interns, usually idealistic and energetic people in their twenties, became like family. They helped raise the children. By age six, Emmet had gained the confidence to explain to them when they were pulling weeds the wrong way. On hot summer days he was deployed on his bicycle to the Mercantile, where—in a rare exception to Luci's rules—he filled glass jars with ice and Pepsi for the crew.

Perhaps the greatest challenge was in raising children at the height of the digital age. Luci was maddened by the school's focus on computers. "They teach a lesson about global warming while every light and every computer in the school is turned on," she said. "And nobody connects the dots."

She taught her children responsibility and self-discipline, to show them they need not rely on fossil fuels and electricity. If Wendell needed to submit a paper online for school, he biked his laptop to the public library or bank and used the WiFi. Even after he got his license, he was not permitted to drive that mile in the car. If Luci found her teenagers plopped on the couch fiddling with some iThing (also bought with their own money), she asked, for the hundredth time: "Is this contributing to truth, beauty, and justice? Is this contributing to your self-improvement? If not, put the fucking thing away. Now."

"The Internet has been a major disservice to the culture," Luci said, "because we are humans and we can't control our impulses that don't help us be better people, but they help us be lazier, dumber, fatter. We need an edge, we need to be hungry. Then we're healthier and smarter, and behave better."

She was equally intolerant of pop culture. One day while she and Steve sorted heads of garlic outside the storage fridge, she told me, "We don't immediately take the kids to all the stupid-ass movies."

"Well, some of us do," said Steve with a laugh. "I grew up loving comic books. I love it when I hear there's a new Spider-Man movie."

In this marriage, Luci was the cop, Steve the buddy. "I'm not going to lose any sleep if they drink a Coke," he said. But he had not drunk one himself in decades. If he was out with just the kids, he would treat them to a natural soda. If Luci was there, they got juice, or worse yet, kefir. Sometimes he had to remind them: "The thing about your mom is that she's right."

The kids came to accept this. When Ali's request for a ride into town was denied, she pointed out that in the biodiesel Jetta the gas was actually free. This provoked a lecture from Luci: someone had to drive to the mall to get the used fry oil, someone spent their time refining it, and the car had to be bought, as did its tires, and even though the fuel came from vegetables, it still released carbon dioxide. It was most certainly not free.

"The high-volume tirade that I'd get from my mom for coming home with a Pepsi is not worth the Pepsi," said Emmet. She would tell him how Pepsi was part of a multinational corporation, how high-fructose corn syrup destroyed the American farm and the American metabolism, and how plastic bottles never decayed but floated in the Pacific until the end of time. "She's right, and everyone knows she's right, and she knows she's right," said Emmet. "My mother is the most aggressively rational human being in existence."

For years Luci and her mother bickered over boxed cake mixes. As a girl, Luci baked the cake mixes that her mother bought. But on her own, Luci began to bake from scratch.

"Why don't you buy cake mixes?" her mother demanded. "You can't bake a better cake."

But the boxes were filled with chemicals, processed sugar, bleached wheat, God-knows-what-else. "We've been sold the lie that easy is better," she said. "When we embrace *easy*, we're not examining what we give up."

There would be no cake compromise. "She couldn't figure out why I couldn't buy cake mixes," said Luci. (Steve knew the reason. "Ain't nobody on God's green earth that would prefer boxed cake mix to Luci's zucchini cake or beet cake.")

When Wendell was in high school, he wrote an essay with a line that read, "At home, the farm always comes first." Luci asked if he was bitter, and he said, "Maybe a little." But overall, the kids didn't complain much. "As humans, we accept what is reality," Steve said, "and in this household, *this* is reality. And, as I sometimes have to remind them, they get tradeoffs. They have a fucking hockey rink."

Did the Elliott children appreciate this? Sometimes. They told me that when they first entered public school they were jealous of other kids' haircuts. They envied the plastic-packaged cheese and crackers in the lunches of friends. "The containerization is always cool," sixteen-year-old Wendell said wistfully. Quick foods were perhaps the most obvious casualty of life in the Brieger-Elliott household. "I tell my mom we don't have any food," said fourteen-year-old Ali. "And she says, 'We do—you just have to make it.'" But once they actually started to eat other people's food, they realized how good they had it at home. Ali recalled her disappointment the first time she ate store-bought burgers on white buns at a friend's house: "It tasted like . . . nothing."

Alongside the stream of wide-eyed, curious, idealistic twenty-something apprentices, the children led a farm life. They shot rock chucks with a .22. Ali mowed the grass atop the John Deere, and after a blizzard skied to school. Wendell loaded the truck with rubbish and hauled it to the landfill.

One required chore was planting lettuce, for which Luci and two kids and an apprentice sat on the transplanter that Steve towed through the beds with the tractor. One day I got roped into helping, and took one of the scratchy fiberglass seats on the trailer. "Grab some lettuce," hollered Steve. "Chop-chop." Each of us had a tray of lettuce starts. As Steve drove, every twelve inches he pushed a button that squirted four jets of water into the row. We reached between our legs and plugged a lettuce into the wet spot in the soil. I felt like Lucille Ball wrapping chocolates on the conveyor belt: once I got behind, I reached desperately for more baby lettuces to shove into the ground, but of course the tractor did not slow down. Luci was the fastest, and she not only planted her own row but helped the others keep pace when they lagged behind.

Fifteen

After two years in the city, saving money, Emmet was ready to enroll at Parsons. His AmeriCorps educational award, his partial scholarship, and his parents' college fund of about $10,000 were enough so that he wouldn't have to take out loans. But he would still need to cover living expenses. Now he had to pop the question to his parents: How much would they contribute? By then, his parents had saved more than $100,000. But they had other plans for it. They wanted to buy another farm—an incubator farm, to lease to former apprentices who didn't have the capital to buy land. It would be a way to preserve agriculture in the valley.

"Why are you starting this incubator farm for these apprentices," Emmet asked his mother, "and not doing something for me?"

"It's not for them," Luci told him. "It's not about the people. It's about the idea."

Steve and Luci had stepped off the economic escalator three decades before and created a life where a large income didn't matter. But the money they saved on clothing and even health care was pocket change compared with Emmet's tuition. And it was unclear whether any of the children would follow their path and become farmers. What was clear was that Steve and Luci simply would not—could not—encourage or enable their son to live beyond his means. Luci remained firm. They meant to buy forty acres of barley. Emmet would have to figure out how to pay for the cost of his education in excess of the money they had allocated for him. The discussion resulted in a few tears, followed by jokes about the tears, then laughter.

"It took a couple of hours of bitterness," Emmet told me, "but I haven't thought about it much since then. They weren't buying the land because they wanted it, but for their moral duty. Their mission."

Ultimately Steve and Luci did not consider this a question of money so much as one of values. They wanted to teach their children the value of working for what they get. "I'm not sure we'd do anything differently if we had all the money in the world," Luci said. "I'm not sure paying for everything is the best strategy. I want this kid to have a dog in the fight."

I asked what she would do if, instead of asking for tuition, Emmet had wanted money to buy a farm. "We'd say: Go buy it!" she said. But she wouldn't give him the money. She would want him to figure out how to finance it himself, just as she and Steve had done.

If his parents tease Emmet about being a hipster, he teases them back about being land barons. Upon learning that they had bought the forty-acre farm, purchased raw land in New Mexico from Luci's father, and inherited a portion of the Texas ranch, Emmet quipped, "Well, the sun never sets on Lifeline Produce."

Household might be defined as the intersection of family and work. In the household Luci and Steve had created, in some regards work trumped family. They would support their son, but only to a point. And they would continue to pour their resources into their own vision, even if that meant directing their money away from family.

"I want them to have as good a life as I've had," Steve said, "and I don't think they can have it if they don't work. My parents were products of the Great Depression, and they wanted me not to suffer. They tried to do everything for me. But that didn't exactly work out. I appreciate what they gave me, but I wanted to earn my own way. And I want my kids to have that experience."

Emmet took a job at the pub, working nights, about forty hours a week. He lived cheap by New York City standards, paying seven hundred dollars a month to share an apartment with three others. He subsisted on bodega sandwiches and ninety-nine-cent tacos. He rode his bike everywhere, paying for the subway only in the worst of storms. He never again broached the topic of paying for college with his parents. Over the course of three years in New York, he occasionally asked them for emergency cash, accruing a debt he now calculated at five grand, but Steve told him not to worry about paying it back until graduation.

"I don't want to be in debt to them," Emmet said. "It's too personal, and now I'm attached to the idea of paying for my own college."

Sometimes he resented his classmates, most of whom had never worked. "They talk shit about art theory until they're blue in the face, meanwhile not doing anything worthwhile." He preferred the late nights at the pub, bullshitting with the kitchen crew who—much more than his fellow art students—resembled the people he grew up with.

When he gave it a lot of thought, Emmet approached some hard truths about the world. "I come from a family that works and does stuff that matters for the world, and I have to work for my tuition while others don't. So I have a bit of a chip on my shoulder. I may look like it, but I'm not one of these privileged kids of New York City." Their privilege consisted of never having had to work. "My privilege is having been taught to work."

Haunted by his parents' uncompromising pursuit of an ethical life, he found himself asking if his parents would find his work valuable. Generally he thought they would not. "That's my existential crisis." And whenever he was not productive, he heard his mother's voice: *Is what you're doing contributing to truth, beauty, and justice? If not, put the fucking thing away. Now.*

So, *did* his parents find his work worthwhile? As in many families, this sort of hard question went unanswered. "I told him I wouldn't think my opinion would matter to him," Luci said with a laugh. "But it's going to have to all be paid for, so good luck."

"It's unimaginable that he doesn't know that we are ambivalent," said Steve. "But ultimately we don't hold our kids or our friends to the same standards as ourselves."

When I asked Luci if she thought she was depriving her son of what he most wanted, she spoke more broadly about American society. "Having our children chase after their dream," she said, "we're not looking at the backside of that. There's a lot of wisdom in trying to control a little bit. Or at least give them some reasonable bounds. People can really choke on their freedoms."

And in the long run, Luci and Steve were providing for their children, in accordance with their values. Eventually the Bitterroot farm would belong to Emmet, Wendell, and Ali. Luci and Steve just didn't think that a college degree was as valuable as the land they call home.

CEDAR WAS ACCEPTED to a university in Colorado. She drove down to see the place before making a decision. My feelings were mixed. If she rejected the offer, we would default to the desert plan I wanted. We would move to the property in Utah, pay no rent or mortgage, plant some trees and build a straw-bale studio, and settle into the simple life. It would be nowhere as hard-core as the way Ethan and Sarah lived—we'd have running water and electricity and cars and supermarkets—but we would at least be committing to our own piece of land and breaking free of the lion's share of our monthly expenses.

When Cedar returned from Colorado, she looked glum. "I liked it," she said, "but I don't think I'm going to do it." Getting a degree in poetry was surely a money-losing life choice. All I had to do was agree. All I had to do was nod my head, and just like that, I would get what I wanted. But here was the odd thing I was learning about love. I actually wanted her to have what she wanted. And she was not fooling me. She wanted to pursue her talent, and she wanted it badly.

I thought about my own education, of my parents refinancing the house to send me to college when I was too immature to even understand or appreciate their sacrifice. And I thought of Cedar declining to go to private college because it cost too much. What was money for, anyway? Which was more important: education or land? And to my surprise I found myself coming down on the side of my own parents.

"You should go," I told Cedar. "You have the chance, and we'll find a way to afford it. If you wait, you may never go, and then you'll regret it for the rest of your life. It's just money."

When summer came we packed up a U-Haul, but instead of lighting out for the territory, we lit out for civilization, for a rental house tucked between other rental houses, schedules and payments, power bills, supermarkets. The simple life would have to wait.

AMID THE BOOM IN ORGANIC FOOD, Luci and Steve felt as if they had won the battle and lost the war. In 1990, Congress passed the Organic Food Production Act, which authorized the Department of Agriculture to oversee certification. After decades on the margins, organic was finally recognized by the Feds as worthy. As the official stamp began to appear on packages in 2002, the industry exploded. In 1999, Whole Foods opened its hundredth store, and would pass four hundred stores in the next fifteen years.

The boom was as evident in Missoula as anywhere. In 2003 the Good Food Store moved to yet another building, more than quadrupling its size, a cathedral to healthy, delicious eating: shimmering aisles of plump artisan bread loaves and steaming mugs of fair-trade espresso and a buffet of blackened slabs of wild-caught Alaskan salmon. Shoppers munched tempeh Reubens in the café and learned to roll nori in the back classroom. It was an orgy of the senses, grass-fed T-bones and cave-aged Camembert, heaping troughs of Castelvetrano olives and Marcona almonds, a far leap from the musty oat bins in the ill-lit sprout shop of yore. The Good Food Store upped its orders from Lifeline, buying nearly half of Steve and Luci's produce, ten boxes of carrots in a single week.

Lifeline could command a premium, and it had stopped selling cheap to grocery chains. That same year, it joined the newly formed Western Montana Growers Cooperative, which supplied local organic food across the state, ending once and for all the need to ship to the West Coast. Ernie Harvey's ranch and dairy half of the business was thriving, its cheeses, bacon, and beef distributed to the entire state. Meanwhile the farmers' market scene approached mayhem: on a typical Saturday morning Steve and Luci grossed $2,000, their annual income just two decades before.

The organic infrastructure grew across sectors. In 1996 a nonprofit called Garden City Harvest began to till community plots all over the city. Volunteers pulled weeds in exchange for produce, neighbors invested in a weekly basket of vegetables, and tons of fresh food were donated to soup kitchens and food banks. The University of Montana Environmental Studies department partnered with the group and—a decade after Luci dropped out—created the Program in Ecological Agriculture and Society, built around a working farm where students learned to grow organic. The university established a farm-to-college program to procure local beef, grains, produce, and oils for its institutional food service. Eventually Montana would rank third on the national "locavore index," with Missoula leading the way, joining

Santa Cruz, Madison, Portland, and Burlington as a bona fide local-food town.

It would appear that Luci and Steve's vision had been fully validated. They had succeeded by the standards of organic farmers, as well as by the standards of mainstream America. Three decades after arriving by bicycle at Lifeline and quitting her career path, she was a wife and the mother of three children, and the owner of a beautiful home and a business poised to reap the benefits of a sweeping societal change. Luci and Steve's story combined two of America's most beloved myths. It was the fable of the visionary dropout who, like Steve Jobs, must depart the establishment in order to prove that his innovation will work. It was also the myth of the rags-to-riches entrepreneur—also like Steve Jobs—who only by risking it all manages to cash in.

And yet they were not satisfied. They had envisioned—and manifested—agriculture that was not just organic but also local, small-scale, family-owned, and sustainable. But Big Organic was largely composed of corporations with different priorities. Organic lettuce in the supermarket was grown on vast fields of mono-crop in Mexico, packed in plastic, then shipped thousands of miles in refrigerated trucks. Behemoths like Pepsi and Kellogg unveiled organic versions of their processed snacks and bought out old-line hippie brands like Kashi and Odwalla and Ben & Jerry's. And the fastest-growing shelves—in both health food stores and in Safeway and Kroger—were prepared foods, organic frozen pizzas, and organic microwave burritos, which to Steve and Luci seemed more problem than solution.

"When people buy organic, they believe they are buying it from a small farmer, who probably has a family," said Steve. "They are buying tradition, food safety, and an old value system: the barn, the fields, the cows. Organic does not assure them that, so I consider it false advertising."

For Steve and Luci, eating organic was never the whole point. "To install an off-gassing carpet in your house and then demand certified organic food doesn't work for me," said Steve. The point was to build a household that provided satisfying work and made the world healthier and just. Not using chemicals was only one of many means of achieving that.

"The organic movement settled for getting rid of pesticides," said Steve. "Which is noble, and great. But there are more pesticides on golf courses than in agriculture."

In short, organic certification seemed to them to do as much harm as good. Although strictly organic from the start, Steve and Luci had always opposed certification. They lobbied instead for mandatory labeling, in which the petro-fertilizers and pesticides used on your potato chips would be listed right there on the package. That way the consumer, instead of the government, would be responsible for what he ate.

Few agreed with them. In the late 1980s, when organic farmers in Montana instead formed a certification association, Steve and Luci joined against their own instincts. Lifeline received a checkmark for doing what it had already been doing. Steve joined the board, and when he inspected another farm, he helped the farmer comply with the standards. Though not the system Steve and Luci would have chosen, it was adequate, and had the effect of encouraging organic methods.

The 1990 act created more laws, regulations, agencies—and the potential for misrepresentation. The USDA replaced the self-regulating Montana group. In Steve's mind, the consumer had basically hired a third party to check out farms. He chafed at the idea of inspectors snooping through his barn looking for poisons. He would rather have had the customer come see for himself. In what was likely not an effective slogan, he extended this invitation to shoppers: "Get your ass down here and look at our farm."

Under the old system, inspectors were there to offer advice and mentor farmers into compliance. But under the federal system, the correct techniques were considered proprietary, and inspectors were forbidden from freely handing them over. That rankled Luci. The whole purpose of her years of experimentation was to share her methods.

As conventional farmers elbowed into the premium market, they certified some fields for a better profit while leaving others as is. To accommodate this, each field had to be inspected separately. To Luci and Steve this was absurd. You couldn't have an organic field next to a conventional one, because the pesticides sailed over fences and seeped into the soil. And now Lifeline was required to do more paperwork—and pay more fees—to certify each field, to comply with a system that allowed others to follow the letter of the law while undercutting its spirit.

Why should Lifeline play along with a process that allowed—even encouraged—industrial farms to wreck the land as they edged onto the high-dollar shelves? They valued small-scale, locally owned, in-season crop diversity, as opposed to large-scale, corporate-owned, out-of-season monocrop. "When you start to eat organic grapes in the winter that are shipped in from Peru," Luci said, "you have to question what good you think you are doing."

"The question should not be organic versus non-organic," Steve said, "but corporate versus noncorporate. When you support big corporations, you don't spread justice to humanity."

In 2006, Walmart leapt into the organic market. It didn't take an MBA to figure out that an operation like Steve and Luci's could expand production and ride the gravy train. Instead, typically, they bolted in the opposite direction.

"We certified for seventeen years," Steve said. He remembered thinking, "I'm fifty-two years old. Ain't doin' it no more."

Steve and Luci and a handful of other farmers quit organic certification. They launched the Montana Sustainable Growers Union, branding their produce with an ornery stamp: HOMEGROWN. There were no outside inspectors. Members regulated one another, and when someone wanted to join, instead of simply giving them a pass or fail, the union mentored that farmer to compliance, which basically amounted to following the organic rules.

"Relationships are what govern society," Steve said. "And the relationships between farmers are what govern this movement. We are not going to let each other down, three hundred sixty-five days a year instead of the one day of the inspection. Peer-group pressure is a better way of assuring you that you're getting what you think you're getting. Our way is better."

Ironically, by opting out of getting certification, a strictly organic farm like Lifeline would not be able to supply a chain with a dubious commitment to agricultural health, like, say, Walmart. Indeed, some stores requiring the official seal stopped carrying Lifeline's produce.

Quitting certification was the latest in a string of decisions that might not have made strict business sense but dovetailed once again with Luci and Steve's deepest motivation, which was not to make a fortune or to run a business or, for that matter, to be farmers. They had set out, after all, to make a household. And while one element of household was to grow organic food, another was to do satisfying work, to avoid what Wendell Berry called the "specialization, degradation, trivialization, and tyrannization" of the marketplace—even if that marketplace happened to be organic. Steve and Luci did not want to follow unfair rules or to be bossed. And because there was no model for running their type of farm, they were free to improvise.

In the mid-nineties, with a baby in the teepee and another on the way, Steve had paid the small fortune of $5,000 for an Italian spader— a tilling implement pulled behind a tractor whose American cousin could be found secondhand for a thousand bucks. Some considered this sports car of tillers a farmer's midlife Lamborghini. Yet Steve was convinced that it would improve his soil. The American chisel plow and disc tilled nine inches of topsoil but compressed what was below, leading to a condition known as "plow pan," in which the compacted soil resisted water and roots. The Italian tool softened the topsoil without compaction. It was expensive, and slow, and required a pricier tractor geared to haul it. But after two decades with the spader, the soil was far more productive.

Two years after Ali was born had come that $40,000 inheritance from Steve's aunt. They had spent the money on land—their neighbor's eleven acres of unusable land, to be precise. Why? Because the neighbor put his cows in the creek. "It was heartbreaking to see that whole riparian area completely denuded," said Luci. Erosion ran into their pond. Steve took a Platonic view: "Our farm was incomplete without it." (Emmet offered a somewhat different interpretation: "They bought the new land to make the ditch better. The only thing that would have suffered from not buying it was the hockey pond.") They let the ditch recover, controlled erosion, and soon the creek flowed clear and clean. The new land never paid for itself in income. But neither did the creek degrade to where it ruined their water—or their rink. They wanted their house in order.

As it turned out, the financial loss of quitting certification was negligible. Lifeline's largest buyer, the Good Food Store, supported the move. The other half of their produce went to farmers' market customers and the Western Montana Growers Cooperative, both of which had more faith in Steve and Luci than in the organic stamp.

And yet, local farmers were victims of their own success. The number of vendors at the farmers' market more than doubled, cutting into Steve and Luci's Saturday earnings. Moreover, the distribution network they had helped create was so successful that local organic produce could be found seven days a week at supermarkets, so fewer people waited until Saturday for their weekly shopping.

Once again they had to innovate ways to earn money, to become smaller and more efficient. Luci determined that bedding plants—that is, plants that the buyer transplants to her own garden—were more profitable than produce. A cabbage start, raised in the greenhouse, sold for two dollars, the same as a full-grown cabbage. She never had to transplant, weed, or harvest it. And while the start occupied only four square inches of shelf space at the market, the cabbage was four times as big and four times as heavy. Soon, bedding plants brought in about $10,000 per year, a fifth of Luci and Steve's income. They continued to prosper. After spending Steve's inheritance on the watershed, they saved up and paid cash for another eight acres, bringing their total acreage almost to forty. In 2009, Lifeline officially split into two businesses: Ernie's dairy and Luci and Steve's vegetable farm. In 2014, the couple began paying back the emergency loans they'd taken from friends and family thirty years before. The farm was wholly theirs.

As Steve turned sixty, they began to contemplate retirement. Emmet showed no interest in the farm, and the younger two children were still in high school. The farmers' market was a family outing, and a welcome trip to the city, even though it was hardly worth the effort anymore. Wendell and Ali helped with the setup and takedown but spent the hours in between hanging out with friends. As soon as Ali graduated from high school, it seemed, Lifeline's three-decade run at the farmers' market would end.

Steve and Luci understood that their success was not exactly replicable. Their excellent relationship with the Good Food Store was the result of decades of personal loyalty. Were they to sell the farm to someone else, the new owner would likely lose that preferred status and have to compete with the dozens of other organic farmers (many of them former Lifeline apprentices) who had sprung up in western Montana.

They continued to be out of sync with the nation—even as the nation came around to some aspects of their vision. They had to face the fact that the world they had helped to create was not precisely the one they wanted. As local and organic food became cool, the rallying cries were not liberty and justice but micro-roasted, small-batch, single-source, and nose-to-tail.

The unintended consequences of the changing nation were evident in Missoula. Downtown at Charlie B's, the walls were still lined with black-and-white photos of its former regulars, loggers and miners and hobos with gin-blossom cheeks and cauliflower ears. The portraits emitted a whiff of tobacco smoke, even after cigarettes were banned in bars. You wouldn't see folks like that in Charlie's, or in most of Missoula, anymore. Those old-timers looked as antique as a casting call for *The Grapes of Wrath*. The new patrons were bluff, toothsome fellows in sandals and shorts, fresh from a day on the river, sunglasses dangling from their necks on colorful straps, hats and shirts emblazoned with the logo of a fly rod or a kayak. They gulped pints of malty syrup called Moose Drool or Olde Bongwater (brewed right in town with actual hemp). Although the clientele was scrubbed and collegiate, Charlie B's was still a dive compared with the rest of Higgins Avenue, where you could hardly turn around without bumping a BabyBjörn.

Steve Elliott liked that the new Missoulians bought his beets and voted Democrat. But that didn't mean he actually wanted to live next to them. (He'd returned to the ballot booth after realizing his absence wasn't actually changing the world.) Each year in the Bitterroot more farmland was subdivided into tract homes for Missoula commuters, or developed as second homes for out-of-state millionaires. Huey Lewis moved in, for Chrissake, and fenced the local fishermen off his ditch. Amid the local-food boom, the number of cultivated acres in the Bitterroot actually declined, as did the tons of food produced and the number of farmers making a living at it. After Gramps retired his forty-acre potato plot, he was replaced by permaculturists with advanced degrees who grew an acre of arugula and basil.

Even though Steve served as a precinct captain of the Ravalli County Democrats, his years in a valley populated by militias, preppers, and sovereign citizens had had an effect. "What I like about right-wingers is they know something is really wrong," he said. "That's not always the case with liberals. There's a school of liberalism that says if we can just tweak it, we can fix it. Whereas I agree with the right-wingers: I think things are drastically wrong."

From his years hanging paper by the square foot, he agreed with the hard-right preference for contract work over an hourly wage determined by government or unions. And to my mind he embodied a certain strain of conservative values: Steve Elliott was, after all, an entrepreneur who practiced Jeffersonian small-scale agrarian democracy, who placed individual responsibility above government regulation. "I just want to be left alone," he said. When he built his home, he neither applied for nor obtained permits. "If there was such a thing as a libertarian who thought the role of government was to take care of its weakest members of society, I'd be it."

But he could not support the conservative agenda to gut ecological and labor law. "Since we're clearly not going to live by a *moral code*," he said with a laugh, "we might as well have some regulation." A child of the Vietnam War who never trusted government, he found himself in the maddening position of siding with Washington bureaucrats over his neighbors. "We'd be better off with a smaller government with active citizenry that respected each other," he said. "Security and environment and health care should be left to the Feds. But it clearly wouldn't work in the situation we have now, so I don't advocate for it, even though I think it would be better."

"The stated goal of our culture—life, liberty, and the pursuit of happiness—has always taken a back seat to economic interests," said

Steve. He doesn't believe that all resources will one day be equally distributed, but he thinks we need to try harder to move in that direction. "We don't have a viable plan of achieving the goal. The easy way out is to just hand people a check, and the other alternative apparently is to pull yourself up by your bootstraps. Those are the two alternatives in our society, and neither of them work." He believed that the human species had all the knowledge and technology to build a just society but simply didn't make it a priority.

Luci was more conflicted. Despite her lifelong doubts, she still *wanted* to believe in the power of government to do right, and *wanted* regulation to work. She compared government to a vehicle: when the brakes go out, you fix them; you don't junk the whole car. She could rattle off a few USDA programs she supported: invasive weed eradication, subsidies for small-scale wool producers. Yet she did not employ them on her own farm. The weed management required herbicides. The sheep subsidy, a few hundred dollars for a flock as small as hers, was not worth filling out the paperwork for. She rolled her eyes when her husband waxed libertarian, yet she agreed with him that their farm functioned best without outside aid. Luci sat in limbo: a passionate advocate for an ideal government who found the actual government too corrupt and incompetent to bother with.

"The foxes are guarding the henhouse," she said, "and until we can get the money out of politics, I don't think we can change it. Any time a law comes around to get the money out, it becomes a parlor game in Congress to dismantle it. And they'll say, Yeah, you have to vote for different people. You lost when your candidate lost. Of course we don't have candidates that run the gamut of policy choices. It's going to take a bit of a revolution."

Epilogue

A few weeks before Cedar and I left Montana, we drove over to Idaho for a weekend retreat with a monk from the Buddhist order that Cedar and her family belong to. Just six attended: Cedar's parents, their friends, and us. In the mornings, we meditated; in the afternoons, we worked in the garden; and in the evenings, the monk gave a talk about dharma.

I had been to a retreat with Cedar and to one on my own at a monastery on the West Coast. Those required four meditation sessions per day. I wasn't very good at meditating, tending to twitch and nod off. One of the monks pulled me aside and told me a bit sternly that I was distracting the others. I preferred the "working meditation," which involved following a monk through the woods as he downed timber with a chainsaw. My skepticism toward anyone addressed as Reverend Master was offset by my respect for the skill with which he handled the Husqvarna.

Meditating for long sittings felt to me like intentional suffering. I knew I would never make it as a monk. And I probably wouldn't make it as a homesteader or farmer, either. I don't love it enough. What unites Ethan and Sarah, Greg and Olivia, and Luci and Steve is not what they've quit but what they have gained. They find true joy in their work. They aren't just suffering and renouncing. By living within limits, they find the sort of abundance that so many of us long for. And after that, the need for money and cars and big homes just seems to fall away. Of course one reason so many people quit the simple life is that they just don't like it, or it prevents them from pursuing their true calling. But these people found their calling, and heeded the call.

At the end of that retreat, Reverend Master advised that I try to meditate for shorter periods. It was better, he said, to sit for one minute a day and to enjoy it, to look forward to it, rather than to suffer through twenty minutes of narcolepsy. Since then I had followed his advice and had practiced regularly, working my way up from five minutes to ten.

Reverend Master drove to Idaho to oversee the retreat. After the first morning meditation, in which I was once again fidgeting and nodding off, he offered to give me tips on posture that would make it easier. After the others filed out, he and I sat on the carpet and he demonstrated the proper way to tip my hips, to curve my spine.

I told him about my progress since the last time I'd seen him, my ten-minute practice. Then I told him that many mornings I skipped it because I was anxious to get to my office. I told him that before moving in with Cedar my commute from bed to desk took about fifteen minutes. Now, mornings usually required some housecleaning, a bit of garden work, and then the forty-minute bike ride into town, so that some mornings I didn't get to work until eleven. I had fallen behind on the book. I said that my window of concentration lasted from about nine to one, hours during which I felt a clear sense of purpose and the time slipped past unnoticed. If I lost the first two of them to housework and commuting, I grieved that I could never get them back.

The monk, shaved head and brown robes, knitted his brow. He had known Cedar since she was four years old, and in addition to being her teacher, he was as close to her as an uncle. He asked what the book was about, and I told him about the families I'd met. Without further prompting, I found myself loquacious, telling him about how inspired I'd been at the Possibility Alliance, with its mix of simplicity, activism, and spirituality. I recounted how when I gushed about it to Cedar, she said she already had a spiritual community, and what a neophyte I'd felt, one whose own path never really mattered.

I found my heart racing. I hadn't spoken of this to anyone. I suppose it was like being in confession. I wanted to tell him everything.

He didn't seem particularly interested in hearing any more, but I kept going.

"And sometimes we have these stupid fights over whose turn it is to wash the dishes, and it throws me into a bad mood before I even get to work, and then the whole day is a loss. And when we talk about it she suggests I meditate more, because that's what she does when she's angry or anxious, but I'm thinking: If I have to clean the kitchen, then I don't have time to meditate."

Reverend Master nodded in his pleasant, inscrutable monk way and said, "Let's put these cushions away."

I trudged up the hill to my tiny cabin. As is the tradition of this order of monks, men and women boarded separately, so Cedar and her mother were sharing a bedroom in the house, and I shared the outbuilding with our dog. The path was wet with rain. It was the first time I realized how bothered I had been by my wife's snub. I had wanted to do something together, but her spiritual practice was frankly too hard, and she wasn't hopping on the first train to Missouri when I called.

Later that afternoon, Reverend Master pulled us into the sanctuary. "This is as close as I'll ever come to marriage counseling," he said. He sat us on the floor and directed his attention to me.

"You don't have to do this," he said. "There are a lot of paths out there, and this one, Zen Buddhism, is probably the most difficult.

Unless you really think this is the only way, you shouldn't even try it. I followed this path because it seemed to me that the only other path was death, and until you reach that point, I'd say stick with something easier. And definitely don't do it to please Cedar. That will drive you both crazy.

"The work you do—the writing, the researching—that's your practice. You have to do it. That's what gives you purpose."

I realized I was weeping. Not some tight-throated biting back of tears, but full, chest-heaving, cheek-streaming sobs. And it wasn't grief for being kicked out of Buddhism. The opposite. Far from judging me as an artistic or a religious failure, this man beamed at me with a smile of unconditional acceptance, bringing me maybe the closest I'd ever been, the closest I'd ever be—undisciplined agnostic who squirms at the vocabulary of the sacred that I am—to believing that, there's no other way to say this, maybe God did love me. I felt dizzy joy that this man I hardly knew seemed to understand me more fully than I did, and in a few short lines had said the thing I'd wished that the Committee could say, that the searches would reveal: *You're doing the thing you love, so keep doing it.*

IT WOULD BE ANOTHER TWO YEARS before I was brave enough to put to Cedar the question that Ethan had put to me back at the Possibility Alliance: What had been going on for her that she'd responded that way?

Cedar didn't hesitate. "I felt abandoned," she said. "We'd only been married for two weeks and already you were off traveling, meeting all these fascinating people, and I was stuck at home by myself, writing reports."

I was surprised, not just to learn how she felt, but to realize that I hadn't even noticed. I had gone searching for how I could forge the good life as part of a family, but I had tried to do the searching by myself.

It's true, as the Zen masters teach, that life is like stepping into a ship that is bound to sink. Before marriage, I didn't think much about the final stop, and when I did, I confused the apprehension of death with death itself. The paradox of matrimony is that while the bond feels eternal, it tethers us to the finite. The people in this book believe—and show—that sacrifice leads to abundance. And that's the same allure of marriage, that by giving up one element of freedom we gain something greater.

MISSOURI

On a cool October evening I was topping off tires to ride into Kirksville. Black clouds darkened the skies above La Plata. The fourteen miles would take ninety minutes, and we wanted to arrive before dark. But instead of mounting his bike, Ethan was tiptoeing through the herbs and puddles searching for baby poultry. A brood of five chicks had hatched just a few days before, but now there were only four. An overnight freeze was expected. He must find the runaway.

Just then his neighbors Don and Dana Miller strolled up the driveway. "Batten down the hatches," Don told me. The Weather Channel had predicted a major storm racing in from Kansas City. "They're calling for an inch of rain and gale-force winds."

The Possibility Alliance had a hand-cranked radio that received exclusively the government weather station, but without television or Internet they often got their forecast the old-fashioned way: hand-delivered by the Millers.

I was watching the clouds roll in from the west, but before we could start riding, the phone rang and Ethan was called inside. I followed. The caller was none other than Jerry Mander, one of Ethan's heroes, author of *Four Arguments for the Elimination of Television* and *In the Absence of the Sacred*. Ethan was considering riding the train to New York to attend a conference Mander was sponsoring. Ethan picked up the phone, holding one hand under his sweater against his chest. "Your book was seminal," he gushed. He asked Mander to describe the gist of the conference, to determine if it was worth the train ride. Mander directed him to go look at a webpage.

"Actually," Ethan said, hand still under his sweater, as if gut-shot, or reciting the pledge. "I don't look at screens."

Jerry Mander laughed. "I'm glad someone is actually living this way instead of just talking about it!"

They chatted for a few minutes, then signed off. Ethan decided not to go to New York after all. And soon after, he and Sarah would decide not to move to the coast, and instead commit for the foreseeable future to the Possibility Alliance in Missouri.

At last he removed his hand from beneath his sweater. A ball of downy feathers quivered in his palm. It chirped.

It was the lost baby chick.

A CHANGE OF CLOTHES in our backpacks, we donned fluorescent vests and pedaled off. We rode three miles toward the setting sun on a straight country road that dipped and rose through farms. At a four-lane highway we turned north. The shoulder was wide enough to ride two abreast, but eighteen-wheelers blasted past at a distance of three feet, seventy miles per hour.

We were headed for a meeting of Neighbors United that Ethan was supposed to facilitate. The group had sprung up in opposition to a proposed high-voltage power line slated to slash through northeastern

Missouri, just a mile from the Possibility Alliance. The power line was supposed to run electricity from wind farms on the plains to customers in Chicago and beyond, but Neighbors United contended that most of the power would actually come from fossil fuels. Ameren, an Illinois corporation, sued the State of Missouri to be granted status as a public utility, which would allow it to seize private property through eminent domain. The towers would be erected mostly on farms, with or without the landowners' consent.

During the most recent craft night at the Millers' house, they had made protest signs to hold outside the state courthouse in Jefferson City. Don and Dana would be going to the action, taking a few PA residents along with them. Ethan had carefully orchestrated the carpools; he didn't think the Chelsea Manning advocate should ride in the same vehicle as the Millers. Ethan and Sarah, avoiding cars, would not attend. Tonight as we cycled, other PA members were hitching rides to the meeting with Brian and Teri and the other homesteaders.

Ethan and I were just three miles shy of Kirksville when the storm hit. The skies burst open in torrents. Headlights flashed across the slick asphalt. We crossed the highway median and waited for a break in oncoming traffic to scoot onto a surface street, where rainwater filled the gutters. I splashed through puddles that soaked my thighs. Goose bumps rose on my forearms and I hoped we wouldn't get stopped by a red light because I was too cold to stop pedaling. And also: it was glorious, like swimming through the sky. I felt alive. By the time we arrived at SuperStretch's apartment on the Kirksville square, my feet sloshed in my shoes. We locked the bikes on the sidewalk and climbed a dark staircase to the apartment above a restaurant. Stretch opened the door, took one look, and then passed us a pair of towels. "Why don't you just leave your clothes out there in the hallway?" he said.

After changing into dry clothes and eating a quick potluck dinner—Ethan and I had packed a disc of goat cheese and a bunch of kale—we headed to the community hall. All the folding chairs were taken, and dozens of people stood against the walls. The mean age was about sixty, and the assemblage looked straight out of central casting for farmers: Big Mac overalls and trucker hats that said "LG Feed." American flag pins were in evidence. The younger guys wore Wranglers and Mossy Oak camouflage. There were a few students from Truman State and a handful of homesteaders, but overall the farmer-to-hippie ratio was about ten to one. Clean-cut Ethan, in jeans and a flannel shirt, blended right in.

A minister led us in prayer, asking for wisdom and strength in the battle against the corporation. One woman announced that if all this energy was going all the way to Massachusetts, maybe Ted Kennedy and his fancy friends should stop blocking wind farms off Cape Cod. (Kennedy was already deceased, but the point went uncontested.) Speakers voiced opposition to the federal government meddling in their affairs. They blamed Obama. They complained, correctly, that the power lines were subsidized with federal dollars. They didn't like an Illinois corporation pretending to be a Missouri utility so that it could claim eminent domain. Ethan allowed all to voice their concerns. Although he was one of only three in the room who didn't use electricity, you wouldn't have known it. He never uttered the words *conservation, sustainable, global warming*.

"We are on a big case," he said. "God and Spirit have put us on it to fight for justice." He quoted the Book of Amos and exhorted everyone attending the demonstration in Jefferson City to not be violent or antagonistic toward the police or toward people who disagree with them. "We will love everyone as children of God."

There was a discussion of what the next step would be. What if the state granted the power of eminent domain to Ameren? What to do then?

"It's too soon to go up to the Iowa border and lay down in front of the bulldozers," Ethan said. He trailed off a moment, then regained himself and flashed a smile, "But if we do, I'll be the first one on the ground."

MONTANA

Steve Elliott mellowed. He had the ability not only to adapt but also to embrace, rocking the iPod from the seat of the tractor. He took his kids to concerts: Galactic, the Decembrists, Michael Franti. Still proud of his Los Angeles roots in a state where Californians are often resented, he cruised Missoula sporting his Dodgers jersey, blasting Afrobeat on the truck stereo. "I'm the reason this valley has gone to hell," he said with a laugh. "Even after being here thirty-five years."

A few years back, Steve had gotten a call from the son of his father's former business partner. When Steve's dad had died, his mother had sold his share of the company to the partner for a small sum. Shortly thereafter, the partner sold the business to a corporation and became an executive. His son took over from him. The phone call—which was only about some minor legal matter—gave Steve a chance to reflect. If his own dad had not died, perhaps it would have been Steve sitting in that corner office of a Los Angeles skyscraper.

Of course, he would not have switched places if he could. He preferred being on the tractor, or chasing down cows that broke through a fence. "Ours is a relatively easy path," he said. "I've got it better than ninety-eight percent of Americans. All we have to do is work really hard. We underestimate how difficult office work is on you."

Steve's dad had dreamed of being a rancher, and in many ways Steve had fulfilled that dream. Funny thing is, he never meant to. "The act of farming forced me to be the person I wanted to be." He ran as far as he could from his father's life, and somehow he'd ended up with the life his dad always wanted.

Steve never forgot his first glimpse of Emmet, the day he was born in the teepee: the baby had eyes that stared right through him. His own father had gone to the office every day, and after he went into the hospital, Steve never saw him again; looking back, Steve thought that maybe he was ashamed of his weakness. Steve got to see his own kids every day. "You might call it a luxury," he said. "I call it freedom."

Luci Brieger did not mellow. She remained a crusader, a warrior, never in doubt, never backing down. "You think she'd be the mellowest person in the world because she lives a nineteenth-century hippie life," said Dan Baum. "But maybe she lives this life because she's so incredibly pissed off at everything."

Luci, who calls herself a "happy pessimist," saw a lot out there to get angry at. "The world is too big, and there are too many choices," she said. "Some people can spend half an hour trying to pick out toothpaste and would say that's freedom, that's what's great about America. But it's stupid. Stop it."

As her children got older, Luci joined the local school board. In Emmet's graduating class of twenty, three of the ten girls had been pregnant. Luci tried to develop a sex education class. Her proposal was defeated. When she learned that the school had no plan to dispose of old computers, she contacted the university to see how to recycle them. There was no functional way to do it. The university had an entire floor of a building filled with old computers, waiting for a way to get rid of them.

"They talk about online security, but not the ethics," she said, "not the epidemic of obesity and nearsightedness. They're all myopic. And the machines are obsolete in five minutes. No one talks about planned obsolescence or the landfills. No one is talking about heavy metals, about cell phones causing brain cancer. No one is talking about addictive behaviors, the fifteen hundred clinics in China opened up to treat people with Internet addiction."

When one of Luci's apprentices arrived late, he suggested that there had been a misunderstanding. "There was no communication breakdown," Luci said with a laugh. "You screwed up!" Then she announced to anyone within earshot, "You gotta call kids on their shit." An apprentice had nicknamed Lifeline "No Mercy Farm." "She is strong medicine," said Dan Baum. But Luci retained a singular ability to bluntly criticize while maintaining a tone of genuine affection, and she rarely offended.

The one relationship in which she had not achieved this balance, perhaps, was with her own mother. Even as she was aware of the dynamic surrounding boxed cake mixes, for example, Luci continued to bake cakes from scratch. "For a daughter to reject some of her values—there's a lot more at stake," Luci said. "She felt judged."

"As the years went by, Luci became a bigger mystery than I was," said Steve, "so her mother would talk to me about Luci."

Luci agreed. "My mom eventually liked Steve a lot more than me. He's not quite as rigid."

While Luci is not precisely proud of her inflexibility, neither does she seek to change it. "If you think you're right about something, first you have to see that you're making assumptions, and then you have to examine them, and once you've done those things and thought them through and come to your conclusions and stuck to that, then are you rigid? If you've made a decision that you like? Depends how you define *rigid*. I'm sure my kids would say I'm rigid."

Asked if it was important that her parents approve of her life choices, Luci blurted out, "No!" She said she was driven to live up to the standards of her husband and children, however. "When you're married to someone you respect, you have to earn their respect," she said. "Even more so with kids. You have to do your ethical best. It's good to be with someone that makes you a better person. Sometimes I worry I've failed my children, my husband, my family. But I don't dwell on it. I just move on."

In 2013, Luci's mother fell ill. Luci went to Texas. In the hospital, the first thing her mother said was how nice Luci looked. The compliment was such a shock that Luci marched out of the room and dialed her sister.

"Mom's a goner," she said.

A few weeks after the funeral, Luci was transplanting onions with her apprentices when a friend stopped by. They did not use a high-tech method to plant onions. They sat or squatted in the dirt, poked a hole with a finger, stuck in the onion reed. It could take all day. Certainly there was a machine to do this, but Luci would never buy it.

Luci wore purple tights beneath a skirt and clogs, long brown hair with bangs that flopped over wraparound sunglasses. She was trim and wiry, and from a distance could be mistaken for a teenager. Up close, streaks of gray were visible. Her palms were callused, fingers bent like claws. A mutual acquaintance told me that the only other place he'd seen hands like that was on peasant farmers in Poland. Luci had just turned fifty-seven.

Luci recounted her mother's final days to her friend, how her mother had told Luci she wasn't required to come back at the very end. But Luci came back anyway. "And I can imagine myself saying the same thing to my kids. And I can also imagine being a bit lifted if Ali showed up with her own kids. I can imagine really wanting to see their faces. They have such beautiful little faces. And hear their voices. When I told my mom I was glad I was her daughter, that she'd done a good job, she said, 'Well, I tried.'"

There in the onion patch, snow shimmering behind her on the mountains, Luci discovered that she had choked up, her sunglasses steaming. She looked away and gestured toward the apprentices. "These boys have had to listen to me bleat on about this all week."

The young men continued to plug onions into the soil.

"When you become a parent," she told them, "you really need your kids' approval."

From the distant end of the farm came the roar of Steve firing up the tractor. On Emmet's last visit from New York, he had noticed that, for the first time he could remember, his mother had sat still in a chair for an entire hour and watched a full episode of a television show.

She began recounting some of the debates she'd had with her father over the years about the ethics of the oil industry, in which he spent his career. "He took it so personally, like I blamed him. I was too stupid to understand that he would take it that way."

Luci said that at the memorial service, her mother's longtime companion asked, "Aren't you happy that your mother never told you that you couldn't do what you wanted?" Luci told him that she was. "I took it, during her life, that my mom wasn't terribly concerned. She was not a worrier. But he said that she consciously made the decision that whatever I wanted to do was going to be fine. He wanted me to understand that. *'Aren't you glad she did that?'*"

Luci was crying again, fog on the lenses. "He admires what Steve and I do. And he only gets his information from my mother." She swallowed back the ache. "So, she never said this to me, but I think she ended up very much admiring what we did with our lives."

DETROIT

"You got to Detroit just in time," Olivia Hubert told me when I caught up with her at her table at Eastern Market. It was my third visit, in the fall of 2013. "They're about to liquidate our assets. They're going after all the art at the DIA."

"I thought you meant personal assets."

"Oh, we don't have any assets," she said, flashing a smile and patting her belly. "Except the baby. And nobody would want a mixed baby. Maybe if it was white, it would be worth something."

Olivia and Greg did not move to the country. Eventually they would buy the house next door in North Corktown, deepening their Detroit roots even further.

Despite the pockets of renewal, Detroit was still in free-fall, the floor not yet reached. As Whole Foods opened its glimmering doors, Detroit's mayor and council were unable to pay the city's billions in debt, and the governor appointed an emergency manager to rule the city. His first act was to declare bankruptcy. Residents wailed in protest, fearing that a settlement would pay the banks while robbing pensioners and looting what remained of Detroit's jewels—Belle Isle and the Detroit Institute of Arts, with its van Goghs and Matisses and epic Diego Rivera mural financed by the Ford family. After a series of appeals, the manager emerged victorious. The birthplace of the automobile, the arsenal of democracy, the Paris of the Midwest, was bankrupt.

The ruling had little immediate bearing on Greg and Olivia, who were busy preparing their home for the Fritz, as they called their future offspring. They spackled holes in the walls and painted the nursery. Olivia found a midwife and planned a home birth. She'd timed the pregnancy for a winter delivery. "I'd read about pioneer women being pregnant in the heat of summer," she said. "I didn't want that."

They joined with some friends to start a charter school. The farm fared better than ever, and they were able to pay the note on their new land as well as purchase health insurance and car insurance and pay down Olivia's student loans. Slogging through morning sickness, she circled the block searching for Buffy, the disappeared chicken. She suspected it had been carried off by the neighbor's dog. Greg texted the neighbors to keep an eye out.

"This is what it's going to be like when we have the baby," she moaned. "It'll disappear. Greg will text the neighbors to see if they've seen the Fritz. I'm going on hunger strike until Buffy come back."

They partnered with a young chef to start a weekly café in a silver Airstream down the block. Customers paid seven dollars for Moroccan tagine or Korean tacos, brown-bagged a beer, and sat around a campfire, the roar of the freeway not far off. It was spontaneous, loose, festive—and totally illegal. But the old neighbors didn't complain. They liked it, especially after their teenage granddaughter was hired to help in the kitchen.

"In this new economy we can't just take out a loan to get to the next level," said Greg. "Trust is the new currency. Instead of credit we use trust and credibility to leverage things we need. We need each other."

Greg and Olivia joined a neighborhood association that gave microloans to help fix up houses, and also formed a block club with the six remaining families on the block, hoping one day to plant a food forest and even build a shared sauna.

As they risked all their wealth on their farm, they became less patient with those from nonprofits and committees who preached radical change from the security of a day job. They were wary of the grant money pouring into the city. "It's not sustainable," said Olivia. "Corporations hide their money by giving it away to nonprofits, and if any blip happens to their bottom line, that money will disappear. And then what will all these nonprofits do?"

After the initial thrill of media acclaim, the couple became irritated by film crews arriving unannounced and demanding interviews.

They were exhausted by young dreamers bending their ear about some pie in the sky that would revitalize Detroit, a scheme that generally involved more social networking and fundraising than crouching over crops like a peasant.

"A lot of people like the social element of being in the city, being able to go to the art gallery or museum," Olivia said. "But that's kind of some *bull*, because if you're *farming*, you don't have time to go to the art gallery or the museum every time there's an exhibition."

Spend enough time in Detroit and no conspiracy theory seemed far-fetched. Olivia's mother had long posited that forces were at work to plunder the Belle Isle Conservatory so that the state could steal it from the city. In early 2014, Lansing did just that, creating a state park with an entrance fee, effectively placing it off-limits to the city's poor. That same month, nine foundations pledged $330 million to save the city's art collection from the auction block. A bankruptcy plan was approved that cut the pension of Detroit's retired schoolteachers and clerks and bus drivers by 14 percent, and repaid bondholders at fifteen cents on the dollar.

That January a historic cold snap punished the city. "Detroit winters are not like 'White Christmas,'" Olivia told me. "It's Donner Party shit, like that movie where the plane crashes and they all eat each other."

While land in Detroit might be cheap, you got what you paid for: unplowed streets, miserable public schools, broken streetlights, and ambulances that did not arrive. When Olivia's mother took a vacation, someone broke into her house. "You can't go anywhere," said Olivia. "You can't have anything nice." In the suburb of Dearborn, a young black woman's car broke down late at night. She pounded on the nearest door for help. The white man inside shot her dead.

"Detroit is like a movie where writers set up an impossible situation for the hero," Olivia said. "Too many villains. You got white-collar criminals, robbers, drug dealers. There's not enough non-villainous people."

Each day she wondered if the benefits of being a citizen of her own hometown were worth the sacrifices. Most days she decided they were.

"If you think it's doomed, it's already too late," she told me. "You may as well go lie down in the street."

Forces of history—industry and agriculture, race and class, the production of internal combustion engines along the River Rouge and the harvest of coca leaves in the Peruvian Andes—continued to collide, beyond the grasp of those at their mercy.

Forces of nature, too. The polar vortex, subzero weather displaced from the Arctic by unprecedented warming, bore down on Detroit. Greg bundled up on the tractor seat with the snowplow, hustling for a hundred bucks. Olivia stuffed the stove with split firewood. Buffy the chicken never returned.

Amid it all, a baby was born, a girl, a child of Detroit, a daughter of America, descendant of enslaved Africans in the Mississippi fields and dogged Europeans on the Model T line. With the first signs of thaw, snowmelt pooling and icicles crashing, her parents were in the greenhouse, pressing another row of seeds into the soil.

ACKNOWLEDGMENTS

This began when my agent, Richard Abate, told me to find and read a book by David Shi called *The Simple Life: Plain Living and High Thinking in American Culture*. I am indebted to Richard for another nudge in the right direction, and to the author. From there my thoughts matured to the literary equivalent of a line scrawled on a cocktail napkin. I could not at that point articulate what sort of people I was looking for, only that once I found them, I knew they would be the right ones. Gratitude to my editor, Rebecca Saletan, who bravely signed that napkin and sent me off searching. Her own curiosity and faith in that which we could not yet see allowed this book to exist.

I am grateful to the three families who let me into their homes to record their extraordinary lives. Also to Ina May Gaskin and the late Stephen Gaskin, Cliff Davis and Jennifer Albanese at Spiral Ridge Permaculture, Malik Yakini, Brian Thomas and Teri Page, Scott and Barbara Brant, Isan Brant, Richard and Rosemary Sundeen, Rich and Joanne Sundeen.

Early readers and advocates: Rae Meadows, Robin Wasserman, Amy Irvine, Lydia Peelle, Greg Martin, Mathew Gross, Mel Gilles, Wiley Cash, Leslie Jamison, Sarah Eisner. And Fred Haefele and the rest of the Wednesday-night Missoula nonfiction squad: Jeremy

Smith, Mary Jane Nealon, Larry Mansch. Research assistance: Brian Kevin, Dena Saedi, Drew Webster.

I was generously supported by the Montana Arts Council and the MacDowell Colony. I'm grateful to Benjamin Nugent and Diane LesBecquets at the Southern New Hampshire University MFA program, and to Sharon Oard Warner and Eva Lipton at the University of New Mexico Summer Writers' Conference.

Authors and books that shaped my thinking:

Wendell Berry, *The Unsettling of America*
Thomas Sugrue, *The Origins of the Urban Crisis*
Stephen Gaskin and The Farm, *Hey Beatnik! This Is the Farm Book*
Ina May Gaskin, *Spiritual Midwifery*
Richard Fairfield (with Timothy Miller), *The Modern Utopian*
Kelly Coyne and Erik Knutzen, *The Urban Homestead*
Lanza Del Vasto, *Gandhi to Vinoba: The New Pilgrimage*
Gary Snyder, *The Gary Snyder Reader*
Helen and Scott Nearing, *Living the Good Life*
Mark Binelli, *Detroit City Is the Place to Be*

At Riverhead: Michelle Koufopoulos, Jynne Dilling, Helen Yentus, Karen Mayer, Liz Hohenadel, Glory Plata, Anna Jardine, Katie Freeman. For my publisher, Geoffrey Kloske: Fool you twice, shame on me. Fool you three times . . .